SO

MUCH

WASTED

•

Perverse Modernities

A series edited by

Judith Halberstam

and Lisa Lowe

SO

MUCH

WASTED

•

Hunger, Performance,

and the Morbidity

of Resistance

PATRICK ANDERSON

Duke University Press

Durham and London

2010

© 2010 Duke University Press

All rights reserved

Printed in the United States

of America on acid-free paper ∞

Designed by Amy Ruth Buchanan

Typeset in Carter & Cone Galliard

by Keystone Typesetting, Inc.

Library of Congress Cataloging-

in-Publication Data appear on the

last printed page of this book.

for four:

Shannon Jackson

Della Pollock

Ruth Wilson Gilmore

and

Kaja Silverman

contents

•

acknowledgments

•

Septembers and Octobers in Berkeley are always surprisingly hot. The heat shouldn't really be a surprise—it happens every year—but when it descends upon the Bay Area after a deceptively cool summer everyone moves a little more slowly than usual, as if rehearsing for the staging of a William Faulkner novel. What makes the heat endurable is the light, which Janet Adelman once described to me as "filtered through honey." It is relentlessly beautiful, mesmerizing in the broadest sense of that word.

Septembers and Octobers in Berkeley also seem to constitute an informal earthquake season. There's nothing geologically true about that claim. But I have felt the ground shake most furiously during the fiercest heat waves. I always jump toward the nearest doorway (no longer considered the safest place to be during an earthquake, but the Doorway Method is too ingrained in me to allow for any other) and, when there, notice that I am sweating not from nerves, but from the searing heat. There are earthquakes during other times of the year, but in my experience the fiercest come in the aching intensity of a Berkeley fall.

So I count myself lucky to have pursued my graduate training in a place where I was so severely physically unsettled during the same months that I was mentally roused from the slumber of summer vacations. This was a helpful reminder, every year, that learning is deeply embodied, and that the body is exceedingly smart. As with everything else I know, I learned this from others; like Berkeley autumns, my relationships to those who have helped me craft this book are textured with trembling heat, the kind of quivering flush that Bataille might have called *ecstasy*. I am endlessly fortunate in my collection of colleagues, mentors, and friends — my chosen families — to have found and forged relationships with people who not only occasion in me both vulnerability and pride, but also welcome my stuttering but persistent attempts to profess gratitude with a wholly insufficient ineloquence.

This book is not really mine to dedicate, but I dedicate it nonetheless to four women who have changed me in earthquake-y ways. Shannon Jackson, who set out on the long haul of advising me when I was an undergraduate at Northwestern and then when I was a graduate student at Berkeley, has been supportive and demanding in all of the traditionally academic ways, but has buoyed me in many other ways too. Our long history and shared intellectual vocabularies set the scene for our work together, but her wit and endless kindness filled that scene with warmth. She is family, friend, colleague, and forever trusted mentor. Della Pollock has embodied the ironic (and often disturbing) sense of loving humor required to be a conscientious academic. She is, quite simply, one of the smartest and most generous people I have ever had the privilege of knowing. Ruthie Gilmore, whom I first met shortly after one of those precipitous minor earthquakes, looked me in the eye, laughed lovingly, and told me everything I was doing wrong. She is the personification of what David Román calls "critical generosity," and I am convinced that I learned from her how to teach and how to engage with the work of others. Kaja Silverman taught me how to read and how to care about what I write. More important, she has shown me how caring for oneself can be a radical form of caring for the world, and vice versa, which has clarified my relationship to the horrors of U.S. politics after September 11 and to the trauma of private pain. Kaja is family too, the best kind.

Other mentors have been similarly uncompromising in their guidance and care. The late Dwight Conquergood, my first true mentor, grabbed me early in my intellectual life and showed me the importance of rigorous political action, humble ethics, and difficult compassion. I think of Dwight almost every day, and I profoundly miss his harsh, uncompromising care. I can only dream that he would have heard the echoes of his own voice in this book. Bill Worthen, also a longtime mentor, taught me how to work with tireless abandon, never forsaking the meticulous geekiness we share; he is always, always ready to share a laugh, a priceless quality in a quintessential academic. D. Soyini Madison taught me how to speak the language of generous, gracious questions, one of the hardest intellectual lessons I have ever had to learn. Chris Berry exemplifies the calm hand and steady eye of someone with real patience — all too rare in this line of work — and showed me how the academic's life must not be limited to exercises of the mind. Caren Kaplan was tough on me when I thought I knew what I was doing; I will forever be grateful to her for once saying, "Okay, fine, you're done with that. But here's what's next." Mary Zimmerman taught me how precise a body can be and also gave me the chance to learn how to stay standing on a slippery slope in a pool full of cold water. This has turned out to be an unusually adaptable skill.

I was fortunate to pursue my doctoral training in the context of an extraordinary interdisciplinary culture at Berkeley. I was particularly inspired by conversations with my various cohorts, including Marlon Bailey, Mona Bower, Sarah Burgess, Catherine Burriss, Renu Cappelli, Gretchen Case, Reid Davis, Kate Drabinski, John Fisher, Peter Goodwin, Katie Gough, Dan Grausam, Beth Hoffmann, Priya Kandaswamy, Sara Clarke Kaplan, Laura Levin, Joshua Linford-Steinfeld, Marissa Lopez, Joyce Lu, Jane McGonigal, Eve Meltzer, Andrew Moisey, Omri Moses, Stuart Murray, Joe Nugent, Zabet Patterson, Dylan Rodriguez, Maya Roth, Jared Sexton, Lara Shalson, Adriano Shaplin, Kristina Hagström Ståhl, Monica Stufft, Joanne Stoddard Taylor, Andrew Uroskie, Daniel Ussishkin, Heather Warren-Crow, Don Weingust, and Frank Wilderson. I must also thank Mary Ajideh, an extraordinary woman who managed the daily administrative affairs of Berkeley's doctoral program in performance studies with grace, humor, and abiding care.

My colleagues and students in the Department of Communication at the University of California, San Diego — we converge from an unusually broad range of home disciplines — have been exceptionally supportive of my teaching, thinking, and writing, all in the context of a rigorously collective political conscientiousness. Robert Horwitz and Dan Hallin have chaired our department through some tumultuous institutional times since my arrival at UCSD; I am grateful to them for both their departmental stewardship and their individual guidance and advice. I have been privileged to work with many graduate and undergraduate students who have taught me much more than I have taught them; these include Samia Abu-Samra, Lauren Berliner, Jakeya Caruthers, Erin Cory, Patricia Davis, Beth Ferholt, Aaron Gurlly, Deniz Ilkbasaran, Robert Lecusay, Warren Mark Liew, Kelli Moore, Matt Moore, Ciara Murphy, Yumi Pak, James Perez, Virginia Preston, Ivan Ramos, Renee Skarin, Thea Gold Tagle, Jenifer Vernon, Michaela Walsh, Nia Witherspoon, and Alvin Wong. Katrina Hoch, Laurel Friedman, and Fatma Ulgen have generously provided invaluable research assistance and deserve full credit for several footnotes, translations, bibliographic entries, and rhetorical questions found throughout this book.

I have also been fortunate to find a number of excellent readers in addition to many of the people listed above. Janet Adelman, Srinivas Aravamudan, Wendy Brown, Leo Cabranes-Grant, Lisa Cartwright, Sue-Ellen Case, Giovanna Chesler, Emily Colborn-Roxworthy, Renee Alexander Craft, Jill Dolan, Laura Edmondson, Mel Gordon, Judith Farquhar, Emine Fisek, Susan Foster, Marcela Fuentes, Brian Goldfarb, Mark Griffith, Lynette Hunter, Jennifer Johnson-Hanks, E. Patrick Johnson, Suk-Young Kim, Sonja Arsham Kuftinec, Jill Lane, Daphne Lei, Peter Lichtenfels, Eng-Beng Lim, Lisa Lowe, Michael Lucey, Carol Mavor, Jon McKenzie, Jisha Menon, Paige McGinley, D. A. Miller, Jules Odendahl-James, Natsu Onoda, Peggy Phelan, Öykü Potuoglu-Cook, Tim Raphael, Janelle Reinalt, Bryan Reynolds, Ramón Rivera-Servera, Janice Ross, Jon Rossini, John Rouse, Kelly Rowett-James, Rebecca Schneider, David Serlin, Shannon Steen, Diana Taylor, Charis Thompson, James Vernon, Frank Wilderson, Linda Williams, Simon Williams, Patricia Ybarra, Harvey Young, and Elana Zilberg have all encountered portions of this text at various stages of its emergence and have been fabulous interlocutors. I am grateful to all of them for their enthusiasm and their feedback, and I beg their forgiveness for any moments when I neglected to follow their careful advice.

Without exception, everyone at Duke University Press has been engaged, attentive, and thorough in helping me maneuver the many transitional stages between manuscript and book, but especially the wonderful Ken Wissoker, Mandy Earley, and Mark Mastromarino. Ken is the ideal editorial interlocutor, and I am endlessly fortunate to have had this opportunity to work with him. He is a shrewd reader, an elegant conversationalist, a meticulous thinker, and a sharp and intuitive listener, the Tim Gunn of academic publishing. Mandy and Mark have been helpful and attentive with every step, and I could not have managed without them. I have also been privileged to enjoy the sharp, witty, and exceptionally generous feedback from Lisa Lowe and Judith Halberstam, who jointly edit the Perverse Modernities series of which this book is a part.

Harry Elam and Peggy Phelan invited me to spend a wonderful year in the Department of Drama at Stanford, which gave me profoundly valuable time to focus. In addition to Stanford's Humanities Center, I have presented portions of my research at the following institutions and organizations: Carleton College, the Leslie Center for the Humanities at Dartmouth, the English Institute at Harvard, the Townsend Center for the Humanities at Berkeley, the Departments of Theatre and Performance Studies at Northwestern, the American Anthropological Association, the American Society for Theater Research, the Association for Theater in Higher Education, the Modern Language Association, the National Communication Association, Performance Studies International, the University of California Multi-Campus Research Group in International Performance and Culture, and the University of California Performance Research Group. I am grateful to my hosts, colleagues, and audiences for their attention and engagement in all of these settings.

I have previously rehearsed several of the arguments staged in this book in the pages of academic journals whose editors, readers, and publishers I would also like to thank. Chapter 1 is a substantial extension and rethinking of my essay "Anorexia Nervosa and the Problem of 'Men,'" published in *Women and Performance* 18, no. 2 (2008); similarly, chapter 2 draws from an early essay on Henry Tanner and Chris Burden, "Trying Ordeal," published in the *Radical History Review* 98 (spring 2007). Chapter 4 was previously published and includes several small revisions here as "To Lie Down to Death for Days" in *Cultural Studies* 18, no. 6 (2004). In the introduction and afterword I have included several sections from a short comment piece published as "On Feeding Tubes" in *TDR* 49, no. 3 (2005); and a short portion of the conclusion was published as "There Will Be No Bobby Sands in Guantánamo Bay" in *PMLA* 124, no. 5 (2009). I wish to acknowledge Taylor and Francis, the MIT Press, and the Modern Language Association for permitting me to reproduce revised and extended portions of this work here.

To strike a more personal chord: I am especially indebted to the many friends and medical specialists who assisted with my own acute experience with mortality in the early years of the twenty-first century. Clinics, hospital rooms, operating theaters, and the dark, noisy interiors of MRI machines were the places where I truly absorbed the personal and political significance of death. I am equally grateful for extended conversations with Chris Berry, Mona Bower, Lisa Cartwright, Giovanna Chesler, Catherine Cole, Reid Davis, Anne Finger, Nadine George-Graves, Nitin Govil, Val Hartouni, Larissa Heinrich, Georgina Kleege, Sam Martin, Joe Nugent, Monica Stufft, Richard and Barbara Tittle, and especially Kaja Silverman, all of whom have helped me to understand (and to endure) that experience in unexpected ways. But my extraordinary mother deserves all of the credit for my survival. She gave up months of her life to be with me when I most needed her; just as significant, she set aside her own need to mourn so that she could bear witness to mine. These are unspeakably selfless gifts from an enormously strong and sensitive person, and I can only hope to live up to her example.

Finally, my most effusive thanks I give — in spirit, if not sentences — to George, Izzy, and Kashew, for helping me build something like *home*.

Patrick Anderson
San Diego, California
August 2009

hunger in the event of subjectivity

•

The nutritive soul, in beings possessing it, while actually single must be potentially plural. . . . There is one function in nutrition which the mouth has the faculty of performing, and a different one appertaining to the stomach. But it is the heart that has supreme control, exercising an additional and completing function.

—Aristotle, *On Youth and Old Age,*
On Life and Death, On Breathing

I see you. I don't see you dying. I see you. I don't see you living. I see you. I don't see you.

— Joseph Chaikin, *The Presence of the Actor*

I begin with the image of a dying man. He lies on an iron-framed bed, a red bandanna tied around his forehead, his friends and family standing nearby, photographs of others like him hung in a grid on the wall behind. He is gazing off slightly to the left of the camera; he looks startled to be at the center of so much attention, as if he has awakened in a place other than where he fell asleep. His emaciation is extreme, and one can see through the sheets draped across his body the gaunt, weakened limbs beneath. He smiles, or nearly smiles, at nothing in particular, or nothing we can see.

The terms that we attribute to this image will depend upon the scene of its enactment—for example, a hospital ward, a gallery space, a prison cell—and upon the colloquy that imbues its composition. But the conditions of the image are clear: this man is starving, and because he starves, he is going to die. Knowing that the man has chosen to starve, actively refusing to satiate a hunger that has become profound beyond description, complicates the way we see him. Is this an image of psychological distress, of performance, of political resistance? What will allow us to distinguish between those three conditions of cultural practice? How will the image change, its meanings becoming more refined, when we are finally able to categorize it? What does it hope to do?

This book is about self-starvation. One of the most recognizable and diagnosable symptoms of what has historically been called nervous disorder, self-starvation has simultaneously been an extremely disturbing and yet alluring cultural practice to behold, an exceptionally compelling demonstration of political argument, an immensely pious mode of religious prostration.[1] As a form of cultural practice unkind to the blind hope that life continue unfettered by the intervention of death, the meaning of self-starvation oscillates wildly between perversity and pleasure, devotion and resistance, hope and despair, love and loss. Indeed in its various articulations and in the many representational forms that attempt to frame, commemorate, or embody it self-starvation works against the drive to wrench these terms into opposition.

More chilling and more compelling, self-starvation works to disrupt what is arguably *the* oppositional pairing underwriting the troubled but relentless project of humanism: what Sigmund Freud evocatively narrates as the move between *fort* and *da* and what we know more colloquially as the conflict between life and death.[2] Pushing the limits of the climactic vanishing point of human possibility, embracing the potential of *disappearance* for the experience of *becoming*, self-starvation represents the most extreme domain of what Michel Foucault called subjectivation and what Martin Heidegger called *Dasein*, through a radical and paradoxical embrace of mortality.[3] Hovering at the very brink of disappearance — we might say, *aimed* at the death of the subject[4] — self-starvation conceptually and methodologically obtains its significance as cultural practice not simply in gesturing toward absence, but in viscerally and affectively summoning us to bear witness to the long, slow wasting away of human flesh.

In this book I explore the political economy of self-starvation in several specific cases, staging a critical intervention around what I am calling the politics of morbidity. Although I begin from the most base definition of self-starvation as an expressive and extended refusal to eat,[5] I do not attempt to engage or explain every practice or category of practices that involves temporary or long-term fasting. Instead I summon into conversation three institutional domains in which self-starvation achieves its most historically pronounced presence: the clinic, the gallery, and the prison. I seek to examine the manner in which self-starvation stages the event of *subjectivation*: the production of political subjectivity in the context of subordination to larger institutional and ideological domains. What does it mean for the clinic, the gallery, and the prison when one performs a refusal to consume as a strategy of negation or resistance? How does self-starvation, as a project of refusal aimed (however unconsciously) at death, produce violence, suffering, disappearance, and loss differently from other practices? What are the meanings of those registers, and against what forces might they be positioned? How is the subject of self-starvation — simultaneously the *object* of self-starvation — refigured in relation to larger institutional and ideological drives? How is that subject refigured in relation to the state?

These questions are at the heart of my writing. In pursuing them I argue that practices of self-starvation perform subjectivation by staging and sustaining the ultimate loss of the subject occasioned by death.[6] Indeed self-starvation reveals death to be at the core of what it means to forge subjectivity in the context of a specific political world. Death and dying *haunt* self-starvation, just as mortality attends the most intimate experience of subjectivity. This latter argument, staged in various articulations across the disciplines, builds on Freud's work on instincts and the death drive and Heidegger's account of *being-toward-death* and coalesces into what I am calling the politics of morbidity:[7] the embodied, interventional embrace of mortality and disappearance not as *destructive*, but as radically *productive* stagings of subject formations in which subjectivity and objecthood, presence and absence, life and death intertwine.

The conceptual starting point for my exploration of these practices is where Louis Althusser, Michel Foucault, and Judith Butler converge in reflecting upon the condition of subjectivity — perhaps an obvious place to begin, but one that bears some explanation. Subjectivation, the term I am using to consider the modes through which self-starvation obtains its most profound political impact, has become the preferred translation for Foucault's *assujettissement*, a concept that folds subordination and agential subjectivity into the very same function. The word *subjectivation* is intended to preserve both aspects of that function, suggesting that subjectivity, classically conceived as a somewhat pure form of human agency, is underpinned by subjugation to more dire forms of institutional and ideological power. In his clearest and most pithy articulation of this argument Foucault reminds us that "there are two meanings of the word *subject*: subject to someone else by control, and tied to his own identity by a conscience or self-knowledge. Both meanings suggest a form of power which subjugates and controls."[8] Resonating deeply with Althusser's notion of interpellation, an iterative "hailing" by which subjects are summoned into belonging to a given structure of state power, Foucault's concept of subjectivation implies that we experience ourselves as subjects insofar as we have been summoned into such a belonging and insofar as we recognize ourselves as such within the context of a given set of institutional power relations.

In a passage strikingly similar to Foucault's, Althusser stages the subject within an unresolved drama of determination that stipulates *freedom* only within the context of subjection:

> In the ordinary use of the term, subject in fact means (1) a free subjectivity, a centre of initiatives, author of and responsible for its actions; (2) a subjected being, who submits to a higher authority, and is therefore stripped of all freedom except that of freely accepting his submission. . . . The individual *is interpellated as a (free) subject . . . in order that he shall (freely) accept his submission*, i.e. in order that he shall make the gestures and actions of his subjection "all by himself." *There are no subjects except by and for their subjection*.[9]

Althusser articulates this argument in what he calls a "little theoretical theatre," a street scene in which a policeman accosts a person with a simple phrase — "Hey, you there!" — whereupon the subject turns (a "mere one-hundred-and-eighty-degree physical conversion") in response.[10] In answering the policeman's call the subject becomes a subject: interpellated by the policeman's hailing, she or he is *subjected* in both senses of the word.

It is critical to note the triply textured condition of this scene. For Althusser interpellation functions through discourse (the linguistic summons), embodiment (the material street, the corporeal turn), and ideology (a *faith* in sociality that invests the policeman with the presence of authority and that compels the subject to turn in response). In other words, Althusser's iterative hailing stages interpellation and performs subjection along the intersecting axes of the discursive, the embodied, and the ideological. Foucault's attention to the modes through which power is produced through everyday disciplinary practices hinges on precisely this point. Especially in the context of his institutional studies (prisons, clinics, etc.), for Foucault the subject is made and remade as discourse, the body, and ideology (in Foucault's vocabulary, "knowledge") converge to facilitate and to provoke power's production.[11]

Here Judith Butler intervenes to explore further the relationship between subjectivity and freedom that Althusser all but forecloses under the sign of ideology. In her highly influential *Gender Trouble*, a book that has had such impact that it is difficult now to consider the question of subjectivity without summoning it into conversation, Butler proposes a model for gendered and sexual subjectivities based on the performative. First proposed by the linguist J. L. Austin in 1955,[12] performativity refutes a Cartesian metaphysics that divides the discursive and the material by demonstrating the social, cultural, and political *force* of language, by tracking the deeply consequential and material effects of language upon various arrangements of subjects into a "social." For instance, in Austin's classic example the institution of marriage is utterly and completely dependent upon the "felicitous" execution of certain speech acts, "I do" and "I now pronounce you . . . ," whose very performance conditions and provokes that which they describe: the union of subjects into a domestic, familial unit. I will not trace or name the many social, cultural, and political effects that obtain once the contract of marriage has been performatively instituted, except to note that they are in fact *many* and to recall that those effects alter and condition the subjectivities of the parties involved in the speech act of the wedding.

For Butler the value of the performative as an analytic lies in its potential to explain further the power of the discursive function in subjectivation: if indeed Althusser's interpellant "Hey, you there!" describes an instance of subjectivation, it functions as such through the performative force of that incantation. Likewise for Butler the *promise* of the performative is in the potential for agential presence within the speech act. That is, the performativity of Althusser's scene depends not only upon the policeman's call, but also upon the passing subject's response: it is in this moment of turning, this "one-hundred-and-eighty-degree physical conversion," that the performative effect of subjectivity obtains. But Butler cautions, "The source of personal and political agency comes not from within the individual, but in and through the complex cultural exchanges among bodies in which identity itself is ever-shifting, indeed, where identity itself is constructed, disintegrated, and recirculated only within the context of a dynamic field of cultural relations."[13]

In *Gender Trouble* performativity emerges as a compelling model for the production of gendered and sexual subjectivities. "Genders can be neither true nor false," Butler writes, "but are only produced as the truth effects of a discourse of primary and stable identity."[14] Lest this argument be misconstrued, around, say, a confusion between theatricality and performativity,[15] to suggest that gender mimics theater (a set of staged practices in which subjects take on gender roles much as actors put on costumes), Butler begins her next book, *Bodies That Matter*, by clarifying the terms of her argument and by reclaiming its stakes. Gender is not a "taking on of masks" but "that reiterative power of discourse to produce the phenomena that it regulates and constrains." She reminds us again of the "paradox of subjectivation," rephrasing Althusser and Foucault to emphasize the centrality of the *normative* in the subject's emergence: "The subject who would resist [ideological] norms is itself enabled, if not produced, by such norms."[16]

It is important to recall that for Butler discourse never bears a wholly oppositional relationship to the materiality of, for example, the body. Insofar as discourse can be said to produce the matter it simultaneously names, delineating between this matter and that, and thus creating the demarcations that make meaning legible, the matter of bodies is neither fully limited by nor fully subsumed within the domain of discourse. *Bodies That Matter* thus takes up the question of *mattering* — precisely, that is, the question of value, and how it comes to be attributed to some bodies but not others. The "power" that "produces and constrains" does not treat all subjects the same, and here the question of subjectivation becomes a distinctly political problem.

In *The Psychic Life of Power* Butler foregrounds the politics of subjectivation yet further, in terms of the psychic processes — here we find a return to the consciousness to which Althusser and Foucault gesture — by which political subjects come to incorporate a desire *for* the very subjectivation that constrains, and paradoxically comes to *mean*, freedom. In a haunting articulation of this argument that dramatically restages Althusser's street scene Butler writes:

> Power that at first appears external, pressed upon the subject, pressing the subject into subordination, assumes a psychic form that constitutes the subject's self-identity. The form this power takes is relentlessly marked by a figure of turning, a turning back upon oneself or even a turning *on* oneself. . . . The turn appears to function as a tropological inauguration of the subject.[17]

In a bold move that, much like the subject on Althusser's street, pivots on a turn, Butler reminds us that subjectivation involves a psychic shift, an incorporation of the call to power that comes to shape what Foucault and Althusser both describe as the consciousness of the subject. That is, the subject on the street, summoned into the social exchange of interpellation, does not merely *acknowledge* that she or he is the *referent* of the call; she or he comes to *recognize herself or himself* through the currency of the call and response. To put this a different way, subjectivation emerges as the very condition of referentiality.[18] The law of power "is not literally internalized, but *incorporated*, with the consequences that bodies are produced which *signify* that law on and through the body; there the law is manifest as the essence of their selves, the *meaning* of their soul, their conscience, the law of their desire."[19] I will return in a moment to the deployment of psychoanalysis in considering the politics of subjectivation. But first I would like to dwell upon the question of referentiality and its relationship to subjectivation by turning to another scene on another street.

Bertolt Brecht's essay "The Street Scene" (1938) proposes a model for epic theater, a technique for staging theatrical narratives aimed at producing "a socially practical significance" for audiences and artists, by describing an encounter at the site of

> an eyewitness describing to a collection of people how a traffic accident took place. The bystanders may not have observed what happened, or they may simply not agree with him, may "see things a different way"; the point is that the demonstrator acts the behaviour of driver or victim or both in such a way that the bystanders are able to form an opinion about the accident.

In performing the accident as she or he witnessed it, gesturing to show the location of events, portraying the parties involved, the "demonstrator" converts the accident into a representational form and bestows upon the onlookers accountability for determining its value. That is, in performing the scene of the accident, the demonstrator *becomes* the representation and the onlookers are compelled to bear witness to the demonstrator's referential power to name, define, and assess the accident "as it occurred." Crucial to this "theatre for a scientific age" is the technology of representation: the demonstrator's portrayal. What defines Brecht's model for representation is its referential relationship to the event of the accident. The demonstration must not cast itself too acutely or too broadly as "the engendering of illusion"; Brecht clearly and succinctly stipulates that "the street-corner demonstrator admits it is a demonstration (and does not pretend to be the actual event)."[20]

At issue in Brecht's model for the epic theater is precisely the status of representation — in particular, performed representation — and its relationship to referentiality. What Brecht proposes in his model is a loosening of faith in the ideology of the reference, or more strongly put, a demonstrative, documentary form in which representation itself becomes *both an intervention and an undoing*. The demonstrator in Brecht's scene reveals the technology of representation — his own portrayal, his performance — and in so doing invests it with agential presence. In short, Brecht's demonstrator *bears witness* both to the accident he aims to represent and to an action of representing that will stir the onlookers to action, clearing space for "a socially practical significance." What is *undone* in Brecht's epic demonstration, seen in the broader context of theater history, is the tight signification that goes under the broad epistemological name of realism. Divorced from the demands of strict referentiality and resonating with Austin's "I do" the demonstration becomes performative: "We are *doing* something . . . rather than *reporting* something."[21]

Brecht's story of the street scene and its demonstration recalls the scene of recognition described in Althusser's account of the policeman's hail and the subject's response. Central to the experience of subjectivation, though this experience is typically an unconscious one, is a moment of *recognition*: the subject identifies herself or himself with the policeman's call and so turns to respond, "Yes, me." Althusser links this turn to the "Subject *par excellence*" of ideology, what I will cautiously call the Subject-ideal. It is from and on behalf of this Subject-ideal that subjectivation proceeds, and it is through the attachment to this Subject-ideal that subjectivation obtains. Subjectivation thus involves a convergence of recognition and aspiration and depends upon faith in referentiality, binding and bound: "*a subject through the Subject and subjected to the Subject*."[22]

I gesture to Brecht's street scene first to suggest that Althusser, Foucault, and Butler are similarly involved in a kind of witnessing to subjectivation itself, and second to suggest that the practices of self-starvation explored in this book stage similar modes of undoing and intervention. Even as these practices involve performances that *subject* their practitioners (in both senses of the word), they also bear witness to the function of subjectivation described by Althusser, Foucault, and Butler. Subjectivation thus marks and eventuates a crisis in referentiality, in part through what Butler calls the "citationality" necessarily at work in the performative, and in part through the production of the subject recognizable and indeed demonstrable as such, even as it is exceedingly referential. In his haunting description of yet another scene on yet another street, Frantz Fanon highlights the political resonance of this productive, potentially violent undoing:

> Sealed into that crushing objecthood, I turned beseechingly to others. Their attention was a liberation, running over my body suddenly abraded into nonbeing, endowing me once more with an agility that I had thought lost, and by taking me out of the world, restoring me to it. But just as I reached the other side, I stumbled, and the movements, the attitudes, the glances of the other fixed me there, in the sense in which a chemical solution is fixed by a dye. I was indignant; I demanded an explanation. Nothing happened. I burst apart. Now the fragments have been put together by another self.[23]

In the context of these tracings of the subject, what, and how, does self-starvation *mean*? And what, and how, does self-starvation *matter*? The "turning back" or "turning *on*" oneself marked by Butler as a key function of subjectivation is psychically and somatically epitomized by practices of self-starvation, which reflect an eminent moment of agential presence even as they conceptually and symptomatically eventuate the death of the subject. The manner in which self-starvation performs subjectivation begins from the basics of the practice itself: a structured and sustained refusal to rehearse and perform normative eating, resulting in emaciation (among other physical effects) and, in the end, death. The meaning of self-starvation extends from the surface of the body inward to organs that begin to consume themselves before finally shutting down entirely, and outward into a given space that was the context for the commencement of the fast and that is the staging ground for continuing negotiations of the fast's social, aesthetic, and political impact. The surface of the body takes on resilient significance as the inside it protects begins literally to decompose. But that shrinking surface also becomes the icon of devout resistance emblazoned on or sutured to the outside in which it is produced. This book thus concerns a *loss* of bodily integrity, but a particular kind of loss out of which a powerful form of political subjectivity is produced and embodied, and *resistance* to an outside force, but a particular kind of resistance that imagines the death of the subject as its potential final effect. In a blazing articulation of indelible presence the self-starving body marks and maps the complicated, contradictory *presence* of subjectivation, a presence defined by the discursive, the embodied, and the ideological, a presence defined by the fact of its gradual, relentless fade.

The surface of the self-starving body fully takes on the paradoxical significance suggested in the pairing *loss/resistance*, for as it literally shrinks into oblivion it becomes larger and larger in the vernacular of its political effects. There is no slack in this paradox. The tautness of the starving body's significance is a direct result of the sustained performance of violence by and upon the body; that violence both restages the effects of institutional and ideological power and reverses the production of those powers at the hand of the faster herself or himself. Playing perilously with the binaries subject/object and active/passive, self-starvation produces political subjects who attain positions of such demonstrative power precisely because they seize these techniques of bodily violence and hover treacherously on the brink of self-destruction. The meaning of self-starvation, and the force of its effects, rests on the rearticulation of what is conventionally the *object* of bodily violence as both subject and object.

In the words of Allen Feldman, self-starvation "fus[es] the subject and object of violent enactment into a single body."[24] In each of the cases I explore in this book that fusion results in a production of subjectivity that both reproduces and refuses the power of the state. But to be clear: what I am calling the state is not a single centralized force, power, institution, ideological construct, order of discipline or restraint, law, legal text, elected official or vicious demagogue, moment of injury, genealogy of violence, image of ideal citizenship, family unit, skyscraper, map, currency, economic system, economic theorist, prison, or cop. I imagine the state instead to be an assemblage of forces and drives, techniques and tactics, often organized as violence, performed in discrete sites and scenes typically organized as a national location. The state reproduces itself by enabling the production of political subjects and reinvents itself by describing and defining those subjects according to a dogma of rights that in turn reflects an impression of (and solicits faith in) values such as freedom, security, and property. On one hand the state is highly regimented, always in the process of refining its techniques and apparatuses of domination; on the other hand the state is extremely diffuse, unable to be named with any precision except in terms of its moment-by-moment production. The state is thus *retroactively* recognized as such, often as a sort of ghost form, invisible agent, man behind the curtain who both was and was not there. It operates through this set of contradictions but appears as a unified force; indeed *appearing unified* as a single stage, structure, or system that can be resisted, attacked, or overthrown is the state's most insidious function. It can thereby respond to any threat with the ultimate bait-and-switch, appearing here as a policy that can be amended or nullified, there as a prison warden with a well-worn truncheon, there again as a schoolroom history textbook whose pages go by the name *amnesia*. It is both all of these things and not exactly any of them.

The state as I am defining it is also specifically a nationalist project, requiring the creation and maintenance of geographical borders, civic works, legal systems, rites of citizenship, disciplinary institutions, and ideological codes. These requirements represent the continuous production of designated insides and outsides, rules of identification and abjection, practices that define belonging and enforce exclusion. It is specifically through the production of political subjects that the state is able to maintain any integrity whatsoever. For the purposes of this project I imagine the subject to be not the embodiment of a psyche, not a single and discrete unit of any given social, not a particular arrangement of bodily surfaces, organs, and functions, but the point of engagement between the three, a production resulting from the interface between psyche, social, and soma. It should be apparent that my working definitions for the state and the subject are intimately imbricated and mutually constitutive. They produce and are produced by one another; they cannot do without one another; they are kin.

These definitions clearly facilitate my use of the theory of subjectivation. They also suggest that statehood and subjectivity are continuously active as agents of representation: fashioning meaning out of signs and symbols; mediating natural objects and experiences through various abstract and material figurative forms; performatively becoming themselves through reflection, portrayal, reproduction. Representation, in other words, is as much the condition as a symptom of the production of political subjectivity. Self-starvation plays an unusual role in this representational realm: both ontologically and as representation, self-starvation "becomes itself through disappearance."[25] This phrase, borrowed from Peggy Phelan's account of the ontology of performance, both gestures to the durational nature of self-starvation as a cultural practice requiring constant rearticulation of the refusal to eat and reveals self-starvation as a form whose central meaning derives from the disappearance, the death, fantasized and eventuated by its persistent denial of sustenance. In other words, self-starvation becomes itself most fully, and becomes meaningful in the logic of its own image most vividly, at the moment of death of the anorectic or faster or hunger striker. Every representation of self-starvation points forward to the inevitable outcome of a sustained refusal to eat. Every use of self-starvation as a symbol and enactment of resistance, negation, or refusal carries with it the threat or promise of death; death is both the reason and the limit for whatever powers self-starvation may claim as action, idea, or sign. This again is the paradox of self-starvation — and the paradox of subjectivation: death is at the center of self-starvation's capacity to forge a subject whose existence is endangered by the very practice through which she or he produces power.

Earlier I summoned Butler's work on subjectivation to assist in outlining my use of that term. I ended that brief discussion with a citation from *The Psychic Life of Power* making the following claim: "Power that at first appears external . . . assumes a psychic form that constitutes the subject's self-identity." The psychic incorporation of a force that both enables and constrains the subject may go by several names from the linguistic catalogue of psychoanalysis; we may recognize this incorporated force as what Freud called repression, or the preconscious, or in later topographies the superego. If we were brave we might even call that force, or at the very least suspect its psychic effects on, the libido. Much of Kaja Silverman's groundbreaking work has built upon her suggestion that the subject is produced, reflected, and sustained by what she calls "libidinal politics," a more generative and expansive model for considering the vicissitudes of gender and sexual identification. In *Male Subjectivity at the Margins* Silverman invests normative male subjectivity in particular with a profoundly traumatic power to define the experience of subjectivity and its harrowing, often deadly misses for subjects who find themselves in flagrant disabuse of that experiential normalcy, not simply for those who anatomically or otherwise find themselves approximated as male, but for the full stretch of the deeply divisive and variegated range of gender and sexual identifications.

In Silverman's work masculinity and male subjectivity emerge not as dependably stable categories of cultural experience, though they derive much of their power from pretending that they do, but as flawed, often violent projects of ideological and bodily constraint.[26] The very notion of stable male subjectivity (or for that matter, unimpeachable masculinity) is what Silverman calls a "dominant fiction" of normalcy, suturing individuals, as gendered subjects, to a common faith in the durability and desirability of healthy heterosexual male subjectivity and desire. Her explicit aim in this argument is to develop a psychoanalytic theory of ideology, "libidinal politics," through Jacques Lacan's symbolic order and more precisely through the immense range of representations reflected back to the desiring subject in "the mirror [a subject] looks into for recognition."[27] In this logic male subjectivity is deployed psychically, symbolically, and socially as the central ideological stake to which representations of our own subject formations are tethered.

Tracing her notion of ideology back to Althusser's interpellation and in concert with Butler's use of subjectivation, Silverman contends that subjects are not simply "grafted" onto psychic formations that precede them, but participate in the continual production of an interpellant matrix wherein subjectivity, ideology, and the state itself are perpetually being constituted. The "Hey, you there!" narrativized by Althusser in his account of interpellation, a summoning that occasions a scene of recognition and so writes the subject into the story of the state, can take many forms: acoustic, as a voice that fixes the subject within a discursive structure of language; visual, as an image through which the subject sees herself or himself (or not); tactile, as a seduction into a specifically organized structure of intersubjective embodiment; and others. Althusser called the vast range of such hailings "rituals."[28] The subject is literally surrounded by (and constantly summoned into) such rituals, and the ease with which she or he can respond with a "Yes, me" defines the quality, the very possibility of her or his relationship to what persists as ideological normativity.

Of course for the vast majority of subjects, answering "Yes, me" to every single instance of interpellant hailing (or even most of those that assail us on a daily basis) is impossible, or underscored by disavowal, or cast as a hollow, unattainable dream. This is another way of saying that ideology disbelieves in difference and that the casualty of that disbelief is the subject herself or himself, or more precisely the subject's hope for or faith in any pure form of agential presence. This is the paradox that initiates and defines Foucault's *assujettissement*. In order to participate in what we know as the social, and in so doing to become good subjects,[29] we must resolve to respond to Althusser's iterative hailings as often as possible in the affirmative — "Yes, me"; "Yes, me"; "Yes, me" — and swallow whatever grievance or guilt may arise from knowing that "Yes" often to be, if not exactly a total lie, at the very least a fabrication, at the very *most* a hopeful gesture toward a *we*.

That swallowing, Butler teaches us, is so central to the production of subjectivity that it takes a psychic form, which is to say it becomes an unconscious part of our everyday performance, an alienation, an event only *just* approximated by what Freud called repression. Freud recognized — more strongly put, his entire corpus of work is built upon the recognition — that repression is central to the development of personhood (in all its troubled, neurotic glory). It is on this point that we find a subtle intersection between two potentially incommensurate languages: philosophy and psychoanalysis. For Foucault subjugation enables subjectivity; for Freud repression initiates psychic development. Indeed the ease with which I have thus far moved between the words *psyche* and *subject* implies a correlation where one has not conventionally been assumed, an implication that obviously underwrites my definition of the subject as the interface between psyche, social, and soma, but that also bears some explanation. On this point I turn to two more representatives from the discursive frames of philosophy and psychoanalysis: Martin Heidegger and Jacques Lacan, respectively.

If I seem to be painting a forlorn portrait of the subject, then turning to Heidegger may make the picture seem yet bleaker. But alas, it is here that Heidegger's work on Dasein intervenes as an insistent call to reconsider the experience of being and its relationship to finitude, the ultimate extension of our paradox to the precipice of human possibility. For Heidegger, being, what he calls Dasein, is for most polluted by a continual alignment with the *they*: a rough equivalent of Althusser's ideology, but characterized by Heidegger as a homogeneous bloc of other subjects with whom we are expected to identify, into whom we are meant to accede, and through whom we are compelled to recognize ourselves. True Dasein emerges for Heidegger in what he finally calls *being-toward-death*.

In *Being and Time* Heidegger introduces Dasein as the meaning of existence, the "average everydayness" of our lives. He explores the "totality" of Dasein, its fullest and most intense articulation, as *care*, the manner in which others — other objects, other creatures, other people — come to matter to us and invite us to matter to them. "Authentic" Dasein, which we may reductively summarize as a life lived in full, depends upon death. That is, for Heidegger death does not merely define the *end* of one's life, that moment when one ceases to be; death paradoxically comes to *mean* life, and life becomes meaningful within the context of dying.

Death is defined not as a moment of ceasing to be — not, that is, as an event that will occur sometime in the future — but as the "possibility of the impossibility of Dasein," an imminence. However:

Many things can be imminent for *Dasein* as *being-in-the-world*. The character of imminence is not in itself distinctive for death. . . . A thunderstorm can be imminent, remodeling a house, the arrival of a friend. . . . Imminent death does not have this kind of being. But a journey, for example, can also be imminent for *Dasein*, or a discussion with others, or a renouncing something which *Dasein* itself can be — its own possibilities-of-being which are founded in being-with others. Death is a *possibility of being* that *Dasein* always has to take upon itself. With death, *Dasein* stands before itself in its ownmost potentiality-of-being. . . . It is *an eminent* imminence.[30]

As a "possibility of being" that defines Dasein's "ownmost potentiality-of-being," however, death as a phenomenon escapes the "everydayness" of Dasein; it is not comprehensible within the consciousness of the everyday. Just as death is essentially private — when it happens, it happens to us alone — it is not and perhaps cannot be understood as such. It "happens to other people," and we know it only when we see it as a "case of death":

Someone or another "dies," be it a neighbor or a stranger. People unknown to us "die" daily and hourly. "Death" is encountered as a familiar event occurring within the world. As such, it remains in the inconspicuousness characteristic of everyday encounters. . . . The fleeting talk about this which is either expressed or else mostly kept back says: "One also dies at the end, but for now one is not involved."[31]

The *they* here represents not just a collective but a rabid seizure of Dasein, a consumption of the *I* that refuses to disclose the possibility of death and its hold on any personal significance whatsoever. The *they* convinces us that "one dies," but not us, not here, not now. Death becomes subsumed in and by the *they*, absorbed into its own "potentiality-of-being," meaningful in the context of "being-with-others," but "not yet objectively present for oneself."[32]

Being-toward-death orients us to the possibility of death not just as that which will, in Silverman's words, "have the last word in determining who we will have been," but also as that which will individuate us from the *they* and will thus literally make us ourselves. In orienting ourselves to this possibility, not living in fear of the event of death but coming to terms with the freedom from the *they* that it will occasion, we become conscious of our situation within the *they*. Being-toward-death includes embracing the constraints of the *they* by incorporating the phenomenon of death into the meaning we make of our lives. Silverman continues, "By embracing our limits, we participate in the determination of what we will have been, and thereby transform them into a kind of agency."[33]

Being-toward-death is thus a form of care — care for the self, ironically, but also care for the world into which we have been thrown. For Heidegger being-toward-death individuates us by "silencing the empty speech through which the 'they' manifests itself," and in so doing allows us to realize not only our own "potentiality-of-being" — in a word, the *value* of our own lives — but also to register and act upon our "responsibility for, or indebtedness to, other creatures and things."[34] Being-toward-death individuates us by allowing us to see how important others are to us, how dependent we are on them and they on us, and finally how enormous our capacity to care for others can be. In individuating us being-toward-death does not exonerate us from the situation of our lives or from those who are in the world with us. Here again, individuation comes to mean both a detachment from the "empty speech" of *they* and a reorientation to the potential we have to care for ourselves and to care for others. In Heidegger's astonishing words, "Dying is grounded in care."[35]

The cases I explore in this book represent both a particular practice of being-toward-death, though not necessarily in the fullness of its Heideggerian inflection, that similarly grounds them in care. The individuation that extends from these practices corresponds to subjectivation: it is an individuation that is characterized not by simple isolation, but by grounding in a radically altered *being-in-the-world*. In each of these cases self-starvation is typically received by its audiences not simply as oppositional to the very notion of care, but as a perverse practice met with institutionally sanctioned forms of treatment — heavy monitoring, psychological counseling, force-feeding — presented and defended as their own forms of care. These institutional responses are care of a different sort, at times grounded in sincere (and often urgent) attempts to alleviate suffering and prevent an imminent demise, at other times grounded in the expectation that subjects and their bodies will conform to a naturalized "thrown-ness," a being-in-the-world that is consumed with its unseeing associations with *they*. Identification in this form of care is radically uncaring, unsympathetic, and ultimately undone by those practices that seize upon its failing imperial drive to master difference and practice abjection through the rhetoric of humanity.

As I discussed earlier, in Foucault's logic subjectivation describes the manner in which we come to experience ourselves as subjects, defined by our free will, in the context of such ideological and institutional powers that regulate and constrain us. I might also call the process of becoming a subject, never fully preempted by the power of the state but never fully complete in spite of it either, performative, dependent upon the citation of recognizable structures of meaning, but effective in producing the moment-by-moment sense of agency that we experience as individuality. That is, the subjectivation that Foucault works to complicate in his historical studies of ideological domination and claims to resistance is emblematic of performativity.

Performativity also describes what Lacan marked as the "death of the real" initiated by the accession of language. To put it simply, Lacan claimed that the act of naming is simultaneously an act of killing: the transformation of an object, say, into a word, or of an affect into a phrase. But this is in effect a mercy killing, for as the real evaporates from its phenomenological fullness in the process of being given a name it also enters the domain of language, where it can be summoned and sent forth in the context of a given social scene. Language, Lacan says, makes the real "impossible" as such but simultaneously *produces* the real as an accessible field: it is a "presence made of absence"; it "creates the world of things . . . by giving its concrete being to their essence." But this function too condemns the real to meaning attributed by its transaction: the "signifier *enters* the signified and . . . anticipates meaning by unfolding its dimensions before it."[36]

Such "unfolding" is especially complicated in the naming and the experience of hunger. Hunger itself is produced from a void, the empty stomach, and initiates a series of somatic complaints, growls and hunger pangs, that in turn call for action, the action of eating. In Enzo Cozzi's words:

Hunger is the pressing presence to an organism of the absence of sustenance. . . . The very first graphism for "hunger" is the incongruous letter "H," the alphabet's mark for absence, a consonant that has lost its sound, or a vowel yet to be formed, and in any case the presentation of a void. It indicates pure hissing and gasping, breath uncontaminated by sound. It means pre-linguistic air that has known the lungs but has had no communion with vocal chords. It is either the sign for voicelessness or a substitute for it, a decoy at the fringes of verbality, simulated speech.[37]

In Cozzi's formulation the act of naming hunger is itself a performance: a graphic embodiment of the intense longing that precedes language, the most bodily experience of need, the superlative primal instinct. Naming hunger fails to satisfy its insistent call and serves only to move its meaning from the pit of the stomach to the tip of the tongue.

Real hunger may appear as that which can only ever be approximated by physical craving: a hole in the stomach, the absence of that satisfying warmth that suffuses the digestive tract when the craving is filled with food. Real hunger can perhaps be heard in growls, screams that come in fits and starts, hunger pangs. It includes, but can only be summarized by, visceral desire locatable in a void: the empty stomach. It ceases to be real as soon as it is uttered as such, and at this point enters the domain of the symbolic. Within the symbolic hunger becomes infused with meaning. This meaning is displaced from the real that initiates it; as we articulate hunger's symbolic significance we detach ourselves from real hunger, re-situating ourselves before a sign that can only be theorized as such. Imaginary hunger — that is, the dispatch of the reality of hunger yet beyond its symbolic reflection — might then be mapped as and into both fantasy and the unconscious. Imaginary hunger constructs and is enlivened by a hunger-ideal and thus hunger at its most extreme: the extension of an anorexic state of affairs, the projection of those final few moments before starvation yields to death, the satisfaction of hunger through cannibalism or, worse, Erisycthon's consumption of his own starving flesh.

My fragile divisions are structured in concert with Lacan's distinctions between the domains of the real, the symbolic, and the imaginary. I suggest this formulation for three reasons: first, to foreground questions of representation as productive rather than merely reflective of subject formation; second, to recall Freud's development of a theory of instincts through the model of hunger; and third, to situate the absence of sustenance at the heart of that inscription. To put the last of these intentions into a more supple incantation: hunger depends upon its potential refusal. If there were no inanition, no threat or promise of anorexic effects, there would be no need to name hunger itself. Hunger adheres to an always present anorexia lingering in the shadows or at the lamp of its spotlight; hunger calls because anorexia persists.[38]

I have journeyed a long way from the image with which I began this introduction. In those opening moments I asked of that picture of an emaciated man lying down, surrounded by the photographs and bodies of family and friends, Is this an image of psychological distress, of performance, of political resistance? What will allow us to distinguish between those three conditions of cultural experience? I have since proposed a model for the politics of morbidity, a model in which the subject and the state are entwined as coproductive, in which the specters of death and dying underwrite our most intimate experience of subjectivity, and in which mortality itself becomes a powerful mode of producing the very subjectivity whose final demise it will also eventuate. Morbidity, as distinct from mortality, connotes an enduring state of decline and is "characterized by excessive gloom or apprehension, or by an unhealthy preoccupation with disease, death, or other disturbing subject; given to unwholesome brooding."[39] Morbidity is thus marked both by dying *and* by a preoccupation with dying. To cast this more evocatively: morbidity is consciousness of the profoundly affective significance of one's own mortality, a reflection of Heidegger's being-toward-death in terms of its most political possibilities.[40]

Reading further down the OED's characteristically exhaustive list of possible definitions for morbidity, we eventually find a surprising reference to the domain of art production: "of a flesh tint; painted with morbidezza." Dutifully following that last word to its own entry we find "lifelike delicacy in flesh tints" and, surprisingly, "delicacy, softness, especially in musical performance; sensibility, smoothness. Also occasionally with negative connotation: unwholesomeness, effeminacy, sickliness." Of course any reference to "flesh tints" gives us pause, given the historical tendency of that phrase to connote the broad, expansive range of structural, representational, and political inequalities commonly mapped under the rubric of white privilege.[41] Our interest is similarly piqued by the correlation of "unwholesomeness, effeminacy, sickliness" and death, a lethal cocktail of associations with a similarly long cultural genealogy.

Those readers familiar with the relatively young canon of performance studies will no doubt recall a discussion similar to this in Eve Sedgwick's and Andrew Parker's introduction to *Performativity and Performance*. In that essay Sedgwick and Parker rediscover the word *etiolated* in Austin's *How to Do Things with Words*, the father (or superego) of all texts on performativity. Tracing the meaning of this obscure word not to the OED but to their more populist Merriam-Webster they find a strikingly similar set of connotations and so contend that "the performative has thus been from its inception already infected with queerness."[42]

For Sedgwick and Parker the correlation of queerness and performativity leads to a compelling discussion of the U.S. military's "Don't Ask, Don't Tell" policy forbidding lesbians and gay men from serving in the armed forces. For the purposes of my argument I take this denotational aside as a reminder of the close affinity of sexuality, especially nonnormative sexual practices and identities, with death in public consciousness of the modern era. But I also signal a final turn in this introduction: to trace a connection between sexuality and *hunger* proposed explicitly in much of Freud's work on the instinct. In the opening lines of *Three Essays on the Theory of Sexuality* Freud asserts a metaphorical and metonymical relationship between sexuality and hunger: "The fact of the existence of sexual needs in human beings and animals is expressed in biology by the assumption of a 'sexual instinct,' on the analogy of the instinct of nutrition, that is of hunger. Everyday language possesses no counterpart to the word 'hunger,' but science makes use of the word 'libido' for that purpose."[43] Much of this early work on the instinct would later be revised by Freud in "Instincts and Their Vicissitudes" and especially *Beyond the Pleasure Principle* to stress the importance for the subject of what he would eventually call the "love-instinct" and finally the "death drive." Not only does Freud situate hunger as, to use Jean Laplanche's word, a "paradigm" for the instinct,[44] but he also eulogizes the refusal to satisfy hunger as an originary moment of psychic development. In *Life and Death in Psychoanalysis* Laplanche suggests that for Freud the primal scene of eating, when Mommy and Daddy offer spoons of food to the child, initiates the role of the social in subjective development: the satisfaction of instinctual need, "whose paradigm is hunger," becomes psychically manifest as intersubjective.[45] The refusal of those spoons, a moment of "turning away" (coinciding with Butler's "turning *on*"), emerges as central both to the development of psychic subjectivity and to the radical rearrangement of its given social context. Indeed Laplanche's derivation of hunger relies on anorexia as a founding concept and posits all nonanorexic ("normal") eating as essentially neurotic. Following Laplanche I hesitantly substitute the word *anorexia* for *self-starvation* for the duration of this brief discussion.

I propose that hunger, and spectrally anorexia, is central to Laplanche's argument and to Freud's thought on the development of sexuality, which, in the language of psychoanalysis, corresponds with the event of subjectivity. Anorexia initially appears in Laplanche's argument that sexuality can be "secreted" by *all* vital processes. This implies, in the time of subject formation, a stage prior to autoeroticism, a stage marked by a "coherent vital order" wherein needs are organized succinctly into a constellation of instincts that seek satisfaction in nourishment. It is in the insufficiency of the vital drive, that is, in the inability of the vital drive to find that originary lost object of subsistence, what Laplanche calls "that milk," that sexuality "breaks out . . . infest[ing] and sustain[ing]" the vital order itself, and thus the child herself or himself.⁴⁶ Laplanche imagines what appears to be an originary anorexia, a refusal to eat based on the incommensurability of a presently proffered nutritional object with the lost object passionately desired by the child. In this example, a story told around "a spoon for Mommy, a spoon for Daddy" being offered when the child will not otherwise eat, the solicitation of Mommy's and Daddy's love (which Laplanche pithily equates with sexuality) both invades the practice of eating and reverses that initial refusal, blocking its search for satisfaction.⁴⁷ That is, in equating Mommy's love with the spoonful of undesired (because not "that milk") but much-needed food, this specifically socialized love demands the satisfaction of hunger, and in so doing sexualizes the *scene* of hunger.

I mean to mark how anorexia is situated as fundamental to sexuality's sustenance of the vital order, the impetus, as it were, for the swerve to the sexual drive. Laplanche's little story posits the response to the vital order's insufficiency as a refusal to eat at all, which then is reversed only when sexuality introduces itself as the parental scene of spoons and love. According to this formulation, sexuality sustains the vital drive precisely by reversing its refusal, and sexuality becomes linked to the vital through the negation of that reversal—that is, through the suddenly always present possibility that anorexia will intervene and through sexuality's fragile power to defend the vital drive from anorexia's invasion.

Further Laplanche argues that the impossibility of refinding the original lost object of nourishment translates into the *unpleasure* of anything that is *not* "that milk." The implication is that all eating is experienced by the unconscious as unpleasurable and unsatisfactory precisely because it can never again live up to that first experience of sated warmth. Sexuality mitigates this unpleasure by facilitating the substitution of the many erotically charged persons and objects that constellate the space of a psychic life for the unrecoverable originary object of satisfaction. But the unpleasure experienced in eating persists, if in a diminished form. Freud's famous line "The finding of an object is in fact a re-finding of it" implicitly places the original lost object, as well as our repressed desire for it, in the domain of the unconscious.⁴⁸ Eating anything *not* "that milk" is thus represented as a source of unpleasure for the unconscious, which relentlessly strives for the satisfaction found only in the object relentlessly lost.

From what medical and other accounts tell us, those who starve themselves find some pleasure in their refusal to eat and unpleasure in being forced to eat; those of us who refuse to refuse food tend to find conscious pleasure in eating. If, as Freud through Laplanche suggests, eating anything other than "that milk" is experienced by the unconscious as unpleasure, then we arrive at the following formulation:

Anorexia: Conscious unpleasure in eating = Unconscious unpleasure in eating

Eating: Conscious pleasure in eating = Unconscious unpleasure in eating

To narrativize this little equation: Freud suggests that eating anything other than "that milk" is experienced unconsciously as displeasure; in anorexia this displeasure is matched by the conscious discomfort experienced when eating. In the best kind of normative eating we experience nutritive satisfaction pleasurably. In its converse form, this equation becomes:

Anorexia: Conscious pleasure in not eating = Unconscious pleasure in not eating not-that-milk

Eating: Conscious unpleasure in not eating = Unconscious pleasure in not eating not-that-milk

This recalls Freud's own suggestion that neurosis is "the negative of perversion":[49]

Perversion: Conscious pleasure = Unconscious pleasure

Neurosis: Conscious unpleasure = Unconscious pleasure

Aligning these equations results in an unexpected conclusion: if anorexia can be called perverse, then all eating can, by the same logic, be called neurotic.

I have obviously departed from the domain of real hunger, and in so doing have begun to chart hunger's inflection in the domains of the symbolic and the imaginary. I do so to recommend revisions in thinking about how and why self-starvation aligns itself as a kind of disease, a rupture in the vital order, whether psychological, behavioral, or somatic. Such conceptions (for example, anorexia nervosa as disorder, staged fasting as masochistic, hunger strikes as terrorism) imply that these practices are grotesque disruptions of normalcy, intrusions upon health, evidence of a dramatically disorganized sense of self. I advance a contrary argument in the cases that follow. The proliferation of cultural meanings attributed to the practices explored in each of my chapters, the many ways in which those who starve themselves are understood and represented, speaks more to the practical and formal power of self-starvation than to any psychological, behavioral, or somatic anemia in those who perform it.

With these premises underwriting my theoretical orientation I embark upon a vigorous exploration of the *disappearance* foundational to live performance as proposed by Herbert Blau and Peggy Phelan and as reconsidered by Rebecca Schneider and Diana Taylor.[50] I propose, differently within each case study, that practices of self-starvation demonstrate how disappearance *articulates* (in both senses of that word) the ontology of performance and the ontology of subjectivity precisely through the experience of the live. To return to the discussion in the opening pages of this introduction: these practices obtain such profound aesthetic, social, and political significance by summoning us to bear witness to disappearance as a *productive* rather than *destructive* force in staging the venue of subjectivity. These practices occupy the harrowing and resplendently mortal interstices of perversity and pleasure, devotion and resistance, hope and despair, love and loss; as such they materialize the troubled event of subjectivation as theorized by Foucault, Althusser, and Butler.

So Much Wasted consists of four chapters followed by an afterword. These chapters are not organized genealogically or taxonomically, but rather reflect the practice of self-starvation in three domains—the clinic, the gallery, and the prison—of key significance for what I have marked as the ideological and institutional production of the state. In highlighting these three domains I am obviously relying upon Althusser's demarcation of "ideological state apparatuses"—"Ideologies [are] *realized* in institutions, in their rituals and their practices"—while broadening his focus on "class antagonisms" to other registers of difference.[51] I mark the rituals and practices described by Althusser as *performances*, highlighting their embodied, durational, spectatorial, and intersubjective qualities. I further trace the consequence of these practices simultaneously through the aesthetic, the social, and the political; indeed I propose that these stagings of self-starvation demonstrate the profound imbrication of those three registers of cultural practice.

But in all of the chapters that follow the *demarcations between* the clinic, the gallery, and the prison flicker in and out of focus as discourses indigenous to each of these domains cross-reference one another, feeding and increasing the cultural impact of self-starvation in its wide variety of forms. A subsidiary purpose of this book is to demonstrate that self-starvation is replete with representational currency across institutional divisions and to argue that self-starvation obtains its cultural significance in part from its legibility across institutional instantiations. In this respect I follow the lead of (and am greatly indebted to) the work of Foucault and Althusser, but also Theodor Adorno, Cathy Cohen, Kimberlé Crenshaw, Douglas Crimp, Ruth Wilson Gilmore, Saidiya Hartman, Steven Miles, Vincent Pécoil, and many others whose research has similarly sought and disclosed the flows of power between and among institutional domains.[52]

In chapter 1, "The Archive of Anorexia," I begin with a critical history of anorexia nervosa both as a clinical manifestation of disorder and as a topic of intense feminist concern during the second half of the twentieth century. I propose a reading of anorexia as an archival project, that is, as a practice that has motivated compulsive historiographical scrutiny and as a practice that corporeally archives its own loss. Restaging the complex archive of anorexia by focusing on the nontraditional diagnostic constituencies of men and boys, I trace the role of men and the figure of masculinity in the development of diagnostic standards for anorexia (and its related predecessor, hysteria). Taking up Elspeth Probyn's evocative call for a renewed investigation of the anorectic's "taste for power" I argue against one of the most conventional interpretations of anorexia as a digested form of misogyny. I track the implications of anorexia's historical development as disease entity into the contemporary era, focusing in particular on clinical presumptions about the interrelationship of male anorexia and homosexuality, which represents one mode through which differently sexualized bodies are negotiated relative to normative consumption in the broadest sense. I close this chapter with a discussion of Jacques Derrida's *Archive Fever*, relating his use of Freud's death drive to Wernicke-Korsakoff syndrome, which sometimes results from long-term anorexic practice, in order to draw connections between self-starvation and what Herbert Blau calls the "amortization" of presence epitomized by performance.[53]

In chapter 2, "Enduring Performance," I begin with a familiar scene in the historiography of anorexia nervosa: New York at the turn of the twentieth century. I focus specifically on Dr. Henry S. Tanner, who attempted to align himself with the case of the famous Brooklyn "fasting girl" Mollie Fancher by staging a long-term fast in a New York medical college in 1880. Tanner's fast, designed to prove that extended self-starvation was both possible and beneficial, was attended by a broad swath of medical professionals, journalists, and a captivated public who widely applauded his efforts, even as they were dismissed as "performances" by allopathic doctors and other critics. I track the implications of this story forward into the mid-twentieth century, turning in particular to the period now commonly recognized as the beginning of the U.S. avant-garde, the 1960s and 1970s. I focus on the performance and sculptural work of the U.S. artist Chris Burden, paying special attention to those works for which Burden starved himself for extended periods of time. Now historicized as the bad boy of the avant-garde and most often noted for daring performances in which he put his life at risk, on several occasions Burden fasted on stage, summoning his audiences to bear witness to their own spectatorial responsibilities in producing a scene of artistic encounter that would potentially endanger the life of the artist. I propose that Tanner's and Burden's "trying ordeals" reveal the deep imbrication of the economy of the body and the economy of the spectacle and stage a familiar model of masculinity deeply rooted in the masochism of such endurance exhibitions.[54] Here self-starvation works both to trouble conventional conceptions of gendered looking of the sort described by Laura Mulvey as "the male gaze,"[55] and to attempt to reassert masculinity in its most stalwart and sturdy form.

In chapter 3, "How to Stage Self-Consumption," I follow this trajectory along slightly different and differently gendered lines to the work of the artists Adrian Piper, Ana Mendieta, and Marina Abramović. I position these artists within a genealogy of avant-garde performance in which the conventional commodification of the art object was radically undermined, distributed both as and into the stuff of everyday life. Beginning with a discussion of that anticommodification turn within the avant-garde and of Michael Fried's antitheatrical criticism of mid-twentieth-century art production, I focus in particular on Piper's *Food for the Spirit*, Mendieta's *Siluetas*, and Abramović's *The House with the Ocean View*, performances that demonstrate the productive plentitude of disappearance as an index for radical, and radically situated, political presence. In *Food for the Spirit* Piper fasted for several months while contending with Kant's propositions on the material manifestation of consciousness. In her now famous *Siuleta* series Mendieta deployed what I call allegorical self-consumption both to eviscerate the objectification of women's bodies as spectacles laid bare for the gaze of men and to reimagine her geographical displacement as a Cuban-born U.S. citizen. Abramović's *The House with the Ocean View*, produced after 11 September 2001 in New York City, staged self-consumption as a gift in the aftermath of a tragedy with both local and global implications, structured around ideologies of abjection and exclusion. This chapter considers how these works inhabit the interstices of subjectivity and objecthood, presence and absence, here and gone in order to explore the grounded materiality of the live.

In chapter 4, "To Lie Down to Death for Days," I turn my attention to hunger strikes staged in prisons across Turkey in the early years of the twenty-first century. On 20 October 2000 the longest and most deadly hunger strike in modern history began in response to the government's plans to develop and construct new so-called F-type prisons (in which prisoners are isolated from one another, from legal advocates, and from family members) and in response to recently enacted antiterror laws. In a country where political prisoners make up roughly one-sixth of the total prison population and where a long history of prison torture has been criticized by a wide range of outside human rights groups, the hunger strike saw little chance of achieving its goals: convincing government officials to repeal the official legislation and to reconsider its shift to the F-type prison system. Nonetheless the strike continued for well over two years and claimed at least 107 lives. This chapter explores the political effects and performative value of a mode of resistance not only founded on the eventual death of many, if not all, of its practitioners, but also ineffective in eventuating its desired changes. I begin by asking how and why Turkey has been positioned at the border of the West, simultaneously signifying "ally" and "other" for Western identification and expansionism. I then explore the rhetoric, both official and local, surrounding the strike and consider its performative value in producing new, viable models for resistant Turkish subjectivities.

In the afterword, "The Ends of Hunger," I turn to a site of intense international significance, especially since 11 September 2001: detention centers at Guantánamo Bay, Cuba, and the hunger strikes staged by foreign nationals detained there as enemy combatants. I argue that it is precisely through the refusal to recognize the power of hunger striking that the state produces its own power, not in taking the lives of marginalized subjects, but paradoxically in enforcing their continued survival. This refusal manifests as both a carceral and a clinical practice by camp officials, and so I also turn to a second highly publicized and politicized event in the early years of the twenty-first century: the death of Terri Schiavo. I argue that Schiavo's representation in the mass media and her death represent a moment in which the sovereignty of the state, defined as the right to control who *must* live and who *may* die, is radically confounded. I explore in particular the rhetoric surrounding Schiavo's illness (and its possible connection to an eating disorder before her convalescence), asking how this narrative informs our reading of her ad hoc living will, used by her husband to justify the removal of her feeding tube. I then query the manner in which Schiavo's case was taken up both by the U.S. religious right and so-called right-to-die activists, asking how we may approach Schiavo's death in the light of the many representational forms that circulated around the time her feeding tube was removed. In the context of Schiavo's story and the concurrent deterioration of Pope John Paul II's health, which also necessitated the use of that alternately valorized and demonized medical apparatus, I argue that the feeding tube takes on resilient significance as the means through which the state attempts to exert its sovereignty over "bare life."[56] The afterword thus draws lines of ideological affiliation from the carceral institution of Guantánamo Bay back to the clinic, and so returns to the site with which I began the book in chapter 1. My purpose in the afterword is neither to summarize nor to conclude the previous studies, but rather to concentrically complete my tracking of the political economy of self-starvation in its exchanges not only within but also between ideological and institutional domains.

Some readers may be surprised not to find images reproduced in this book, and I offer the following explanation for that decision. Many of the performances, installations, and films I describe are widely available in public libraries, galleries, and museums and online and have been reproduced in many other scholarly and popular books. But many of the cases explored here are not. For example, clinical encounters, which may be documented using a broad range of visual technologies, are dependent on confidentiality in patient records; this is particularly crucial for those who seek medical assistance with body image concerns. Similarly images of incarceration facilities and prison populations are typically tightly managed by correctional staff and administrations; this is especially true for the specific institutions and facilities I discuss. Given this disparity in the availability of images from the cases I explore, to reproduce images from some domains (theater, gallery, film) but not others (clinic, prison) would imply a taxonomy in genres of performance, indeed would risk marking some scenes as performances over and above the others, which I neither intend nor endorse. I have thus chosen not to reproduce the more accessible images in the interest of steering clear of a notion of performance that relies too intuitively upon the function of the visual.

Following Peggy Phelan's work in *Unmarked*, I write toward, not in spite of, the "disappearance" of bodily presence eventuated by self-starvation. But how to write (about) self-starvation? How to cull these longings to disappear, these enactments of refusal, these performances of violent loss, into a document that depends upon the weight of words? How to write *toward* disappearance without imposing unity of meaning or form on a set of practices that defy the logic of self-preservation underwriting conventional impressions of the production of subjectivity? If, as I have suggested, self-starvation is not only a powerful cultural practice, but also its own representational form, how to translate between it and this text?

First, and most important, my research for this book has involved collecting and reading texts from a broad range of genres. Self-starvation is extraordinary in the variety of texts it has produced: case studies, clinical records, experimental films, performances, curated objects, memoirs, sociological surveys, newspaper articles and exposés, documentaries, autopsies, missives smuggled out of prisons, historiographies, sculptures, photographs, and more. Conceptually I treat each text as performative, as actively involved in both describing and producing various images or notions of self-starvation. Some of these texts — clinical records, photographs, newspaper articles — produce the image of self-starvation as an emaciated body. Others — films, for example, and memoirs — focus on the meaning of self-starvation as a narrative of loss or refusal. My intention is to allow such differences in textual productivity to speak to my suggestions for the relationship between self-starvation and subjectivation through the live: I aim to consider the distinctions between the representational work being done by these many texts as differing but related fronts in the production and continual revision of self-starvation's many cultural and political meanings.

Second, the structure of this book assumes but does not concretize the differences between the forms of self-starvation I explore. In many cases, such as the image evoked in the opening of this introduction, these three practices overlap with one another in telling ways. What does it mean, for example, when anorectics are described as being on a kind of hunger strike, when artists who fast on stage are colloquially diagnosed as anorexic, or when a hunger strike is journalistically described as if it were a theatrical production? I explore these questions by reading across textual genres, moving from clinical record to autobiography, from film to photograph, from historiography to diagnostic code. In so doing I intend to interrupt the taxonomy of self-starvation in order to explore the political economy of self-starvation. In other words, I do not mean to suggest that there is any stability whatsoever in the category I designate with the term *self-starvation*. While I define self-starvation at its most basic level as an extended and expressive refusal to eat, I simultaneously recognize that eating habits, and indeed hunger and refusal, are infused with often inaccessible meanings within their particular cultural and political contexts. To eat, or not, in a Turkish prison will mean something very different from eating, or not, in a gallery space on the Lower East Side. Collapsing such distinctions would relegate self-starvation to the field of meanings we anticipate as eminently coherent and closed, and would furthermore infuse the act of critical writing with a colonialist drive to master difference and enforce streamlined coherence, a drive similar in form and content to the function of ideology outlined earlier.

Instead I am interested in how and why self-starvation as practice and as representational form can bear the weight of such differences without losing its extreme significance. What links the cases I explore perhaps more significantly than the fact of their fundamental refusal to consume is the power with which they command attention and the force with which they become politically meaningful. Focusing on the political economy of self-starvation, as opposed to a rationalized taxonomic system categorizing its specialized forms, brings that power and that force to the fore, homing in on the complicated relationship forged between those who starve themselves in various forms, for various reasons, and the cultural and political contexts of which they are a part. I am of course greatly indebted to the many scholars and critics who have worked to track the genealogy of self-starvation in many of its current and historical instantiations. But the archives of self-starvation represented here, conventionally written as historical accounts of enduring presence, emerge most profoundly and significantly in the bodies and practices that push forward into the void. It is to these more harrowing, inexorably mortal archives that this book bears witness.

CHAPTER ONE

the archive of anorexia

•

The subject of "dying" gave him much preoccupation at this time.
. . . He said to me that when he died he would move only very
slowly — like this. . . . He also asked if one did not eat for a very
long time would one have to die then, and how long would it take
before one died from it.

— Melanie Klein, *Love, Guilt and Reparation*

By the blindness of the way he has chosen, against himself, in spite
of himself, with its veerings, detours, and circlings back, his step,
always one step in front of nowhere, invents the road he has taken.

— Paul Auster, *The Art of Hunger*

In the opening scene we do not know where we are. The full and shapely lips of an anonymous mouth appear in extreme close-up — like Rocky Horror, like the Rolling Stones, like the gasping lead character in Samuel Beckett's *Not I* — calmly reading a list of procedures: "breast reduction, abdominoplasty, liposuction, body contouring, collagen injection." In a flash the frame slips forty-five degrees, the mouth now set at an angle, continuing to speak, as if reading from a relentlessly hopeful medical brochure: "Often changing how one looks on the outside changes one's perception of the world, giving one an inner sense of well-being and self-confidence." Another flash, the mouth now panning across the screen like a landscape shot: "You will re-enter the world, not only looking great, but feeling great." This is *Tom's Flesh*.[1]

We may have noticed the teeth, wet and unevenly arranged behind the moving lips. We may have noticed the voice's deep tonal resonances — it "sounds like a man"[2] — and wondered how or if it maps onto the body we have yet to see. We may have noticed that once the lips open to speak, they do not again close. But just as abruptly as it appeared, the mouth is gone, replaced by a wandering gaze that sweeps cautiously, tenderly across the spinning lights of a fairground, accompanied by the casual tinkling of a music box. These grainy views will toggle throughout the short film to the slow-motion nostalgia of an old Super 8: children in various states of apparent domestic bliss. But in a viciously gentle game of *fort* and *da*, what the screen gives it will also take away. These idyllic scenes are accompanied by ominous lines from our narrator: "I deserved what he did to me"; "He made me stand in front of them, welted and bleeding"; and from a new, second voice, whispered with a foreboding annunciative accuracy, "*See how lucky you are not to be me.*" In time — we might, after Cathy Caruth, say *in the time of trauma*[3] — these images are replaced by others, at first more difficult to read: segments of skin stretched and twisted into unrecognizable forms; postoperative scars of survival; bodily landscapes that constitute what the voice calls "beauty." As the first narrator tells us, "I've undone everything. I've undone it all."

The ontology of that undoing, described simply on the film's first series of intertitles, begins with a complicated scene of recognition: "Age 7: My father told me that I was fat / I looked in the mirror / He was right." In a dramatic retelling of Lacan's story of the mirror stage — or from another angle, a reimagining of Althusser's street scene — the voice of Tom's father occasions a search for the subject, a visual turn to answer the father's call. Tom looks to the mirror to see himself, and in so seeing he becomes what his father summons. The momentum of that becoming — in Nietzsche's words, that movement "across the turbulent stream of becoming"[4] — accelerates as more scenes from Tom's childhood echo with the father's cruel calls: "*Boys don't love*"; "He slapped me when I said the word *love.*" Moments later we see "Age 11: I weighed 180 lbs." And then, with a soft but resounding climax of commencement, Tom's story turns: "Age 18: I weighed 300 lbs. / I stopped eating / In seven months I lost over 180 lbs. / I became anorexic."

If the emergence of anorexia in Tom's narrative marks the commencement of a certain kind of becoming, a becoming that is itself an undoing, it alone among his strategies of survival remains otherwise unspoken throughout the film. Anorexia is marked within the script of that single intertitle, but it is never again spoken, never demonstrated as openly and graphically as the many other practices — self-laceration, a grotesque kind of play with the wounds from his father's abuse, reconstructive and cosmetic surgeries — that constitute Tom's becoming. These are excessively represented, indeed almost overrepresented, in the images and spoken narratives of the film. But anorexia, so insistent, so haunting in that initial citation, will not likewise be archived within the scopic or narrative space of *Tom's Flesh*; anorexia appears both to index and to archive itself. Or rather — "Age 11: I weighed 180 lbs."; "Age 18: . . . I lost over 180 lbs." — anorexia becomes the force and the law of Tom's corporeally archival work.

Tom's Flesh reveals anorexia, perhaps especially in the silent persistence of its presence in the film, as itself an archival project of undoing and becoming, a deeply (to use Paul Connerton's word) *incorporated* historiography of trauma.[5] At the same time, anorexia exceeds its conventional role as a nomenclature of individual suffering, especially since its introduction into a broader cultural presence in the closing decades of the twentieth century. We might locate that colloquial inauguration of anorexia on a Las Vegas nightclub stage in the fall of 1975, when the popular musician Karen Carpenter collapsed while singing "Top of the World"; or on the morning of 5 February 1983, when news of Carpenter's death from a "starvation diet" was published in newspapers across the United States.[6] As the historian Joan Jacobs Brumberg writes of these events, Carpenter's experiences "fueled interest in the disease [and] focused national attention on the life-and-death drama of anorexia nervosa."[7] Where previously in its troubled history the concept of anorexia, perhaps the very word *anorexia* functioned as a technical taxonomy of disease in rarified spaces (clinics, hospitals, medical theaters), suddenly in the 1970s and 1980s it also became a vernacular, an everyday word, an idiom.

These rhetorical transformations likewise disclose the agility of anorexia as a speech act.[8] That is, as a practice, as a constellation of practices that reveals both the grave performativity of clinical diagnosis and the diagnostic power of cultural representation, anorexia transgresses the boundaries between clinic and world, gathering in its reach a broad range of functions, orientations, and forms. It has been called an "epidemic," a "cage," a "stance," a "phenomenon," a "metaphor," an "aesthetic," and (almost universally) a "disorder."[9] In all of these resonances anorexia is marked not only as a category of psychological distress, but also (and perhaps most significantly) as symptomatic of and fundamental to the capital and corporeal excesses of late modernity. John Sours evocatively characterizes this quality of the contemporary manifestation of anorexia as "starving to death in a sea of objects."[10] Kim Chernin explicitly politicizes this characterization by positioning anorexia as a response to what she calls "the tyranny of slenderness."[11] Both diagnostically and representationally anorexia reverberates with significance, abounds with descriptive promiscuity, thrives on the profusion of its psychic, somatic, and social effects.

In calling anorexia an archival project of undoing and becoming I mean to highlight both the function of anorexia as an individualized practice that archives its own loss and the status of anorexia as a deeply and ardently historicized cultural artifact. Indeed efforts to chart the history of anorexia's clinical and cultural emergence have proliferated in the years since it obtained colloquial standing, coalescing around the practice from a broad range of disciplinary perspectives. Most notable among these historical studies are those authored by medical and public health professionals and feminist cultural critics, constituencies that do not often find themselves mobilized around similarly articulated concerns, orientations, or goals. That is to say, the drive to archive anorexia's clinical and cultural past has itself emerged within a critical dialectic that, from one angle, seeks to track and to treat the complicated nosology of anorexia *as a disease* and, from another angle, seeks to position anorexia *as a symptom* of the radically uneven flows of cultural power that initiate and reproduce expectations for how particular (and particularly gendered) bodies should act and appear.

"We are not the first to look upon this emaciated figure," writes Angelyn Spignesi. "Researchers have been strongly drawn to this figure; they have eyed her carefully. The voluminous amount of research . . . illuminates how vividly the anorexic has caught the imagination. Researchers have been attached to her, perhaps even enamored. . . . For one hundred years, [they] have been attempting to put this female skeleton back into shape."[12] Spignesi highlights the relatively deep history of medical research on the practice of anorexia, the frenzied clinical attempts to track its many variations and to promote methods for treatment or cure; she casts these attempts as infused with a clinical passion that is as "attached," as "enamored" as it is urgent. Likewise, in cultural criticism of at least the past several decades, historians and theorists have worked diligently to track the effects of "impossible standards for beauty" in the emergence and spread of anorexia through and across diagnostic constituencies. Maud Ellmann likens the surplus of writing produced about anorexia to anorexic practice itself: "While there is some debate as to whether the disease of anorexia is on the rise, there can be no doubt that the research is epidemic even if the malady is not, because it has infected every discipline from medicine, psychology, and sociology to women's magazines and literary criticism."[13] In Ellmann's appraisal the urgency to historicize anorexia is itself a kind of compulsion that (like a contagion) infects, mirroring the obsessive desire to starve diagnostically characteristic of anorectics. Anorexia, that is, compels its own archival drive, beckons us to seek the vicissitudes of its histories, stimulates a desire to encounter the ghosts of its historical presence. For Sours "the history of anorexia proves that history does, indeed, repeat itself."[14] For Leslie Heywood "the real of anorexia is the residue of discourses about it."[15] For Spignesi "the Gods of this disease will be reflected in its pathos as well as its logos."[16] Anorexia *compels*; anorexia *is* its own inscription.

At the same time, as the physician Charles Rosenberg remarked in his study of cholera, "a disease is no absolute physical entity but a complex intellectual construction, an amalgam of biological state and social definition."[17] The archive of anorexia, the historiography of anorexia and anorexia *as historiographical practice*, is also an archive of a given social context and its epistemological relationship to the body. In their expansive study of "the history of self-starvation" Walter Vandereycken and Ron van Deth mark this quality of illness as "culture-bound": "The notion of (ab)normality is . . . particularly dependent upon the culture where the behavioural pattern in question is observed. . . . This implies that the syndrome is only meaningful and comprehensible (diagnosis, explanation, therapy) within the psychosocial sphere of a specific cultural context."[18] Vandereycken and van Deth imply that as a medicalized practice, as a diagnostic symbology anorexia obtains its significance precisely as a representational form, a system of signs, meaningful only insofar as it bears some relationship to and holds some possibility for comprehension through the many forms of (clinical, popular, aesthetic) interpretation that define a given cultural moment. As they later claim, illness "becomes a metaphor, a figurative concept which arouses the imagination: it may be romanticized as a bogey or cultivated as a myth. Illness becomes synonymous with inexplicable mystery or inevitable mischief."[19]

For Susan Bordo the "mischief" of illness is precisely its eloquence as "the crystallization of culture": "I take the pathologies that develop within a culture, far from being anomalies or aberrations, to be characteristic expressions of that culture; to be, indeed, the crystallization of much that is wrong with it."[20] Like many others who have taken anorexia to be, in Ellmann's words, "a symptom of the discontents of womankind,"[21] Bordo is particularly attentive to the modes through which cultural expectations for idealized body sizes and shapes are incorporated and adopted as objects of desire, as mirrors through which women aim to see themselves. Along with Jean Kilbourne and Naomi Wolf,[22] Bordo positions anorexia as a practice that reflects women's struggles to conform to such expectations (if not precisely as a complete sublimation of or submission to that "tyranny of slimness"). This interpretation of anorexia as a direct result of implausible patriarchal demands for compliance with those sculpted (and, in print, airbrushed) silhouettes of perfection is dominant in so much of the critical and popular literature that little room has been left for other, more nuanced or rigorously tracked readings of anorexic practice. In an extremely prescient study in 1986 that anticipated the ascendancy of this interpretation, Susie Orbach notes:

> While at first glance it might appear that the anorectic's refusal to eat is an act of conformity, a taking-up of the commandment, the act of refusal contains its dialectical response: I shall not partake of that which is offered for it is not sufficient/not for me at all. The food is the symbolic representation of a world that has already disappointed the anorectic. Entry into it is not the answer.[23]

To be fair to her important and influential work, I should make clear that Bordo does not ascribe to the simplistic and unforgiving interpretation of anorexia as nothing more than submission to bodily ideals internalized from a cultural context that promotes relentless dissatisfaction with one's physical appearance. Insofar as anorexic practice is, to borrow Wang Ping's words, an "aching for beauty,"[24] it represents a profoundly conflicted and conflicting relationship to the incorporation of ideological demands. But Bordo is acutely resistant to any attempt to align anorexia with, for example, the overt political orientation of a hunger strike. She writes:

> The anorectic's protest . . . is written on the bodies of anorexic women, not embraced as a conscious politics—nor, indeed, does it reflect any

social or political understanding at all. Moreover, the symptoms them-selves function to preclude the emergence of such an understanding. The *idée fixe* — staying thin — becomes at its farthest extreme so powerful as to render any other ideas or life-projects meaningless.[25]

This citation represents an uncomfortable moment in Bordo's study: her refusal of the anorectic's ability, however fraught, however failing, to articulate starvation as or within a conscious political stance seems to reproduce the very voicelessness against which she is otherwise so clearly mobilized. To gesture to "any other ideas or life-projects" as "meaning-less" for the anorectic, and especially to deny "any social or political un-derstanding," risks limiting our ability to trace anorexia's function within the life of the subject: more specifically, the Foucauldian notion of the subject that Bordo earlier claims is central to her understanding of pow-er's production at the extremely localized scale of the body.[26]

Bordo's suggestion that anorexia "actually function[s] as if in collu-sion with the cultural conditions that produced [it]," especially the "slen-der pivot" of that "as if," does, however, leave space for the possibility of reading anorexia alongside Foucault: "The body is directly involved in a political field; power relations have an immediate hold upon it; they invest it, mark it, train it, torture it, force it to carry out tasks, to perform ceremonies, to emit signs."[27] It is possible, that is, to understand an-orexia's "collusion with cultural conditions" as simultaneously exemplary — to recall Foucault's framing concept — of the intertwined processes of subject-formation and subordination. Orbach seems to hint at this char-acterization of anorexia as emblematic of subjectivation when she writes:

We can begin to see, then, that the cause she has taken on is that most precious one: the creation of a safe place in the world. She is trying to legitimate herself, to eke out a space, to bring dignity where dismissal and indignity were rife. Her cause is no less imperative than that of the overtly political hunger striker. The resolve of her commitment is equally intense. The political prisoner who embarks upon a hunger strike does so to draw attention to the injustice of her or his incarceration and the righteousness of her or his cause. The anorectic woman on hunger strike echoes these themes. Her self-denial is in effect a protest again the rules that circum-scribe a woman's life, a demand that she has an absolute right to exist.[28]

For Orbach this "cause" is marked by a delirious, desperate kind of hope — for safety and security, for a sense of legitimacy, for dignity, above all for freedom — paradoxically forged within a practice marked (just as deliriously) as hopeless: "The hoped-for goal of denial — freedom — is unattainable."[29] Orbach reasons that that desired (if ultimately "unattainable") freedom promises a release from the demands placed upon women in the distinctly gendered structures and economies of contemporary cultural life.

Orbach's eloquent study of anorexia as "a metaphor for our age," grounded in clinical work with anorectics and their families, suggests that this complicated, seemingly paradoxical constellation of practices is "spectacular and dramatic."[30] In her use of the word "dramatic" Orbach does not mean to suggest, as did Victorian doctors specializing in hysteria, endlessly suspicious of the authenticity of their patients' symptoms, that anorectics consciously fake their experiences. Rather she means to gesture to those qualities of anorexia that depend on intersubjective experiences of exchange, that is, on the complex interplay of gazes and appraisals that define both the ontology and the experience of the anorectic.

In a passage that recalls Althusser's interpellant street scene Orbach describes an imagined encounter with an anorexic woman:

> Unknowingly one moves into the role of the spectator. A sense of bewilderment, linked with a desire to understand, shortly turns to discomfort. One begins to look upon the anorectic and the anorexia uncomprehendingly. Compassion turns to fear and a wish for distance; a need to disassociate oneself from the painful sight. . . . Turning anorexia into an exotic state, with the attendant labelling and judging, substitutes for engagement. By these means a distance is created between oneself and the anorectic.[31]

This passage, replete with a descriptive grace characteristic of Orbach's prose, compellingly illustrates the vexed sense of "engagement" that pervades encounters between anorectics and others. This engagement, she argues, is fraught with the anorectic's embodiment of "anguish and defiance combine[d] in the most curious way" and evokes in the spectator a "simultaneous desire to retreat and to move in closer," both of which impulses are intensified by the potential for the spectator's self-recognition in the image of the anorectic: "There is a painful continuity between most women's daily experience and that of the anorectic."[32] As a result, Orbach explains, this imagined (but nonetheless real) encounter with anorexia produces an intricate, if contradictory affective exchange:

The dual process of recognition and labeling creates a symmetrical split in the way in which one responds, then, to the physical presence of the anorectic. . . . The woman who is suffering anorexia is unable to contain a wide range of feelings within herself. Without realizing it, she flings them out into the world where they are momentarily picked up by those whom she meets. . . . She "hands over" her feelings to another.[33]

This encounter on the street, like other scenes we might recognize as dramatic, is defined by the paradoxical interplay of recognition and estrangement, resemblance and otherness, empathy and disaffection.

Orbach's narrative underscores the nature of the subject's encounter—with anorexia and with herself through the appearance of anorexia—as a scene, as *performed*. I propose that Orbach's (perhaps unconscious) allusion to the language of the theater is not simply allegorical in its significance, but an acute and concrete indication that the function of anorexia—in Elspeth Probyn's words, anorexia's "taste for power"[34]—is founded upon profoundly embodied, intensely spectacular, and inherently intersubjective exchanges between and among anorectics and others. In other words, I propose that anorexia derives, concentrates, and facilitates its clinical and cultural power *as a performance*. I organize this proposal around four key claims.

First, as a condition anorexia is durational in nature. Unlike organic diseases, a diagnosis of anorexia requires its own continuous reproduction: extended enactments of the refusal to consume sufficient sustenance. Anorexia obtains not at the initial "I choose not to eat" but only when that declarative is incessantly repeated over time. This is represented in the medical literature by the diagnostic attention paid to "periods" of weight loss and "experiences" of self-perception; it is also manifest in the standard for treatment in many clinics, where a *minimum* body weight must be achieved before a given patient may be admitted.[35] Anorexia, in other words, does not stand still (*in situ*) and cannot be named except in reference to its enactment through stretches of time.

Second, anorexia is an embodiment of predetermined modes of resistance to a given set of alimentary norms. As embodiment anorexia transforms interwoven cultural and psychic processes of specular self-assessment and critique into a bodily practice that aims explicitly to create the form of an imaginary ideal. That is, anorexia obtains its medical and social significance precisely by staging on a bodily scale the effects of ideological normativity. Paradoxically such significance requires a simultaneous consumption of the normative ideal in its psychic representational form and a refusal to consume what is commonsensically recognized as sustenance. These competing drives, to consume and not to consume, are at the heart of anorexia as both an individually experienced condition and a cultural phenomenon.

Third, anorexia is extensively and increasingly mediated through representational forms in a wide variety of genres. These include medical records and clinical case studies, but also journalistic accounts, documentaries, memoirs, memorials, photographs, novels, staged performances, and descriptive films. Indeed in its contemporary form anorexia appears to depend upon such textual productivity and is most broadly recognizable not as a stable category of illness or disease, but through the image of a radically emaciated body and in the narrative of self-regard reflected on the surface of a pejorative mirror. All of these representational modes circulate around an essentially variable practice that requires continual reassertion of its central goals and, taken together, work to produce a notion of anorexia as disturbance and disorder. That is, the textual promiscuity that so diversely represents anorexia in our cultural imaginary mirrors the psychic disequilibrium clinically assumed of anorectics themselves.

Fourth, anorexia is defined by specularity. The relationship between the visual and the medicalization of the body has been vividly traced by a number of feminist scholars in cultural studies, most notably Paula Treichler, Lisa Cartwright, and Constance Penley, but also specifically in the case of anorexia (and its diagnostic forebears) by Carole Spitzack, Kathleen Biddick, Martha Noel Evans, and Georges Didi-Huberman.[36] As Biddick explains in her analysis of historical photographs of anorectics, "The criteria of the visible [has come] to mark modernity."[37] The role of specularity specifically in constructing and compelling anorexia both as an individual practice and as a social force is intricate and multifaceted. Certainly one could trace the history of anorexia by laying out a genealogy of scopic technologies that document the somatic distress resulting from gradual self-starvation. But documenting the psychic patterns of visualization and display that operate with such relentless force to define consumption and abnegation is an entirely different issue, one that cuts to the heart of what it means to be (or for that matter to *seem* to be) an anorectic. Della Pollock casts this issue in broader terms: "In the alienation of [material body-object from agential body-subject], the subject is a subject insofar as she surveys her own body, insofar as she cuts herself off from the very thing she would own by *looking* — and by looking *good*: by observing well and by being well worth observing."[38]

The alienation of the objectified body from the body-as-subject occurs with astonishing regularity in both the social and the psychic fields. Indeed the systems through which psychic life is experienced as meaningful for, relevant to, or invited into social life typically require a dissociative move epitomized in Pollock's distinctions between "observing well" and "being well worth observing." This is no more evident than in the cold, clinical rhetorics of etiology and treatment that produce and reproduce the figure of the anorectic and in representations of anorexia in popular media, which ask us to watch anorectics watch themselves in anticipation of us watching them. The limits of specularity, especially in the latter example, is forgotten as health professionals and an obsessed public gaze, sometimes overwhelmed with longing, sometimes horrified beyond belief, gape at the "desperate desire to be thin."[39]

As Pollock reminds us, the flip side of looking, or more broadly, of accessing the world outside ourselves and its constituent objects, is having the look turned back upon us, so that we become the object of other gazes, the stages on which others' desires may be played out, whether we like it or not. In a haunting essay published in 1993 Carole Spitzack writes this spectatorial doubling into the story of normative female subjectivity, which she suggests is "contingent on a division in identity: a woman embodies the positions of spectator and spectacle simultaneously."[40] Although this argument (recalling my discussion of Bordo) represents one of the most accepted derivations of anorexia nervosa, a condition whose formation extends from patriarchal expectations that women's bodies conform to an idealized silhouette that most recently has been designated by the word *thin*, Spitzack complicates the description of that incorporated demand by reminding us that it compels not only an object to be seen, but also a subject who sees. In this exceptionally compelling logic, not only is the anorectic objectified as a visual commodity, but the anorectic is also mobilized as a bearer of the look: the anorectic's gaze, Spitzack suggests, is radically detached from a "healthy self-image" as it aligns itself with the unforgiving glare seemingly initiated, in this case, by desiring heterosexual men.

If the rubric of performance assists with mapping the contours of anorexia's cultural and clinical presence, the paradigm of *performativity* will allow a more precise tracking of anorexia's impact. J. L. Austin's powerful notion of the performative, a category of language that enacts the reality it purports to describe, has initiated a wide range of scholarship on the active role that representational forms play in producing the real.[41] As I discussed at length in the introduction to this book, Judith Butler in particular has demonstrated that what we experience as "gender" is enmeshed in and mediated through the performativity of such representational forms, "produced as the truth effects of a discourse of primary and stable identity."[42] Butler's work has shown that the effectiveness of gender performatives, their ability to "land," their success in producing effects, depends upon a profoundly present past that authorizes and initiates the power of the speech act; she calls the relationship between a given performative and its authorizing convention "citational," drawing our attention to the constant, cacophonous interplay of echoes required for the performative to succeed in its consequence. The performative is, by definition, intersubjective; it is also, in practice, archival.

In my discussion about recent writing on anorexia, the authors I (citationally) engaged all assume a particularly gendered anorectic: she is in every case a woman. As I now turn to expand my earlier claim that anorexia is an archival practice and to connect this claim to the archival function of the performative I focus on a relatively new population of diagnosed anorectics: men and boys. Although the affiliation of masculinity, maleness, and men with anorexia is not unique to the contemporary era — indeed the most often cited "first text" in the medical literature on anorexia includes a case study of a young man — the vast majority of clinical practice, cultural criticism, and popular attention has been paid to the presentation of the anorectic, seemingly by definition, as female.

It is important to bear in mind that anorexia has been a consummate example in the work of contemporary scholars who seek to explain the gendered character of medical practice and the ideology of health. Indeed the broader history of eating disorders is conventionally narrativized as emerging from within clinical arrangements that privilege men as the producers of knowledge and women as *sites* on which that knowledge is visualized, examined, and staged. More urgently the vast majority of diagnosed anorectics are women and girls, and although there are reasons to suspect that men and boys are underrepresented in these statistics, eating disorders continue disproportionately to plague communities of women and girls worldwide. My examination of male anorexia is based not on a turn away from those communities, but on the recognition that the history of anorexia implicates masculinity as a key player in the relentless violence that underlies the genealogy of medicine and its relationship to women and women's bodies. I turn to male anorexia in an effort to interrupt the mute implication that anorexia is a symptom of contemporary femininity.

Moreover in designating male anorexia as a topic for research I do not mean to posit that condition as a category of illness that replicates the anticipated stability of (presumably female) anorexia. I mean instead to question the strict identification of anorexia as a woman's problem and the simplistic interpretation of anorexia as a sort of incorporated or digested misogyny. Such assumptions rely on the easily identifiable and immobile category of Woman, stable lines of signification between anorexia and female subjectivity,[43] and the notion that power descends unidirectionally from a centralized force in order to impose itself onto objectified bodies. Such arguments essentially neglect both to conceive of the complicated function of ideological power and to imagine how it might be inverted or indeed converted into a form of agency. Probyn casts this concern evocatively as a "taste for power":

> As I stare at [the anorectic's] sad figure of mute victimhood, I want to shake her image as the feminist emblem of powerlessness. I want to take her from the sphere of a metaphor where she is not allowed to taste, where her refusal of food slides into universalizing discourses of women's oppression. This use of the anorexic can only be performed at the considerable expense of ignoring her developed taste for power. . . . This is not to render her heroic, nor again to give her credence as the metaphor for our times. It is to attend to her tastes. . . . Considering anorexic practices as articulating the very power of taste and the will to taste power may help us displace a common tendency to isolate the anorexic away from the circuits and networks of everyday power that are cathected along the corporeal lines of food, sex, sexuality, gender, class, and race. We ignore at our peril the challenges that she poses; we condemn ourselves to fatuous mouthings if we do not also own up to our own taste and desire for power.[44]

Often cited as the first written record of anorexia, Richard Morton's *Phthisiologia, or a Treatise on Consumption* (1694) describes subjects whose seeming loss of appetite resulted in the slow wasting away of their humors and tissues.[45] A "devoted subject" of the British monarchy, Morton aimed to diagnose and prescribe treatments for various forms of consumption; collated under this heading at the time were maladies including what we would now call tuberculosis, melancholia, and hypochondria. Morton's weighty thesis moves swiftly from case study to case study, gathering in its sweep a dizzying range of conditions and disorders, defining consumption as "a wasting of the *Muscular* parts of the Body, arising from the Substraction, or Colliquation of the Humours, and that either with or without a Fever." Within the general category Morton noted atrophy, "an Universal Consumption proceeding from the whole Habit of the Body, and not from an Distemper of the Lungs, or of any other Entrails, without any remarkable Fever, and is either Nervous, or the effect of Evacuations," and a particular form of atrophy, nervous consumption, "that which owes its Original to an ill and morbid state of the Spirits; . . . a wasting of the Body without any remarkable Fever, Cough, or shortness of Breath; but . . . attended with a want of Appetite and a bad Digestion, upon which there follows a Languishing Weakness of Nature, and a falling away of the Flesh every day more and more."[46] Nervous consumption described behavior in subjects whom many historians have retroactively (and problematically) diagnosed as anorexic, and is commonly recognized as one of anorexia's taxonomic ancestors. But unlike many contemporary historiographies of anorexia, Morton's text fails to specify nervous consumption as a specifically gendered malady. In one of his most prominent examples of the condition he writes:

> The Son of the Reverend Minister Mr. *Steele*, my very good Friend, about the Sixteenth Year of his Age fell gradually into a total want of Appetite, occasioned by his studying too hard, and the Passions of his Mind, and upon that into an Universal *Atrophy*, pining away more and more for the Space of two Years, without any Cough, Fever, or any other Symptom of any Distemper of his Lungs, or any other Entrail; as also without a Looseness, or *Diabetes*, or any other sign of a Colliquation, or Preternatural Evacuation. And therefor I judg'd this Consumption to be Nervous, and to have its seat in the whole Habit of the Body, and to arise from the System of Nerves being distemper'd. I began, and first attempted his Cure with the use of *Antiscorbutick*, *Bitter*, and *Chalybeate* Medicines, as well Natural as Artificial, but without any benefit; and therefore when I found that the former Method did not answer our Expectations, I advis'd him to abandon his Studies, to go into the Country Air, and to use Riding, and a Milk Diet (and especially to drink Asses Milk) for a long time. By the use of which he recover'd his Health in a great measure, though he is not yet perfectly freed from a Consumptive state; and what will be the event of this Method, does not yet plainly appear.[47]

This early case is exemplary in its explicit recognition of the difficulty in locating a somatic center for the symptom of general emaciation. Like contemporary case studies, Morton's narrative situates "studying too hard, and the Passions of his mind" as causative features of a "Universal Atrophy" and "a total want of Appetite." The language here is telling: Mr. Steele's son, apparently suffering from an overactive intellectual life and unnamed "Passions," ceased to consume and so became consumptive. These factors in the etiology of nervous consumption have survived the vicissitudes of anorexia's convoluted history and remain unresolved concerns in the contemporary literature. Further the phrase "want of Appetite," which for Morton implied the atrophy of normative hunger, suggests a desire *for* desire at the core of nervous consumption. Mr. Steele's son was consumptive not only because he wasted away, but also because he deviated from *and longed for* the normalcy of hunger that precedes and defines healthy consumption; he was "*pining away* more and more." We see in Morton's early study the seeds of what will become, especially during the Victorian era, illness and desire conjoined as symptomatic of "a morbid state of the Spirits."

The cultural work of marking some desires or "Passions" as deviant is extensive and relentless, and we might recognize the effects of such work today in those subjects and practices that are ideologically marked at or as the outskirts of human behavior, indeed as the inhuman. Morton's account of nervous consumption suggests rampant passions that overtake the normal functions of the body and act out against the tissues that collectively compose the body's internal structures. The effect of this overtaking is read visually: a "general Atrophy" that has no record in the fluctuations of temperature, pulse, or pulmonary performance. Morton's note that Mr. Steele's son was "not yet freed from a Consumptive state" perhaps unintentionally expands the source and scope of his suffering beyond such immediately individual functions as heart rate and breathing. The pun in the phrase "a Consumptive *state*" gestures to a larger context in which Mr. Steele's son found "the whole Habit of his body" falling into "a total want of Appetite."

As an origin story for the archive of anorexia Morton's text reflects several key components of contemporary medical standards for diagnosing and treating the condition. Most notable are his attention to those deviant "Passions" and his curative command that the young man realign his daily routines with those prescribed more generally for healthy men and boys. These are hardly unusual in the history of medicine, but it is worth noting that in modern clinical practice they have been particularly operational in diagnosing and treating psychological conditions. Even more particularly, the regulation of desire and social behavior was a hallmark of the modern history of clinical attitudes toward hysteria, that broad, indeterminate, and deeply flawed disease entity from which anorexia nervosa most recently emerged.

Hysteria's broad past entails generalized violence against diagnosed (or even suspected) hysterics, performed through clinical and domestic scenes of vague diagnosis and terrifying treatment.[48] In the late decades of the nineteenth century hysteria had become such a broad and versatile compendium of illness that many doctors began focusing exclusively on mapping its intricacies, diversifying its diagnoses, and documenting its many symptoms. Widely theorized, most famously by Sigmund Freud and Josef Breuer,[49] as resulting from disturbances in sexual development, hysteria was recognizable in the opinion of its experts as a series of symptoms: trances, physical tics, ecstatic seizures, masquerades and deceptions, and "improper" eating habits. A system of signs forever gesturing back and forth between its physical manifestations, hysteria depended ontologically on discrete scenes of spectatorship in which (generally) male doctors put (generally) female patients on flagrant display in medical theaters, journalistic exposés, and live performances in which the public was invited into domestic spaces to see the "fasting girls" who had piqued so much scientific curiosity.[50]

Hysteria became the antecedent and the model for modern diagnosis and clinical practice, particularly in its theorized manifestation and representation through a system of symptomatic behaviors. Although it has nominally disappeared from most diagnostic taxonomies, hysteria remains in the shadows of its disordered descendants: anorexia nervosa, kleptomania, multiple personality disorder, schizophrenia, and many others. More important, hysteria lingers in the modern diagnostic manuals as the ghostly precursor to contemporary medical practice, a critical link between the viscera of pain and the trauma of psychic development, indeed the starting point for psychoanalytic theories of the psyche that have so dramatically changed the culture of modern diagnosis.[51]

What set hysteria apart from contemporary illnesses in the nineteenth-century encyclopedia of disorders was its explicit indication of the close relationships between physical health, social subjectivity, and a fraught relationship to the past: "Hysterics," wrote Freud and Breuer in their classic text, "suffer mainly from reminiscences."[52] The problem of hysteria was typically traced to psychological trauma or familial discord, usually involving an interruption in normative sexual development or sexual abuse, and that trauma's continual reemergence in somatic symptoms of suffering; the history of pain, the doctors claimed, was writ upon the hysteric's flesh. Rehabilitation, which took various forms, included reorganizing domestic and romantic relationships and, most famously, Freud's talking cure, in which patients narrativized their past experiences in a clinical setting. Largely because of hysteria's prominence in nineteenth-century medical research, the picture of health became a sign not only of a body functioning properly, but also of a subject properly positioned within the institutions of family, community, and state and a consolidated, fully fleshed-out relationship to one's own archival past.

This sweep in the concept of medical health to include the proper functioning of the body, the social function of the subject, and the function of historicity within that subject's *now* was navigated by the experiments that eventuated contemporary diagnostic standards for anorexia nervosa. The effects of this sweep in the production and regulation of health, from *body* to *subject* and back again, facilitated the extension of medicalized normativity far beyond the architectural bounds of the clinic, asylum, or hospital. Indeed the eventual taxonomic introduction of anorexia nervosa, variously called anorexia hysteria, apepsia hysteria, and other names by its earliest theoreticians, resembled, in the words of several prominent physicians, "the microscope, which opened a whole new world of data."[53]

As I described earlier, it was not until the second half of the twentieth century that anorexia nervosa fully entered the public vernacular in Europe and North America. During this period, especially beginning in the 1970s, diagnoses of anorexia became much more widespread; like hysteria at the end of the nineteenth century it was on a "catastrophic rise."[54] The more recent increase of men and boys among the diagnosed has begun to attract a good deal of medical and popular attention. These diagnoses, which, again, have presented serious challenges to the image of the anorectic as North American or European, middle class, heterosexual, white, and female, have thrown the standards for the condition into crisis, occasioning a flurry of scientific and popular writing on the nature of anorexia and the significance of its spread to nontraditional communities. The recent upturn in anorexic diagnoses among men and boys, an upturn that one popular book mythologizes as "the Adonis complex," has similarly reflected a crisis in conventional masculinity, or more strongly put, has revealed conventional masculinity to be founded upon crisis.[55]

Although the recent emergence of male anorexia may not run precisely counter to the heterosexual male desire I earlier marked as complicit in the circulation and coercion of idealized bodily forms — nor can it interrupt the force with which those forms are imposed psychically and socially upon us — such an expansion in the clinical and cultural presence of anorexia may intervene in how we imagine the ubiquity of that force. The emergence of male anorexia and its recognition in clinical and popular literatures may disclose a deep cultural repression, as J. C. Flugel signals in his notion of the "great masculine renunciation,"[56] of men's anxieties about their own "spectatorial doubling." Simultaneously the emergence of male anorexia presents us with the opportunity to consider disparity in gendered and sexual subjectivities as potentially productive in promoting affiliation *across* rather than *despite* difference. Male anorexia confounds the strict and all-encompassing association of masculinity and maleness with the unseen but ultimately "in charge" voyeur; anorexic men and boys, by virtue of their diagnoses, find themselves potentially aligned with diagnosed women and girls.

What do we do, and how do we know, when we believe a particular man to be anorexic? Or to change the stakes of that question: What do we do, and how do we know, when we believe a particular anorectic to be male? (Angelyn Spignesi bizarrely, but only briefly, foreshadows this conundrum when she writes, "We have to look twice when [the anorectic] appears: female without curves, male with long hair?")[57] We might begin with a turn to the technical, diagnostic classification of anorexia, but finding consistent, and consistently legible, criteria for this "distemper'd System of Nerves" is encumbered by the diverse range of practices and orientations that are retroactively approximated as anorexic. Diagnostic standards, particularly in the inchoate, embodied, interpretive scene of clinical encounter, range from extreme emaciation and a general but completely preoccupying desire to be thin, to the more rigidly described (and deceptively straightforward) criteria collated by the American Psychiatric Association in its *Diagnostic and Statistical Manual* (DSM-IV-TR):

A. Refusal to maintain body weight at or above a minimally normal weight for age and height (e.g., weight loss leading to maintenance of body weight less than 85% of that expected; or failure to make expected weight gain during period of growth, leading to body weight less than 85% of that expected).

B. Intense fear of gaining weight or becoming fat, even though underweight.

C. Disturbance in the way in which one's body weight or shape is experienced, undue influence of body weight or shape on self-evaluation, or denial of the seriousness of the current low body weight.

D. In postmenarcheal females, amenorrhea, i.e., the absence of at least three consecutive menstrual cycles.[58]

At first seeming to propose an objective, almost laboratory inventory of standards, this diagnostic code recalls the echoing interplay of perspectives described in Orbach's imagined encounter with the anorectic. That is, the code requires an interlocutor invested with an evaluative perspective and endowed with the interpretive ability to read a range of affective experiences as diverse as "intense fear," "disturbance," "undue influence," and "denial." This interlocutor is simultaneously empowered to enforce (or "expect") a range of normative conditions, which themselves are harvested from a conventional, if anonymous, *they*.[59] That is to say, the most official and most often implemented designation of anorexia is produced and reflected within the context of an embodied, interactive, and intersubjective encounter in the institutional and ideological domain of the clinic.

This should come as no great surprise; the clinic is but one of many domains (in Althusser's language, "apparatuses")[60] that facilitate the flow of bodily *and* ideological normativity (the various designations of health) through affective, sometimes empathic exchanges. The doctor-patient relationship of a good bedside manner reminds us that the clinic is also simultaneously a site of intimately practiced *care* for a vast and complex range in modes of suffering. But what stands out most prominently from the *DSM* is precisely what Spitzack calls "an acceptance of erasure as the real, . . . a striking unwillingness to accept social definitions of female attractiveness and a refusal to perform the rituals of femininity mandated by observers."[61] That is, the "disturbance" cited in section C of the code—an anorectic's presumed *mis*interpretation of how her or his body appears to its clinical appraiser—suggests a complex interplay of desiring gazes that reflect dangerously back and forth between social subjects and that are mediated on the surface of a pejorative mirror: a mirror eulogized by Althusser as facilitating the flow of ideology and by Lacan as inaugurating the subject's self-consciousness.[62] As Leslie Heywood reductively but hauntingly incants, "The internal violence that becomes anorexia is dependent on three fully functioning bodies: the ghost body (body image, what we perceive our bodies to be); the real body (biology); and the ideal body (the body image we hold in theory as an ideal that we would like our bodies to become)."[63]

It is in this kind of limit scenario, when the subject is met with the paradoxical *convergence and conflict* of ideology and agency, that the question of *liveness* taken up in performance theory becomes most urgent, and potentially most fatal. Peggy Phelan's oft-cited claim that performance "becomes itself through disappearance" argues for the unique ontological power of performance in both its eminent *presence* and its imminent *loss*.[64] Anorexia archives this indelible presence, revealing loss to be "one of the central repetitions of subjectivity."[65] Moreover in the context of the clinical encounters I am citing Phelan's evocative account of "the politics of performance" gestures to the durational nature of anorexia as a practice requiring constant rearticulation of a refusal to eat and reveals anorexia as a representational form whose central meaning derives from the disappearance, the "falling away of the Flesh every day more and more," fantasized and eventuated by its persistent denial of sustenance.

This staging of clinical normativity is also *performative* in shaping the social contexts from which it derives its considerable authority and to which it gestures in defining health. In the turn to diagnose men and boys with anorexia the function of social normativity, that is, the arrangement of particularly gendered subjects within normative social structures of belonging, infuses the practices of naming the disease and charting a cure. For example, often theorized as attendant to anorexia in men is the corresponding identification of gender identity disorder.[66] This astonishing correlation has a contradictory implication: it seems to reassert anorexia as an ontologically female condition and then regards men diagnosed as anorexic as psychically (and abnormally) identified with or *as* women. *This anorexic body* is diagnosed as male but presumed disordered in that approximation, in flagrant abuse of the experiential normalcy anticipated for and upon it as masculine. Any treatment that derives from such a correlation must then respond to a two-pronged threat: the immanence of death for those who continue to starve and a pathologized *impeachment* of masculinity extending from and defined by the very diagnosis as anorexic. In the words of two early studies, male anorectics "fear the masculine role" and exhibit a "notable lack of assertive masculinity or identification."[67]

In other words, male anorexia, with its diagnostic correlation to gender identity disorder, reveals (recalling Kaja Silverman's work on the "dominant fiction") how masculinity is clinically enabled as a model subject formation, what Freud might have called an "ego-ideal," and enforced specifically at the site of the male body.[68] "Enforced" may seem too strong a word to describe the therapeutic techniques enlisted to respond to what is ultimately a matter of life and death. But in the medical and psychiatric literature on men and boys diagnosed with anorexia, another ghostly figure repetitively returns, a figure that was itself included in the *DSM* as its own disease entity until 1973: homosexuality.[69] Strikingly, homosexuality is often explicitly named as a risk factor for anorexia in men.[70] Calling to mind the range of horrific techniques historically deployed in attempts to cure patients of homosexual desire, this slippage in the literature on male anorexia portends another function of clinical intervention: to reassert the social value of normativity and to reorient subjects to their antici- pated, or *enforced*, positions within it.

Sexuality appears most prominently in the very diagnostic code of the *DSM* as its fourth criterion: amenorrhea, or the cessation of menstrual cycles. Obviously this criterion presents a problem for diagnosing men and boys, who are by definition amenorrheal. But where the code ex- cludes men and boys from this diagnostic standard (stipulating "in post- menarcheal females") it also marks its own silence on the question of an equivalent measure. In some studies researchers have claimed a cognate symptom for use in identifying male anorexia: "decreased sexual drive and performance in anorexic males."[71] It is important to note that the proposed male equivalent to amenorrhea includes both sexual *drive*, that is, desire (or "Passions"), and decreased sexual *performance*, that is, the ability to participate actively in an intersubjective erotic encounter, pre- sumably all the way to its bitter, fluid end. Although these studies do not elaborate on the specific manifestations of desire and performance that could be quantitatively or qualitatively measured to *matter* in such ac- counting, this affiliation between amenorrhea on one hand and sexual drive and performance on the other implies that women and men are imbricated — by virtue of their mutual participation in reproductive sex- ual behavior — in this articulation of clinical and social health. Positioning sexual drive and performance in men as equivalent to menstruation in women writes the gendered subject into a larger narrative of consump- tive, reproductive normativity.[72]

In other words, the consumption at issue in anorexia's clinical presence is not only a question of food. Arguing that women's bodies are figured as mothers, housewives, and prostitutes in the master narrative of late capi- talism, Leopoldina Fortunati suggests:

The separation of labor power into two functions — capacity for production and capacity for reproduction — has another aspect. It has a *sexual* connotation — the sexual division of labor — revealed by the fact that the capacity to *produce* has been primarily developed in the *male* worker, while the capacity to *reproduce* has been primarily developed in *female* workers.[73]

The relationship of anorexia to capitalist discourse and exchange has generally, both popularly and theoretically, been described in causative terms, as exemplary of the effects of patriarchal expectations deployed in marketing campaigns to promote dissatisfaction with one's bodily appearance and so to compel a turn to a wide range of commodities, including products and services, for a reprieve; such commodities are themselves posed as cures, not for one's dissatisfaction, but for the imperfections from which that unhappiness derives. Commodity culture both displaces its own ideological tendency to promote displeasure and provides the remedy that keeps satisfaction always just out of reach. Fortunati reveals another deeply buried and vastly more insidious flow within the culture of the commodity: the gendered division of labor around sexual reproduction, which itself functions to produce more and more subjects who will themselves become consumers. Just as anorexia, commonly conceived as a deadly response to the pressures of a patriarchal imperative to commodify the body, paradoxically interrupts the practice of consumption in its persistent self-denial, it also intervenes in the *reproduction* of consumers: a double blow.

Performing a refusal to consume disrupts the continuity with which commodity culture reproduces itself on several levels; most immediately, bodies who no longer consume are no longer consumptive in the strictest sense, and thus are absent themselves from the cycle in which capitalism functions. But just as significant, anorexic bodies, whether amenorrheal or decreased in sexual drive, can no longer produce and reproduce as gendered and sexual subjects are compelled to do, thus disrupting the endless regeneration of new subjects who will consume. Because anorexia weakens the body systematically, anorexic bodies become less and less able to work at all; they simply stop performing.

The emergence of diagnostic constituencies of men and boys within the medical literature has revealed the function of anorexia in archiving the discontents of commodity culture and the profoundly insistent extension in ideologies of health to expectations for cultural identification and social position. And into that slow downward spiral — not simply the physical decline of anorectics, but also their diminishing involvement in social normativity — the clinic and its treatment attempt to intervene. The ideological function of the clinic to attempt restorations in the physical, psychic, and social health of its subjects corresponds with Wendy Brown's characterization of "the man in the state" of liberal democracy.[74] Brown's overarching intent is to trace how the state functions in specifically masculinist modes to solicit faith in its own ability to produce freedom for its subjects. In particular she is concerned with contemporary political claims founded on appeals to state institutions for the bestowal of a consortium of rights ranging from privacy to free expression, protection against invasions of those rights, and retribution for discrete histories of injury. She cautions, "While minimal levels of protection may be an essential prerequisite for freedom, freedom in the barest sense of participating in the conditions and choices shaping a life, let alone in a richer sense of shaping a common world with others, is . . . in profound tension with externally provided protection."[75] In Brown's estimation state power reproduces itself by propagating its self-image as the ultimate guarantor of safety and thus freedom.

The clinic is intimately involved in this complicated political economy of protection through what I have thus far called "diagnosis," "treatment," and "health" and is simultaneously implicated in ideological foundations that privilege and implement a specific construction of normativity. Brown's analysis helps us to make sense of the deeply conflicted relationship that many subjects have with the clinic: the clinic is often essential in mitigating suffering and extending the possibilities for a long and full life; it helps us to thrive. Simultaneously the clinic is neither culturally neutral nor ideology-free. In this respect it institutionally enacts the very paradox of subjectivation by facilitating experiences characterized by both recognition and estrangement, both resemblance and otherness, both empathy and disaffection. In the case of anorexia this is perhaps nowhere more explicit than in one of the most common forms of psychological treatment, in which psychiatrists assist anorectics in tracing the shapes of their bodies onto large sheets of butcher paper, point out the frailty of those silhouetted forms, and finally compose another (presumably healthy) body shape.

A recent HBO film documenting the experiences of anorectics in a residential treatment center includes several scenes demonstrating this technique.[76] Those scenes, indeed the film as a whole, are extraordinarily difficult to watch, largely because we bear witness to the anorectic's struggles to replace one set of internalized bodily demands, incorporated from a larger cultural and familial context, with another set of externally received norms, these from medical and psychiatric professionals working tirelessly to heal their afflictions. The tension between these extremes demonstrates in vivid detail the deep commitment to promote normalcy, the reliance on ideological frameworks in making meaning of oneself in the world, and the tendency to look to others in order to see oneself.

At the opposite end of the treatment spectrum is another instantiation of the very same principle, but imposed with all the force of the direst state intervention. For anorectics who refuse to participate in this mapping of bodily images, or any other tactic aimed to draw an end to their fasts, the authority of the clinic, the family, and the state coalesce into the most dramatic staging of alimentary normativity: force-feeding. When all else fails, the feeding tube intervenes *between body and subject* to force the anorectic to acquiesce and thus to restore some state of normalcy in the consumptive and reproductive potential for exchange in the body (if not the subject). We see in this extreme case an example, in Allen Feldman's words, of "the condition and image of the human body infested with the state apparatus."[77]

Such techniques of surveillance and mastery map directly onto the most conventional impressions of masculinity as the allegorical hero who purports to know better than most how to enforce and to regulate a state of civil, normative calm and, above all, health. We can find "the man in the clinic," just as Brown and others have sought to reveal "the man in the state." This drive to ideological normativity is not limited to endgame scenarios like the one I have just described, but infuses the clinical discourse and practice around anorexia. Against more customary narratives that tell the story of anorexia along discretely gendered lines, I propose that the clinical presentation of male anorexia reveals that discourse and practice depend upon the imbrication of male bodies and female bodies, masculinity and femininity, men and women in order to reinforce normative consumption in the broadest sense of that word.

In this way anorexia archives the melancholy of commodity culture:[78] it entails concurrent conformity to and conflict with the demands and discontents of normativity. That is, anorexia archives its own compulsive rejections, even as the anorexic body disappears, "falling away . . . every day more and more." In his stirring "Freudian impression," *Archive Fever*, Jacques Derrida ultimately poses the archival drive as a similarly paradoxical project of remembering and forgetting, consumption and expulsion, preservation and death. Dependent on the commencement of its originary commandment, for Derrida the archive relies on the authority of its production, its "consignment," its distinction, that is, its *diagnosis* as profoundly as it depends on the materials it purports to house.[79] As such, the archive manifests a concentrated and centripetal site in which the institution of its authority, the melancholy of its remembrance, and the geography of its presence circulate around *hunger*: the wistful but compulsive longing to accumulate the residue of loss. Derrida evocatively casts this archival drive to remember as a *burn*:

> To be *en mal d'archive* . . . is to burn with a passion. It is never to rest, interminably, from searching for the archive right where it slips away. It is to run after the archive, even if there's too much of it, right where something in it anarchives itself. It is to have a compulsive, repetitive, and nostalgic desire for the archive, an irrepressible desire to return to the origin, a homesickness, a nostalgia for the return to the most archaic place of absolute commencement. No desire, no passion, no drive, no compulsion, indeed no repetition compulsion, no *"mal-de"* can arise for a person who is not already, in one way or another, *en-mal d'archive*.[80]

The archive has "the force of a law" and the visceral presence of a fever.[81] Derrida positions the archive against "the death drive," summoning Freud's citation of the "organism's" instinct to reduce conflicting psychic excitations and "to die only in its own way."[82] For Derrida the death drive "is at work, but since it always operates in silence, it never leaves any archives of its own. It destroys in advance its own archive, as if that were in truth the very motivation of its most proper movement. It works *to destroy the archive*. . . . It devours it. . . . It leaves no monument, it bequeaths no document, of its own."[83] But even as the death drive represents a kind of archival *violence*, exacting violence *upon* the archive, Derrida ultimately, and persuasively, positions that violence at and as the ontology of the archive itself—its compulsive, repetitive burn—as archive fever:

> Repetition itself, the logic of repetition, indeed the repetition compulsion, remains . . . indissociable from the death drive. And thus from destruction. Consequence: right on that which permits and conditions archivization, we will never find anything other than that which exposes to destruction, and in truth menaces with destruction. . . . The archive always works, *a priori*, against itself.[84]

Finally "the archive is made possible by the death, aggression, and destruction drive, that is to say also by originary finitude and expropriation."[85]

Likewise oriented both as and against its own preservation, anorexia persists in the logic of a similar kind of fever: to absorb, to cast away; to reflect, to deny; to consume, to refuse. Further, in some clinical studies of diagnosed anorectics researchers have identified Wernicke-Korsakoff syndrome as an effect of anorexic practice and sustained undernourishment.[86] Wernicke-Korsakoff, which is most often associated with heavy, long-term alcohol consumption, is primarily characterized by "persistent, severe anterograde amnesia and significant retrograde memory loss":[87] a diminishing capacity to integrate events from the present into long-term memory and an inability to recall events from the past. What some clinicians summarize as a "disorientation in place and time,"[88] this disintegration of the function of memory enacts an almost literal incarnation of Derrida's archive fever as simultaneous destruction and preservation. To use Herbert Blau's word, it is a radical *amortization* of presence, "the representation of a lack which is the recovery of a loss."[89]

Or, to return to the film with which I opened this chapter, it is "undoing" even as it "becomes." In the final scene of *Tom's Flesh*, suggestively titled "Post-Script," the narrator describes his continuing struggle to reconcile the trauma of his childhood abuse with a present-day relationship with his father, revealing that he is now considering electroconvulsive therapy as a last-ditch effort, not to heal, but to forget, to erase the repetitive echo of his father's haunting voice. In this final scene Tom's voice sounds further removed from the film than we have yet heard it, as if recorded over the failing connection of a telephone conversation, grainy, rumbling, hollow. "It's something that I'm considering to erase the . . ." — here a long pause, full but unmarked — "the memories and the anger, and to let go of it, and to basically kill that part of myself that will not let me continue to want to live." Despite our longing to see Tom in his entirety — the healed Tom, the postoperative Tom, the adult Tom — we are left at the close of the film remembering a series of repetitive reflections, often indistinguishable from one another, spliced among scenes that function like dreams: recalcitrant theaters of the repressed, their surface-level images ghosting a deeply unknowable unconscious beneath. Tom's desire "to kill that part of [him] that will not let [him] continue to want to live," a sentence that mediates self-presence exhaustively with its persistent prepositional phrases, echoes the violent abjection staged earlier by his father's menacing voice: "You're not my son"; "Pack your things. I'm giving you away"; "Get out of here." There is finally no Tom for us to see. We are left only with the knowledge that his becoming, and his undoing, are yet incomplete.

CHAPTER TWO

enduring performance

•

All perfectly formed animals are to be divided into three parts, one
that by which food is taken in, one that by which excrement is dis-
charged, and the third the region intermediate between them.

—Aristotle, *On Youth and Old Age, On Life
and Death, On Breathing*

It is more difficult for boys to withstand fasting.

—Attributed to Hippocrates

The hunger artist lies in a cage on a tiny bed of hay. He is so withered that
he appears skeletal, the contours and etchings of his weak form empha-
sized by the skin-tight clothes he wears. His watchers crowd around,
desperate for a glance. Most of them have come before to see him; some
purchased "season tickets for the last few days and sat from morning till
night in front of his small barred cage." He has fasted for forty days, the
maximum length of time "fixed by his impresario" that he may starve
while on display. Forty days is a comfortable margin: it has been done
before; it casts a vaguely biblical ring; and it provides a suitable crescendo
before the closing ceremony:

> The flower-decked cage was opened, enthusiastic spectators filled the
> hall, a military band played, two doctors entered the cage to measure
> the results of the fast, . . . and finally two young ladies appeared, bliss-
> ful at having been selected for the honor, to help the hunger artist down

the few steps leading to a small table on which was spread a carefully chosen invalid repast.

But soon the hunger artist turns against his audience and his boss. Why stop now when he could go on? "Why should he be cheated of the fame he would get for fasting longer, for being not only the record hunger artist . . . but for beating his own record by a performance beyond human imagination?" Why, in other words, should the hunger artist be compelled to withdraw from his performed endurance, when he feels an equal internal compulsion to persist? Against this urge the faster's impresario brings photographs in evidence, "also on sale to the public, showing the artist on the fortieth day of the fast lying in bed almost dead from exhaustion." With these the hunger artist consents, not from fear that they demonstrate the dangers of his fast, but with the hopelessness of silence: "To fight against this lack of understanding, against a whole world of non-understanding, was impossible." In time he would relent to the impulse to prolong the fast beyond its authorized duration. Later cast to the periphery of the fair, a sideshow to the main event, the hunger artist would lose his audience and, left unobserved, continue to starve long past the forty days. He would shrink from visibility, lost in the dust of that cushioning straw. "Are you still fasting?" they asked when they glimpsed him as they scraped the cage clean. "I can't help it," he replied, drifting then across the precipice of presence, gone.[1]

First published in the journal *Die Neue Rundschau* in 1922, Kafka's story, often described as "a metaphor for the artist,"[2] was drawn against a recent tradition of public fasts staged in a variety of settings. This tradition was marked by the popularity of several famous male fasters and by the concurrent notoriety of well-known "fasting girls": women who claimed to abstain from food for months or years, usually ensconced in domestic spaces and typically diagnosed as "hysterics."[3] The first of these groups, men who publicly starved themselves for weeks at a time, emerged in response to a widely publicized fast set in New York City in 1880. Dr. Henry S. Tanner, a Minneapolis physician who claimed that abstinence from normative consumption could cure disease and prolong life, staged his "Great American Sensation" for forty days during a sweltering New York summer.[4] As Upton Sinclair remembered, "When I was a boy living in New York, there was a man by the name of Dr. Tanner, who took a forty-day fast. He was on public exhibition at the time, and was supposed to be watched day and night; the newspapers gave a great deal of attention to the story, and crowds used to come to gaze at him."[5] Attended by observers, including physicians and newspaper columnists, and cheered by supporters in and beyond New York, Tanner fasted to demonstrate that the human body could sustain its own vital energies without eating. When his fast ended successfully on 8 August 1880 Tanner was presented with challenges from men across the United States and Europe; the most famous of these (and the inspiration for Kafka's text) was Giovanni Succi, an Italian who would stage fasts in cities across Europe at the end of the nineteenth century.[6] Succi in turn would inspire others to exhibit themselves as they slowly starved, sometimes in or near restaurants serving lavish banquets, often (like Kafka's disappearing protagonist) in circuses and traveling fairs.[7] Due to the wide popularity of Tanner's original "scientific exhibition," the hunger artist was born.[8]

Nearly one hundred years after Tanner's "trying ordeal" and long after hunger artists had receded in popularity,[9] staged fasts reemerged in another domain: the gallery of late-twentieth-century conceptual and performance art. Chris Burden in particular would complete extended periods of self-starvation (among other potentially fatal exploits) in his notorious "endurance performances."[10] Although neither his stated intentions for fasting nor the formal qualities of his fasts were identical to Dr. Tanner's exhibitions, Burden's performances elicited similar responses from audience members and critics who were either moved or repelled by the feats of endurance. Like Kafka's hunger artist, who subsisted in part because of his captivated public, for both Tanner and Burden the economy of the fasting body's survival was sustained, reinforced, and intensified by the economy of the spectacle. I consider the performances of both Tanner and Burden as emblematic of this coalescence between the practice and the spectacle of self-starvation.

For both Tanner and Burden staged fasts were founded on a robustly empirical approach, embracing the *experience* (and not just the *appearance*) of self-starvation in crafting meaning of and for themselves. Tanner and Burden thus reflected and deployed the convergence of existential and representational death by implicating their audiences not as passive observers of but as active witnesses to their slow emaciation. That is, these staged feats of endurance compelled and were compelled by their witnesses, even as they resisted straightforward comprehension as mere appearance; to borrow Cathy Caruth's words, they "simultaneously defie[d] and demand[ed] our witness."[11] Further, by demonstrating their durability in undergoing such "trying ordeals" both Tanner and Burden deployed the spectacular imbrication of *endurance* and *masculinity* by staging what Theodor Reik called the "demonstrative" component of masochism, in the broadest sense of that word.[12]

In tracing this genealogy from Tanner to Burden I will shift institutional registers between the clinic and the gallery throughout the narrative that follows. In doing so I implicitly suggest that there is some convergence in the ideologies of *looking* deployed within these two domains. This is not to deny the significant historical, institutional, and representational differences between clinics and galleries, nor is it to ignore the distinct performative effects that retroactively distinguish between diagnostic practices executed in clinical encounters and aesthetic practices staged in gallery exhibitions. But at the same time I do not intend to drive too stubborn a wedge between these institutional domains; instead I propose that the clinic and the gallery coalesce around certain kinds of spectatorial encounters and manifest their historiographical traces on overlapping, at times interwound cultural registers.

On this note, and to return briefly to my note on masculinity and endurance: in her brilliant study of performance artists working in the 1970s the art historian Amelia Jones specifically explores masochism as foundational to what she calls "dis/playing the phallus" in the work of several male avant-garde artists. Jones is careful to stipulate, however, that in her reading of these artists "masochism . . . is to be understood in a metaphoric rather than a clinical sense."[13] But to speak of a diagnostic category as if it did not depend on representational practices is to neglect to recognize how such aspects of lived experience are culturally located, semiotically promiscuous, and historically specific. Likewise to rely on the descriptive value of a diagnostic term without recalling the historical pronouncement of that term in scientific and medical settings threatens to forget or displace the cultural heft of the term's assumed deviance from what it clinically designates as health. I embark upon this study of Tanner and Burden with these cautions in mind, embracing both the representational and the diagnostic significance, or what Mary Russo might call "the aerial and the grotesque,"[14] of self-starvation.

On 18 January 1880 the editors of the *New York Times* were fixated on the subject of hunger. That day's issue includes, in forbidding Gothic font, the headline "Starvation of Children" for an article recounting the tragic story of the Reverend Edward Cowley and his mismanagement of a large Manhattan orphanage. Upon assuming the directorship of The Shepherd's Fold Cowley was accused and convicted of physically assaulting and withholding meals from the children under his care. The article describes the grim appearance of one child in particular, five-year-old Louis Victor, whose "arms, hands, face, and body were greatly emaciated"; he "was nothing but skin and bones." This image of young Louis is strangely set against the description of Cowley himself: "a little, nervous man, about 50 years old, with a gray beard, and a peculiar way of bobbing his head and agitating his body when he makes a statement."[15] In the same issue of the *Times* the editors report on a "revival of monasticism" among the locals. This story describes certain men (of whom "society has tired" or who "have been crossed in love") turning to lay monastic orders, which were "keeping up a continuous rivalry with the theatre, the band, and the casino." Despite their recent popularity such orders were finding it difficult to retain their newer members over time, largely because of their strict regimens in diet, entertainment, and other "worldly pleasures"; even those devotees who survived the orders' attrition found themselves "constantly in disgrace for disobedience."[16]

Directly across the broadsheet page from the story on monasticism, a letter from Minnesota takes up several long columns. Titled "Fasting and Living Death," this letter would initiate a protracted and spectacular battle of wills over the human body's ability to endure extended periods of self-starvation. Henry S. Tanner, graduate of the Eclectic Medical Institute of Cincinnati, a homeopathic college that would eventually succumb to the growing dominance of allopathic medicine in the United States, offers a challenge to William A. Hammond, a former surgeon general and a prominent neurologist in private practice in New York. Tanner offers to repeat a previously completed extended fast under close supervision in order to prove that the "vital chemistry" of the human body can be self-sustaining. He claims this will be neither a negligible nor an inconsequential feat: "I have gone down to the very portals of the tomb, and suffered the pangs of hunger for 42 days that I might gain light and knowledge on this subject, and now if by my efforts I can aid in awakening the slumbering consciences of nations and individuals to thought and action upon this all-important theme, I shall not have suffered in vain."[17]

At the time debates about health circulated between two sharply divided groups of medical professionals, variously identified as homeopaths and allopaths, spiritualists and materialists, irregular and regular. This debate concentrated in particular on the viability and credibility of "fasting girls": women who claimed not just to survive, but indeed to thrive during long periods of inanition. When Tanner's letter was published the most famous and popular of these fasting girls was Mollie Fancher, the "Brooklyn Enigma," who claimed to have endured complete abstinence from eating for fourteen years. An early feature-length article devoted to Fancher's story was published as "A Remarkable Case" in the *Brooklyn Daily Eagle* in 1866; occasional updates in local, national, and international serials would continue to describe her convalescence until her death in 1916.[18] In her youth Fancher had been "a tall, slender and graceful young lady, a decided blonde, and a universal favorite among her schoolmates, teachers, and friends."[19] At sixteen, after a significant loss of weight, she was diagnosed with nervous indigestion and (like Richard Morton's seventeenth-century patients) was told to refrain from reading too avidly and to spend more of her time in the country. Within months of receiving these prescriptions Fancher had gained weight, stopped fainting, and become a "graceless and fearless" equestrian.[20] But the following year, back in Brooklyn, she fell under a streetcar, unable to extricate her crinoline from its undercarriage. When the conductor finally realized what had happened and brought the streetcar to a stop, he found her there, badly injured, unconscious, and wound up tightly in her dress. It was 8 June 1865; this date marked Mollie Fancher's ascendance as a "fasting girl."[21]

During her initial recuperative period Fancher was plagued by a constellation of symptoms, including a temporary loss of hearing, sight, and smell; painful, extended convulsions; and a complete loss of appetite. The last of these was so extreme that her physicians feared her throat was hermetically sealed. For six weeks Fancher was confined to her bed with frozen limbs and severe spinal pain. When she attempted to move unaided around her home, she lost feeling in her arms and legs and collapsed to the floor. Her lungs hemorrhaged relentlessly, leading her family and friends to believe the physicians' prognosis of imminent death; Fancher herself continually kept a finger to her wrist, checking her pulse and declaring, "It beats yet."[22] Eight months after the streetcar incident she began slipping into a series of "trances"; Dr. Tanner would later describe such periods of unconsciousness as "mimicking death," and Fancher herself would write, "I was told I represented the appearance of being dead, and my physician pronounced me so."[23]

During this period of trances Fancher slipped in and out of consciousness and experienced numerous convulsions. For two months she was attended by fourteen doctors and nurses, who stabilized her during seizures and attempted unsuccessfully to feed her to keep her alive. Using accepted standards of care the attendants resorted to a range of treatments, including force-feeding, alcohol rubs, shaving and blistering, shocks from a battery wired to her skin, adjustments made to her bed's alignments with "the earth's magnetic currents," sitz baths, herbal baths, and ice baths. Fancher recalls her response to these attempts to revive her:

> I have a temper, and it was then aroused. Food was forced into my mouth, and I kept it there until I got the opportunity and then I rejected it. My doctor thought I was insane, but, as a matter of fact, I was never more rational in my life. I found every remedy increased my sufferings, and I begged to be let alone. In fact, my spasms and trances were essential to my living.

Rebelling so intensely against the treatment—"My vocabulary was insufficient to express my feelings, and I positively refused to submit"— Fancher urged her family to summon a new physician, Dr. S. Fleet Spier, who "began to recognize the fact that these spasms and trances served an essential part in maintaining life, and if they were discontinued [she] would unquestionably die."[24] Concerned about her inanition in particular, Spier tried a different kind of bath, drawn with beef tea; Fancher promptly lost her remaining senses (some of which would later return) and developed a "second sight, a power or sense of seeing without the use of the natural organs of sight": she became "clairvoyant."[25] When she regained the power of speech she began taking on the personae of friends and family members, performing wedding parties, dances, and barroom brawls. Dr. Spier indulged her, though unconvinced of her newfound gifts: "My theory has long been to do nothing to irritate my patient; I humored her, and have endeavored in that way to get her confidence, to get complete control of her."[26] Until her death Fancher would continue to convalesce in this state, surviving on little or no food for extended periods of time, the longest of which purportedly lasted fourteen years, and garnering in the meantime a good deal of popular and medical attention.[27]

For most medical professionals Fancher's claims to extended fasting were nothing more than a ruse. Most famously William Hammond declared her to be "a fraud" in his expansive treatise *Fasting Girls*, in which he proposed that such claims were indicative of underlying hysteria, with its symptomatic "proclivity to simulation or deception." Such cases of fasting girls—but Fancher's in particular—would provoke an extended debate about the healthfulness, the very possibility of extended self-starvation. Hammond represented the most conventional ("generally accepted by mankind") perspective:

> The body is a machine constructed for the purpose of working. The kinds of work which the body of a man or woman does are many. Every act of perception or sensation is an act of work; so is every thought, every emotion, every volition. The action of the heart or lungs in the circulation and respiration, the evolution of the animal heat, the various functions of secretion and excretion, digestion, motion, speech, etc., are all so many kinds of work. Now as regards work, it is well known that for its due performance force is required, and it is equally well known that for the development of force, matter that can be metamorphosed is necessary.[28]

In Hammond's estimation, which was characteristic of the materialist perspective in nineteenth-century medical circles, the most damning evidence against the feasibility of extended inanition derived from this notion of the body as ontologically defined by the work it performs. For Hammond consumption represented a necessary part of an economy of labor, and that economy defines the human body's very existence, its very *possibility*. That is, *performing work* is both the site and the sign of the body's *being*. Because long-term inanition disrupts that economy, the body not only ceases to be *able* to perform work; it also ceases to have *meaning* as a unit of existence.

But like other economies, Hammond acknowledged, the body produces surplus in the form of "matter that can be metamorphosed." Indeed in the following excerpt he seems to suggest that the body is *constituted* by such surplus, whose use to create the "force" required for "work" will prolong what is nonetheless inevitable: the body's existential and representational death.

> The human body differs from any other machine. . . . When a muscle contracts, it is the muscle itself which is consumed; when a thought is conceived it is the brain which provides the force; when an emotion is experienced, it is again the brain which is decomposed. The body, therefore, lives by the death of its own substance. . . . All bodily force results from [the body's] decomposition, and without this destruction of matter the body would be absolutely incapable of a single functional action. . . . The body can to a certain extent be used up in supplying the force required . . . but there is a limit to this, beyond which it is certain death to go.[29]

For Hammond and the materialists the body survives only insofar as it "functions." And because the body, by virtue of its internal and inherent "decomposition," can itself provide only a small portion of the force required for "work," without an external source of energy it will cease to be "functional": it will cease to *mean*, and it will cease to *be*. With this implication Hammond seems to suggest that the inevitable death eventuated by long-term inanition indicates both a representational and an existential failure: the self-starving body ceases to make sense (it is "nonsense," "humbug")[30] before it finally ceases to survive. It is precisely this claim to which Dr. Tanner objected, but the occasion for that objection would implicate Mollie Fancher yet again, in a controversy with which she had never agreed to participate.

In 1878, the year prior to the publication of *Fasting Girls*, Hammond offered Mollie Fancher a series of challenges to prove the veracity of her claims: first, she must "read" the details of a bank check sealed within an opaque envelope; second, under the strict observation of Hammond and two colleagues from the New York Neurological Society, she must endure a month of fasting. If she should succeed in either of these challenges, Hammond pledged to pay her one thousand dollars and recant his doubt of her claims.[31] Angelyn Spignesi characterizes this ideology of observation, and its precedent as a mode of diagnosis, as an "upperworld classification": "They work with what they see externally and materially (for example, her size, weight, behavior) as well as by the attempt to contain such observations in empirical, personalistic, and developmental formats."[32] Fancher declined Hammond's offer, citing the socially inappropriate nature of such an arrangement: three men watching her continuously in her bedroom. Seeing an opportunity in her refusal Tanner offered himself as her surrogate. Hammond's response — that Tanner's fast could be scientifically significant only if performed under observation in a medical school approved by the New York Neurological Society — received the following reply:

> Believing Dr. Hammond to be actuated in his offer to Miss Fancher by a desire to learn more of the science of life and the laws that govern it, and desiring further light in this direction myself, I was led to make a proposal to him. . . . The proposition to turn me over to the management of a score or more of raw medical students, and to confine me during the test within the walls of a medical college, the atmosphere of which would necessarily be reeking the poison of a dozen or more decomposing cadavers, has

convinced me that I am mistaken in my estimate of the man and the object in view in making his proposal. It is unnecessary to say that I decline to accept the proposal as given to your reporter, for the conditions are such as to preclude all hope of success.[33]

Though he declined Hammond's original offer, Tanner would eventually set the conditions to stage his fast in Clarendon Hall, a former Masonic temple that had been converted into the "irregular" United States Medical College in New York,[34] observed by representatives from both the "regular" and the "irregular" schools. This fast was nothing short of a full-frontal attack on the conventional, materialist theory of the body's internal economies of sustenance. Although he had "long since broke[n] loose from the arbitrary restraints of the Code of Ethics laid down by the American Medical Association," Tanner wrote, "[I am determined] to relieve myself of the odium unjustly heaped upon me by the medical enemies of all righteousness."[35] He was careful to stipulate that "this wonderful test of human endurance" was not merely a demonstration, but also a stark warning against current customs for medical declarations of death followed by quick burials.[36] The fast, in other words, was an event of great importance, indeed a matter of life and death — not only for Tanner himself, but also for those declared deceased by the allopaths. Tanner aimed to prove that the inherent "vital chemistry" of a given human body could not always be measured on the surface of that body; that many who had been pronounced dead may in fact be alive, awakened from their "trances" and clawing at the edges of their tombs; and that the speed with which the "supposed-to-be-dead" are transferred to their graves thanks to the "inductive philosophy" of allopaths and undertakers might indeed be a form of murder. He wrote, "How quietly and submissively we submit to the infinitely more cruel and barbarous custom of hurrying the remains of our loved ones into the grave before we have ascertained to a certainty that the captive spirit is freed from its earthly entanglements. . . . Is there no means known to science by which this counterfeit of death can be detected?" As the editors of the *New York Times* characterized this impetus for Tanner's fast, "He raises his voice in earnest warning against the practice of burying with the haste which is common after apparent death, being firmly convinced that . . . life can be sustained without air, food, or water for weeks together . . . and that there is no absolutely sure sign of death from natural causes except decomposition."[37] For Tanner *external* "decomposition" was the only reliable "sign of death"; for Hammond *internal* "decomposition" marked the body's expenditures of "force" in performing the labor of exertion: thinking, feeling, breathing, moving. The debate between the regulars and the irregulars was thus also a question of representation: how to *read* the starving body; how to *register* the disappearance of "the vital principle."[38]

The significance of Tanner's fast, however, was not limited to the science of interpretation (and the scientific interpretation of *being*); it would also capture the imagination of many beyond the clinical realm. In the voluminous narratives published in American and European newspapers during Tanner's New York fast, physicians, philosophers, politicians, clergymen, historians, newspaper reporters, and everyday men and women would debate the viability of Tanner's feat and its many possible implications. In those reports Tanner himself would be relentlessly, microscopically observed. Every vicissitude in his physical and emotional state — his temperament, his vocal strength, the width of his chest, the strength in his wrists, the force of his breath, the fraying edges of his red blood "corpuscles"[39] — would be tracked with such descriptive flamboyance in the press that an uninitiated reader might assume he was the single most important man alive.

Before traveling to New York Tanner had so thoroughly theorized the dangers of eating that he had begun to run experiments on his own family. After one too many restrictive diets Tanner's wife, Mary, who professed to be a "normal" if "voracious" eater, sued for divorce.[40] After following Mary through several midwestern towns and attempting to reconcile with her, Tanner eventually settled in Minneapolis as a physician. On 15 July 1877 he was summoned by a colleague, Dr. A. Moyer, to consult on a particularly perplexing case that kept them both occupied for much of the night. Tanner was afterward unable to sleep and painfully dyspeptic. With Moyer's assistance he diagnosed himself with "low gastric fever," attributed both to the difficult work of treating Moyer's patient and to the "abrupt change in his mode of living" occasioned by his divorce.[41] He prescribed for himself a fast until his discomfort subsided. Years later he described this precipitous decision:

> I was at such a low ebb physically and mentally at the time that I did not care whether I lived or died, and I determined that, since my drugs gave me no relief, I would starve myself to death ere I again would suffer the physical misery that had been mine for months preceding. I accordingly

told Dr. Moyer, my consulting companion, that I would not again eat food until I was dead or recovered in health.[42]

Under Moyer's observation Tanner abstained from all food for ten days, by which time the gastric fever had abated. But at this point Tanner felt so resilient that he decided to continue. According to his own report on the Minneapolis fast — and with Moyer's certification — he did not eat again until 29 August, six weeks after the commencement of the fast.[43] Of his first postfast repast, Dr. Moyer wrote, "His appetite [became] unappeasable, and . . . although he was taking large quantities at short intervals, he protested that he got no sense of fullness or repletion, that it was simply like 'pouring it down a rat hole'; the more he drank the more he wanted; the hungry system seeming to digest and assimilate it almost instantaneously."[44]

When Dr. Moyer, upon request, published a letter describing Tanner's fast in the *St. Paul Pioneer Press* he prompted a flurry a responses from physicians and scientists claiming that Tanner was a fraud, from advocates extolling the benefits of extended fasts, and from curious others offering anecdotes either supporting or refuting the possibility of long-term inanition. Tanner indignantly (but enthusiastically) participated in the debate, citing in evidence biblical accounts of forty-day fasts, medieval saints who fasted in penance, and the growing notoriety of several fasting girls (including Mollie Fancher).[45] As is characteristic of his later writing about the more famous New York fast, Tanner confidently proclaimed:

> I prefer to call the attention of your readers to *facts* that come under more general observation, and which present positive evidence that animal life can be (and is) prolonged, not for weeks only, but for months, without food. In the forms of animated nature, we have abundant evidence to support the assumption that total abstinence from food for many months does not involve the total extinction of the vital principle.[46]

Realizing that the success of his argument depended on the swivel between "can be" and "is," and feeling strongly that "[his] self-respect [forbade him] to quietly submit to the odium that an unjust, unreasoning skepticism ha[d] reflected on [his] good name," Tanner proposed to "repeat the experiment under the strictest surveillance, for the sum of five thousand dollars."[47]

Although his offer received no immediate response, Tanner became a minor midwestern celebrity, teaching fasting as a therapeutic practice and prescribing extended fasts to patients who presented with a variety of complaints. In late 1878 and throughout 1879, when the controversy around Fancher's case peaked in the press, he offered himself as her surrogate to prove the viability of long-term self-starvation to Hammond and the materialists. He was insistent that his fast be viewed as an experiment, not a spectacle; as he had earlier claimed in a letter to the *Pioneer Press*:

> I am not disposed to play the harlequin for the world's amusement or to gratify an idle curiosity. . . . I am not willing to pass through this trying ordeal simply for fame. I have no desire to be "the best advertised man in America." . . . My highest ambition is, and I hope ever will be, to be a man in the strictest sense of that term. I desire to live up to my highest conviction of right.[48]

Despite such continuing assertions that the fast should be considered a laboratory and not a theatrical performance, the primary focus for much of the concurrent reportage on Tanner's "brutal exhibition" focused on the spectacle *as spectacle*:[49] the "stage" of the lecture hall where he resided during the fast; the "amusements" provided by military bands, visiting pianists and vocalists; the stories read daily from letters received; the pleasure (and dandyish detail) Tanner took in his appearance. Moreover the reporters were obsessed with the question of how and by whom Tanner was surveilled, measured, and appraised. The *New York Times*, *Brooklyn Eagle*, *New York Herald*, and others published daily accounts of the measurements taken of Tanner's rapidly shrinking body and narrated at great length the several observational crises — discrepancies in what individual "watchers" claimed to have seen[50] — that arose during the forty days.

The New York fast began on 28 June 1880 at noon. Tanner was stripsearched at that hour, his watchers carefully examining and measuring his body to guarantee that no food was hidden in the folds of his clothing, and also (especially given his declared intention "to be a man in the strictest sense") to ensure that his body had no peculiarities that might unfairly affect his ability to abstain from eating.[51] The commencement of the fast, drawing a small audience, would prove to be a far less resounding event than its completion; that is, the imprecise moment of *beginning* to stop eating (he had enjoyed a breakfast of cow's milk earlier in the day)[52] seemed less significant than the fixed hour of his return to food, his first hungry meal, forty days later.

This is not to say that the intervening forty days passed with little notice. Indeed as Tanner's body withered from the effects of the fast his literary presence in the press swelled exponentially. Coverage of the fast expanded with such geographical and rhetorical momentum that it would elicit offers of marriage, challenges to future "starving matches," religious condemnation, religious endorsement, and political commentary from a broad range of readers across the United States and Europe. "Dr. Tanner, you know, is unquestionably a man of science — a great genius — and he has a mind above eating," wrote a Milwaukee woman who believed her third husband would soon die of overindulgence. "If there is anything in this world I would rejoice in it would be to marry a man who does not care to eat."[53] An indignant French reader wrote more urgently, "Tanner has done the poor a great deal of harm. . . . This prodigious fast will not fill the stomach of the starving. There is no need to make such experiments; the wretched make them every winter. . . . The familiar appeal, 'My God, sir, pity me; I've eaten nothing for two days,' will never more have any effect on us."[54] In New York a reporter suggested, "The house staff [at Bellevue Hospital] chose a poor time for their appeal to public sympathy [over the poor quality of the food provided to them and their patients]. Dr. Tanner has created so wide an impression of the sufficiency of air and water, that few of the starving can get any sympathy until the forty-first day."[55] From a more vaunted perspective certain clergymen noted that should it succeed, Tanner's fast could present a "very serious blow" to Christianity: "The fast of the Founder of Christianity for the same period in the wilderness [would cease] to be a valuable dogma."[56] As the editors of *Scribner's Monthly* put it, "One thing at least Dr. Tanner has done. He has removed the fast of Christ from the realm of miracle, and made that credible to the disbeliever in miracles which seemed to him like a fable or an idle tale."[57] At any rate, wrote a prescient reporter for the *New York Times*, "there can be no doubt, from the tenor of the letters received, that his success would lead to many more such foolish undertakings, and starving exhibitions might become a popular sport."[58]

Such appraisals, which became increasingly diverse as the fast progressed, were included alongside daily accounts of Tanner's measurements. On the first day, during the close examination of his body and clothes, "he weighed 157½ pounds, measured 40 inches around the breast, 38¾ inches around the abdomen, 22 inches around the upper part of the thigh, and 11½ inches around the middle of the arm. His pulse was irregular, averaging 88 beats per minute; temperature 99° (98⅖° being normal), respiration, 18."[59] These desiderata were updated by the watchers regularly and published in newspapers from the *Los Angeles Times* to the *Times* of London. The economy of Tanner's daily intake (first nothing, then only water) and output (mostly urine but occasionally bile) was also presented to the alternately admiring and skeptical public, who (judging from the sheer volume of letters Tanner received) were obsessed, if not uniformly convinced, by his performance.[60] In an especially bizarre letter received midway through the forty days an anonymous author offered the following derisive bill of fare:

Claradon Hotel
Dr. Tanyard, Proprietor,
Meals at all hours.
Breakfast.
Dreamland Hash.
Dinner.
Promasory steak,
Invisible sauce.
Supper.
One gargle,
Five minutes' snooze.
Extras.
A walk around the block — fresh air.
Desert.
Ices.
Ice a la water,
Ice a la lump.[61]

Tanner himself seemed to oscillate between gratitude for the attention and fury at being so hounded by the growing numbers of visitors to Clarendon Hall. On some days he might be "crusty, somber" or "extremely annoyed at the whispered conversations": "He receives their marks of attention with a very ill grace." On others he was "very much pleased . . . when [a visitor] played on the piano and sang for him."[62] On one occasion, when "regular" watcher Dr. Bradley accused an "irregular" watcher of slipping Tanner a sponge soaked with beef tea, Tanner "cried and sobbed as if his heart would break."[63] But generally speaking, despite the occasional outburst and such variances in his temperament, Tanner "liked passionately to have sympathizing persons around him. He seemed fully sensible that the near presence of individuals that were en rapport tended directly to augment the vital energies."[64] He seemed to believe, that is, that although he fasted alone, his success hinged on the presence of supporters; despite its seemingly solitary nature, the fast depended upon the intangible, intersubjective exchange between Tanner and his audience.

But the success of the fast as a *scientific* demonstration, never uniformly accepted, though even William Hammond would eventually certify Tanner's abstinence,[65] also required the interaction between Tanner and his critics, those regular doctors who persisted in denying its authenticity and its significance. This presented a specific medicolegal conundrum for the watchers, especially those who disbelieved in the benefits of fasting. Given that the materialists in attendance would otherwise intervene to stop a given fast—this was their standard of care—for them both to allow Tanner to persist and to continue participating as observers potentially created a condition of legal responsibility for whatever ill effects he might suffer. Should Tanner die while fasting—and the newspapers regularly posed this possibility—his watchers might be found culpable for that death, particularly (and ironically) if they professed to refuse the feasibility of extended inanition. In a column published near the end of the forty days the editors of the *Brooklyn Eagle* gestured to the case of a well-known fasting girl who eventually died from self-starvation; her doctors "were tried, convicted, and sent to prison for life."[66] A group of clergymen cast this issue as a *moral* quandary: "Should [Tanner's watchers] allow him to die without taking every possible means to prevent such a conclusion of the experiment, such as forcing food into his stomach against his will, a certain degree of moral responsibility must surely attach to them."[67] The editors of the *Gentleman's Magazine* cast this conundrum broadly, suggesting that the ethical and moral implications of Tanner's fast would reveal some medical practices to be "little more than homicide." They broadly predicted, "The technical opinion that will have to be given in our coroners' courts, courts of justice, and other public places and the opinion that will have to be written in our technical and standard works of medical jurisprudence, must, indeed, from this time be considerably modified in many particulars."[68]

These concerns highlight one of the most significant implications of Tanner's fast: the body's economy of survival (debated by Hammond and Tanner in terms of its "decomposition") coalesced with an economy of exchange around the event of *witnessing* Tanner's slow emaciation. That is, the economy of the body and the economy of the spectacle fused as a profoundly vibrant economy of becoming: Tanner's body materialized, in a "maniacally charged present,"[69] not simply as the object of the spectacle, but as the conditions for and the limits of the spectacular. This encounter between watchers and watched, between the witness and the witnessed, reveals its own functional economy as existentially and representationally consequential as the body's economy of consumption. As Dr. Etienne Evitsky claimed near the end of the fast:

> Although life is intimately connected with the consumption of food, or of tissues in case of fasting, the mistake [of the materialist position] consists in assuming that life is the *result* of consumption, while in reality consumption is only the *manifestation* of life. If the former were the case how will we explain the fact that life ceases when the material of consumption is still abundant, as is always [the case] when animals die from starvation. . . . We must look for the cause of death from starvation in some direction other than the failure of materials to satisfy the above-named needs.[70]

Many correspondents would ultimately attribute this "other direction" of Tanner's success to his "will" to *demonstrate* the viability of his claims, to *show* what extended fasting looked like, to "*see and be seen*" while surviving "his dramatic and illusory death bed."[71] Tanner's fast, in other words, staged a theory of the *spectacle* and its effects on the "vital principle" as resolutely as it established the feasibility of self-starvation; indeed Tanner revealed these functions — seeing and being seen, consuming and being consumed — to be profoundly interwoven. Even his critics, especially those most virulently opposed to his exhibition, were compelled to contend not only with Tanner's self-sustained hunger, but also with "the pure aesthetic taste" of its display. As the comic poet Hereward Cockin wrote in 1889:

> INANE, self-glorious lunatic! Thy name
> Has swelled the mulish bray of bastard-fame,
> As that of one who immolates himself
> Beneath the Juggernaut of miser pelf;
> How beautiful the pure aesthetic taste
> That marks thy forty days of tissued waste!
> Thy blasphemous and idiotic fast.
> In lunacy, can only be surpassed
> By fools and quacks, who linger round the bed
> Of one, whose stomach's empty as his head.[72]

Almost a full century after Henry Tanner's New York fast Chris Burden burst onto the international art scene by creating endurance performances in which he submitted himself to a wide range of dangerous, potentially life-threatening acts. Most famously, for a split-second performance called *Shoot* staged on 19 November 1971, Burden stood before a very small audience at one end of the F-Space Gallery in Santa Ana, California, as a friend drew a rifle and fired a copper jacket .22 caliber bullet in his direction.[73] The bullet was intended to just barely graze his skin, but due to an imprecise aim or a fidget it pierced his left arm. Burden said, "[It] felt like a truck hit my arm at 80 m.p.h."[74]

Several photographs remain to document the performance. In the first Burden stares glassy-eyed at the camera as someone tapes gauze over the fresh wound. He is evidently shocked, perhaps speechless, as he sits trapped in the moment of just having been shot. A second photograph, which precedes the first, reveals the mise-en-scène of the performance: the shooter stands firmly in the foreground with the gun aimed, but Burden is caught in motion, his silhouette doubled in a duplicitous kind of half-presence. Neither exposure is fully visible, but both are intractably there in the image. A third photograph, which falls temporally between the first and the second, shows Burden walking away from where he was standing as he was shot. He holds his side, the wound just visible and blood running down his arm; he appears to be calling for help. In the background of this photograph stands a friend, her arms akimbo, smiling as Burden walks away, and a camera perched decisively upon its tripod. The presence of the camera and the spectator in the image highlights the semantic doubling in the title for the piece: Burden was shot by a camera just as he was shot by a gun. What that camera reveals is precisely what distinguished this performance from the tragically countless daily occurrences of someone being shot: its staging in a gallery, its label as performance, its explicit summons of an audience to an aesthetic event. Of course there is also another camera at work in the image: the camera capturing the photograph. Burden is surrounded by them, trapped within the interplay of shoots that are the conditions and the limits of the piece as performance.

This quality of *Shoot*, its positioning of the artist as a victim of both the work and the gaze, epitomizes how Burden has been historicized as the bad boy of avant-garde art produced in the 1970s. Near the end of his graduate training in sculpture at the University of California, Irvine, he shifted the focus of his work to performance. Of this transition Burden claims, "I realized that what I had made [previously] was not a piece of sculpture but something that had to be activated. These pieces were about physical activity, about how they manipulated my body. When I realized that, they stopped being sculpture."[75] The critic Robert Horvitz characterized Burden's earlier work thus: "All of these pieces attempt to establish a delicate sensual interplay between body and apparatus. They are extremely responsive to changes in position and muscle tension and seem to have been expressly designed to amplify these changes. They are not primarily to be looked at: they are to be donned and used."[76] Upon making this "realization," Burden began working with his body as a sculptural "object" that was similarly sensitive to the "changes in position and muscle tension" of a given spectatorial encounter. Jindrich Chalupecky explains:

> [Burden] is transferring his work from the tangible, only to his own body and its behavior. He does not want to create a new work of art, but a new body. It should no longer be a deserted and lonely body, but rather one that is receptive to the world and to other people — a body communicating and being communicated to, a body whose ownership has been given up, sacrificed.[77]

This "giving up" of the artist's body to the work became emblematic of Burden's performances in the 1970s, a period in which, like many of his colleagues in performance and conceptual art, he staged acts that hinged on the delicate, fraught participation of an audience who, by virtue of its very presence, endangered his life. That is, in his iconoclastic performances, Burden staged scenes that could at any moment become disasters; as a result, each of his early performances "flood[ed] its surroundings with an almost palpable atmosphere of anxiety and fascination."[78]

In September 1971, for example, Burden staged *Prelude to 220, or 110.* For this performance he strapped himself to the floor with copper bands, submerged two live wires into buckets of water, and placed the buckets on the gallery floor on either side of his head. If, by some accident or ill will, an audience member overturned one of the buckets, Burden would have been electrocuted. They didn't, and he wasn't, but such scenes stirred in spectators a visceral awareness of their complicity in the artist's predicament and their power to eventuate a bleak and dismal end: the death of the artist, the death of the art. Indeed this would-have-been quality of Burden's performance work, his eloquent evocation of the morbid possibilities of performance, its evaporative liveness, would so jolt his audiences and critics that he would be called, as Frazer Ward summarizes, "masochist; social therapist; existential populist; hero; alter ego of the biblical Samson; helpless victim; heroic victim; anthropologist; scientist, engineer, inventor, tinkerer; victim-by-request; hero of an impossible quest (a modern Don Quixote); voluntary scapegoat; and survivalist."[79] Staged in the subjunctive mood Burden's performances hung on an *if* that conditioned spectators' impressions of him as an artist and simultaneously intensified their experiences of his work as "pure presence." Robert Horvitz, for example, suggests that Burden's performances "work in a level of experience that is conspicuously extra-cultural, primal, atavistic. No piece is ever repeated. No piece is ever rehearsed."[80] Although this suggestion seems to position Burden's work as broadly and humanistically *universal*, a characterization I would strongly resist, it more pressingly implicates the performances in an indelible, unrepeatable, unrehearsable here and now, which accounts for the "palpable atmosphere of anxiety and fascination" they create.

Despite the harrowing *presence* produced by works like *Prelude to 220* and *Shoot*, Burden consistently denied that his intentions were suicidal; he would respond to questions about the danger of his work by insisting, "I don't think I'm trying to commit suicide."[81] Of *Prelude to 220* in particular he explained:

> People were angry at me [for a previous performance consisting of his violently screaming at audience members], so I presented them with an opportunity in a sacrificial situation — to atone for the earlier piece. Not really literally, I wasn't hoping that somebody was going to kick the buckets over, but just by putting myself in that position, it was kind of like a way of absolving myself from the last piece, which was aggressive and hostile.[82]

Such "hostility" was endemic to Burden's early performance work, although it would most often be directed at Burden himself rather than at his audience. In many of his early performances he explicitly submitted his own body to the painful, often dangerous experiments that constituted their dramatic actions. In *Icarus*, for example, he lay nude on the floor of his studio, with two rectangular glass panes balanced from his shoulders to the floor. Two assistants approached, pouring gasoline onto the "wings" and setting them alight with struck matches. Burden stood, sending the flaming sheets of glass crashing to the floor, and walked silently away. For *Trans-fixed* he nailed his hands to the top of a Volkswagen car in mock crucifixion; in *Doorway to Heaven* he plunged two live wires into his chest, setting off a vibrant display of sparks; for *Velvet Water* he stood just offstage (as if to ignore theater's fourth wall entirely) and repeatedly held his head under the water in a sink, gasping for air and nearly drowning.

In several of these early pieces Burden introduced technologies of *looking* directly into the performances. For *Movie on the Way Down* he strung himself up to the rafters of a gymnasium with a rope. An assistant chopped the anchored end of that rope with an axe; holding a small camera, Burden filmed his descent as he crashed to the floor. For *Through the Night Softly* he filmed himself crawling, with arms bound behind his back, through a field of shattered glass; he then purchased advertisement space on a local television station to play ten seconds of the brutal performance between commercials. In these ways Burden both employed a demonstrative kind of masochistic endurance in his work and deployed an evocative critique of the experience of witnessing such acts. In *Movie on the Way Down*, for example, the experience of falling becomes radically imbricated with the experience of watching someone fall. Such moves did not, in the idealized language of theatrical realism, attempt to facilitate empathic exchange; on the contrary, they represented an indictment of the witness, a sophisticated, embodied polemic against the presumption of passive looking that characterizes the most conventional understanding of the gallery. Burden's explicit deployment of the look in such works did not operate as simple allegories for the techniques and technologies of looking that conventionally define the gallery; nor did they function as enhancements of the spectator's ability to empathize with him by seeing as and thus feeling as the artist. Rather Burden incorporated the look, and thus the looker, directly into the act itself: the spectator became a witness.

In addition to such experiments with actions that could conceivably eventuate his own existential death, Burden staged performances that interrogated the representational death at work both in the space of the gallery and as a component of the everyday. Most blatantly, in *Oh, Dracula* he constructed a cloth chrysalis just large enough to fit his prostrate body. He hung the cloth — and himself — to a gallery wall, surrounded by the paintings of "Great Masters."[83] More hauntingly, in *Deadman* he lay down on a busy street outside of a Los Angeles gallery, covered in a black tarp resembling a coroner's body bag and encircled by police flares, signifying a traffic accident or a fatal hit-and-run. As a shocked audience stood watching from across the street, officers from the Los Angeles

Police Department cautiously approached the scene and, upon finding Burden alive, arrested him for "falsely reporting an emergency."[84]

In court the charges against Burden would eventually be dismissed — the jury was hung on his guilt or innocence — largely because of testimony from the gallery owner, Riko Mizuno. Mizuno compellingly distinguished between the criminalized activism associated with bomb threats — the origin for the "falsely reporting an emergency" laws that rationalized Burden's arrest — and the work of an artist by claiming three justifications for an acquittal. First, the actions in question occurred near a gallery and had that gallery's sanction. Second, an audience had been summoned to watch as Burden lay in the street. And third, Burden had a demonstrable reputation *as a performer*. In other words, Mizuno claimed, Burden was innocent of falsely reporting an emergency precisely because he was *performing*: he was in a space marked for performance, he was being watched by an attendant audience, and he could be identified as a performer.[85]

Although these arguments were successful in responding to the exigencies of Burden's arrest — they made sense as a defense — they were radically unfaithful to the epistemological power of Burden's performance work, which continually pushed at the conceptual and experiential limits of spectatorship that define and delimit the gallery. Such performances reveal the complicity of the spectator not simply as a structural component of the designation *performance*, but as an active participant in the event itself. The spectator was made to feel *responsible*, like Burden himself, for the act. In *Deadman* that responsibility was compelled both by the performance event (*as performance*) and by the positioning of death in the public domain: Burden's corpselike form, draped with the tarp and isolated by the flares, initiated and became subject to a particular arrangement of the social. He was surrounded, watched, interrogated, arrested, and tried. *Deadman* was no simple mimetic representation; its performative force in provoking those events matched its profound aesthetic value as performance.

Such deployments of existential and representational death in Burden's work recall William Hammond's discussion of the body's internal economies of consumption and enact, like Tanner's forty-day fast, a similarly compelling intervention. Indeed the strong empirical quality of Burden's performances, their dependence on *experience* rather than *illusion* in crafting meaning of and for themselves, mirrors Tanner's turn to public performance as a mode of substantiating his medical claims. Further Burden's performances, like Tanner's fast, reflect and reveal what I earlier described as the coalescence of the body's economy of survival and the social economy of witnessing. Such connections between Burden and Tanner are especially pronounced in several of Burden's early performances involving spectacular self-starvation.

While still a graduate student at Irvine, Burden staged *Five Day Locker Piece*, for which he secluded himself in a campus locker for five days and nights. In the space above he placed a five-gallon container of water; in the space below he placed an empty five-gallon jug. Both were connected to the small enclosure by a system of tubes that allowed him to take small drinks of water from above and urinate into the container stored below. As word of the performance spread across campus its audience slowly grew — "Viewers could not stay away"[86] — as did the number of security guards and campus administrators who considered forcibly removing Burden from the locker and thus drawing the performance to a close. This they did not do, and for five days and nights Burden remained in the cramped locker, fixed in place without food.[87]

Five Day Locker Piece obviously resembled Tanner's fast formally as a staged enactment of self-starvation, although its duration was significantly shorter. But more significantly the piece was defined not simply by Burden's fast, but also by its framing of a technologically mediated version of the economy of consumption described by Hammond and embodied by Tanner in Clarendon Hall. Tanner's intakes and outputs were daily measured by his watchers; Burden effectively and materially demonstrated those exchanges with the tubes and containers attached to his locker. The performance was resplendent not simply in demonstrating Burden's endurance, his ability to survive a significant period of inanition, but also in revealing his body's economy of consumption. Like the commentators on Tanner's fast, Burden's critics suggested that in *Five Day Locker Piece* he was "test[ing] the capacity of his will."[88] But as Burden himself says of the performance, "I thought this piece was going to be an isolation thing, but it turned into this strange sort of public confessional where people were coming all the time to talk to me. . . . I think that the further away you were from this, the more strange it seemed, and I noticed that when people actually came to talk with me, they were reassured in a way."[89] *Five Day Locker Piece* displayed an economy of social exchange dependent on the proximity of the witness. As those who heard about the performance came to watch it directly they were implicated not only in Burden's continuing ("hungry, cramped, and tired") presence in the locker, but also in a "confessional" encounter occasioned by the audience's presence in the locker room.[90] They, like Burden, were *there*, caught up in the recalcitrant presence of the *live*.

Burden would stage several other performances that similarly implicated an audience watching as he seemed to do nothing. In one of these, *Bed Piece*, he lay on a simple, unadorned bed as part of the Market Street Program in Venice Beach, California. He recalls, "I had a bed put at one end of the room and I stayed there for 22 days. I didn't talk to anyone. There was a portable toilet for me at the front desk, and I [would] run up there after gallery hours, but most of my time was spent in bed."[91] Although the gallery staff would occasionally bring food for him to eat, as he recalls, "A lot of times I didn't get fed because in their minds I had become an object."[92] *Bed Piece* thus hinged on what the art historian and critic Donald Kuspit has called "the austerity of [Burden's] means":[93] the audience watched as Burden endured one of the most mundane daily experiences, being in bed, here swollen beyond its normative duration to twenty-two days.

In his catalogue essay for Burden's twenty-year retrospective at the Newport Harbor Art Gallery in 1988 Kuspit highlights the power of performances like *Bed Piece* to "deconstruct . . . the social contract":

> [Burden's work] calls [the social contract] into question, reminds us that it has many problematic features, and puts us in a position to be able to consider its hold on us, a position which already half frees us of that hold. . . . In a fall from dubious grace, we can no longer blindly accept our condition of illusion. . . . First showing the falseness of the sense of self created by the social contract—its falsifying of selfhood, perhaps its ultimate power—through his violation of various aspects of the social contract, Burden then *turns on* the social contract itself, showing its inherent falseness.[94]

Kuspit goes on to suggest that Burden's performances are significant precisely because they stage a "self-consciousness" characterized as "autonomy," a paradigm that I, in concert with Kaja Silverman's work, would mark as a model of normative masculinity.[95] But Kuspit also gestures to a more supple reading of Burden's work as "show[ing] us the false sense of the body the social contract gives us by denying its vulnerability and mortality, which Burden restores to consciousness."[96] Such an embrace of vulnerability, such a supple incorporation of mortality into Burden's staging of the subject, reimagines the social not as a contract (in the classical Hobbesian sense)[97] but as a form of care.

Bed Piece would prove to be so personally resonant for Burden that he would "reinvestigate" its central themes with a subsequent performance.[98] For *White Light / White Heat* he fasted between 8 February and 1 March 1975 while hidden on a triangular platform built near the ceiling in a corner of the Ronald Feldman Gallery in New York. Because the platform so closely resembled the minimalist sculpture of contemporaneous artists — Robert Morris, Tony Smith, Richard Serra, for example — and because Burden was fully hidden from view, many gallery visitors reported not knowing that he was there at all. Others sensed that "the room [was] haunted" and, upon learning that he was there, were arrested by "his withheld presence."[99] Twenty-two days later — the same duration as *Bed Piece* — Burden descended, having "endure[d] the inactivity, isolation, and hunger to carry the work through."[100]

But it was in Burden's final "imperiling" performance, *Doomed*, that he fully "unmasked the absurdity of the [supposition that by] assuming the role of viewers, we are both blocked and immunized from ethical responsibility."[101] He described the piece, which began at 8:18 P.M. on 11 April 1975, this way:

> [It] consisted of three elements: myself, an institutional wall clock, and a 5′×8′ sheet of plate glass. The sheet of glass was placed horizontally and leaned against the wall at a 45 degree angle; the clock was placed to the left of the glass at eye level. When the performance began, the clock was running at the correct time. I entered the room and reset the clock to twelve midnight. I crawled into the space between the glass and the wall, and lay on my back.[102]

An estimated three hundred audience members waited in line at Chicago's Museum of Contemporary Art for "more than an hour" to enter the gallery.[103] They watched for several hours, but when it became apparent that Burden did not plan to move they grew agitated, throwing debris, clothing, and coins at the glass, screaming "More! More!" and "Less! Less!" and eventually leaving.[104] The following morning he was still there behind the plate glass. The clock continued to tick, but Burden remained completely still but for his blinking eyes.

For forty-five hours and ten minutes Burden remained in the gallery, determined to stay indefinitely. He did not eat, drink, or move; as Kathy

O'Dell writes, his "primary action was inaction."[105] Unbeknown to the audience and the gallery staff, he had set a single condition for the termination of the performance: he would stay there, fasting and still, "until one of the three elements [clock, body, glass] was disturbed or altered."[106] Forty-five hours and ten minutes after the commencement of the performance, after several physicians had been summoned to assess the situation, the curator Ira Licht sent a security guard to place a pitcher of water near the glass.

> We felt a moral obligation not to interfere with Burden's intentions, but we felt we couldn't stand by and allow him to do serious physical harm to himself. There was a possibility he was in such a deep trance that he didn't have control over his will. We decided to place [the water] next to his head and see if he would drink from it. The moment we put the water down, Chris got up, walking into the next room, returned with a hammer and an envelope, and smashed the clock, stopping it.[107]

Doomed epitomizes the tension in all of Burden's early performances as well as Tanner's forty-day fast between the intentions of the subject and the ethical responsibility of the witness. Indeed in *Doomed* Burden's intent to reveal the intersubjective circulation of accountability between himself and his audience became intensely concentrated within an extremely sparse scene, and the burden of action, conventionally attributed to the artist, was transferred across the cordoning ropes that traditionally distinguish the gallery's stage from its observatory. As the critic C. Carr has written of Burden's work, "We, his spectators, . . . know our decisions will have real consequences. While Burden's work exposes power without judging it, his project is not amoral—it forces the moralizing onto us. Sooner or later, we will have to decide. And usually sooner."[108]

At first glance Burden's early performance work seems to be defined by *endurance*, that avant-garde rhetoric of survival that casts the value of a given performance in terms of the artist's will. Indeed many popular and critical responses to Burden have either indemnified or indicted this tendency in his work seemingly to venerate the artist above all else. "Burden survived," such responses seem to cry, "against all odds." Others position Burden at the forefront of avant-garde art production that primarily aimed to eliminate the institutional divisions between artist and audience, illuminating the modes through which spectatorship is actively involved in producing the meaning of the work. Such responses underscore the profound value of these performances in revealing the social nature of meaning itself: artist and audience collaborate in reflecting and determining the significance of a given representational form.

But as Carr implies, Burden's early performance work also demonstrates, and obliges us to participate in, the ethical imperative of the aesthetic encounter. In her illuminating study of masochism and performance, *Contract with the Skin*, O'Dell highlights how, with performances like *Doomed*, Burden "subtly tampered with the institutional logistics and economics of the museum" in order to demonstrate that "the body is always on the line in institutionalized contracts and, more specifically, in the contractual agreements that sustain them."[109] O'Dell's exploration of the contractual expectations underlying all institutional encounters is compelling, particularly in its embrace of the multiple valences of masochism at work in the performance by Burden specifically and endurance artists more generally. But the enactment of a sophisticated, if subtle institutional critique in such "masochistic performance" is complicated yet further in those works that deploy self-starvation as their primary action; in *Five-Day Locker Piece*, *Bed Piece*, *White Light / White Heat*, and *Doomed* Burden not only compelled audiences to grapple with their accountability within institutional structures, but also revealed those structures as manifest *at the scale of the body*. His fasts became both *emblems* and *instantiations* of the structures of circulation that define the gallery. His body was not simply on the line, objectified as at risk by the demands of the aesthetic encounter; it was also sustained by that encounter, made present to itself and others by the sustenance of the look.

Put another way, for both Henry Tanner and Chris Burden performances involving self-starvation exposed the ideologies of looking that delimit and define the gallery and the clinic. But these performances also disclosed the profoundly social, intersubjective character of both the body's economy of consumption and the institutional economy of the spectacle. Looking at these performances both effaced the expectation of passive spectatorship and enacted a vibrant, indeed a *vital* form of *presence*: an experience described more faithfully as being-*with* than being *near*. Tanner and Burden disclosed the capacity of the look to bring forth the presence (and the survival) of others and the generosity of coming into view in forging existential presence. "To look," writes Silverman, "is to care," and "the only domain where Being can emerge [is] the domain of appearance."[110] In Kafka's harrowing tale the hunger artist endures not despite but as a consequence of his performance; when the spectators look away he disappears. From Tanner's and Burden's enduring performances a new figure emerges, one who is bound by the conventions of the institutional domains he has inhabited but who is simultaneously infused with the vulnerability of intersubjective presence. He shrinks from the exertion of his fasts, and in the time of historicity he fades slowly, steadily from view. But in performance, indeed *as* performance, which "saves nothing, it only spends,"[111] he has given himself up to a dramatically open, if deeply contested, *we*.

CHAPTER THREE

how to stage self-consumption

•

It isn't the gesture that lasts.

— Rainer Maria Rilke, "What Survives"

A hazy photograph remains to document the performance. In the center of the image a slim, nude woman stands holding a camera level with her sternum. It is an old camera — boxy, small — and the woman grips it tenderly, as if unconcerned that it might fall to the floor. She gazes expressionlessly into a mirror hung before her, face and features relaxed, while her stare returns back through the lens as if looking at the camera point-blank. There is nothing to see behind her, though at the edges of the image one can just make out the shape of a wall, or a window, or a door upon which the mirror might be hung. With the camera as our guide we see her seeing her see herself.

Adrian Piper's *Food for the Spirit* was a private performance staged in the summer of 1971. During a period of two months Piper devoted herself to a juice-and-water fast, intensive yoga practice, and a close reading of Kant's *Critique of Pure Reason*. She stayed in her New York apartment for the majority of her time fasting, leaving only to run errands and take short walks. Piper writes of reading the *Critique*, "I thought I was losing my mind, in fact losing my sense of self completely. I would read certain passages that were so intensely affecting and deep that I would literally break out into a cold sweat." She became so entranced with Kant's ideas that, "on the verge of hysterics," she would take a break from the reading and, "to anchor [her]self in the physical world," capture a photograph through a mirror while dictating the passage she had just been reading. The photographs, and the recorded sound of her own voice reading Kant's words aloud, archived both her efforts to work her way through transcendental thought and her slow emaciation:

> The sight and sound of me, the physically embodied Adrian Piper, repeating passages from Kant reassured me by demarcating the visual, verbal, and aural boundaries of my individual self, and reminded me of the material conditions of my mental state, that the *Critique* was a book with good ideas in it that I had chosen to study, and not (only? necessarily? really?) the entrance into a transcendent reality of disembodied self-consciousness.[1]

Like the fasting performances staged by Henry Tanner and Chris Burden, *Food for the Spirit* reveals the intimate imbrication of the economies of consumption internal to both the body and the spectacle. But whereas Tanner and Burden aimed to demonstrate their own capacity to endure such "trying ordeals," Piper's intent was to grapple with the material manifestation of consciousness as proposed by Kant. For Piper (following Kant) fasting was deployed not as a mode of empirically testing either the body's limits (as for Tanner) or a given audience's complicity in witnessing potentially fatal acts (as for Burden), but as a synthetic attempt to understand and to experience the nature of being, the *live*, as mediated through the sensual experience of the subject.[2] In *Food for the Spirit* the act of fasting disclosed Adrian Piper to herself, even as she would occasionally "slip away."

In subsequent performance and installation work Piper has continued to experiment not only with the material experience of being, but also with the deeply fraught relationship between subjectivity and objecthood. Before performing *Food for the Spirit* she articulated this interest in the object and its relationship to the viewing subject in 1970:

> All around me I see galleries and museums faltering or closing as the capitalist structure on which they are based crumbles. This makes me realize that art as a commodity really isn't such a good idea after all. That the value of an artwork has somehow become subject to monetary rather than aesthetic interest. That inconceivable amounts of money are lavished on objects, while artists expend their energy in plumbing and secretarial work in order to support themselves and their art. That by depending on a

gallery to package and sell his product, the artist becomes a parasite who produces works tailored to sell rather than innovate. That the artist as parasite necessarily dies when the host dies.[3]

Food for the Spirit, along with Piper's later work, was part of a genealogy of avant-garde art production in the United States and Europe that aimed to confront such parasitism by removing the art object from its protected status in galleries and museums and from the privileged structures of spectatorship that distinguished between the domains of aesthetics and the everyday. John Perreault characterizes this period as defined by the "antigallery, antiobject genres . . . spreading rapidly throughout the art world."[4] Jane Blocker summarizes the era as organized around the following foundational goals: "to eliminate the object, to subvert the artist's authority, and to involve the viewer more actively."[5] Around the same time that Karen Carpenter's collapse on that Las Vegas stage brought anorexia into the public vernacular, a new generation of artists was working in a fragmented field of practice that came to be called performance art. As RoseLee Goldberg and others have documented, performance art was not simply an invention of the 1960s and 1970s; it developed out of previous aesthetic traditions, including Vaudeville, Surrealism, Futurism, Action Painting, and Dada.[6] Such interventions in the strictures of conventional art production corresponded with a more general move, especially in the second half of the twentieth century, to resituate the position and the role of art practice outside of designated spaces of aesthetic production and display and into spaces that constituted a more generally accessible public sphere.

This move was both architectural and philosophical: artists began working outside of galleries and museums, taking their work to the streets, and transformed the stuff of everyday life into artistic media. In Brandon Taylor's words, "The intended result [of such reformulations] was to frustrate the market mechanism by making art objects which were resistant to being sold, collected, and evaluated by conventional means."[7] Many artists, including Allan Kaprow, attempted to resituate both the scene and the content of art as the everyday: public streets, open fields, subway cars, apartments, and Grand Central Station.[8] Others, including Eva Hesse, created works of art that would refuse preservation and slowly decompose.[9] In both cases, Kaprow's "happenings" and Hesse's latex-and-resin sculptural webs, the art object surrendered its status as durable commodity and, in a sense, obtained a life: a period in which it existed as such, but a period defined by its eventual disappearance.

This is not to say that such artistic productions were precisely successful in escaping the economy of commodification in the gallery and other aesthetic domains. Indeed the antiobject turn of the avant-garde generally, and of performance art in particular, eventuated the circulation of new kinds of commodifiable objects. Chris Burden, for example, preserved artifacts of his performances (including the lock securing his confinement in *Five Day Locker Piece*) for display in later exhibitions.[10] More broadly performance artists have documented their work with photographs, films, videos, and sound recordings, which have in turn been used in retrospective exhibitions of their work. The vast domain of critical and scholarly literature about performance produced over the past several decades has become its own kind of commodity, even as it (generally) accedes to its failure precisely to preserve the object itself: performance.[11] In this vein, as Peggy Phelan has proposed, "writing towards disappearance" has emerged as a mode of working through both the affect and the effects of the performance event while simultaneously embracing that performance's ontological fade.[12]

For Adrian Piper intervening in the economy of consumption that underlies conventional art production and reception required not just a turn away from the commodification of aesthetic objects, but also a return to the very notion of objecthood as a radical index for social and political presence; her work was directed not "to eliminate," but to *inhabit* the domain of the object. Piper aimed to plumb the deep complexity of the condition of objecthood in work that was simultaneously relevant on aesthetic, social, and political registers; she demonstrated, with a clarifying audacity, that those three registers are profoundly interconnected. In 1972, for example, she began keeping a list of what she called the "performing objects I have been": self-reflexive journal writer, musical prodigy, fashion model, discotheque dancer, yoga practitioner, student of philosophy, and woman. Each of these roles, she suggested, was intensely involved in "dissolving the subject-object distinction," a dissolution that she would eventually term "the indexical present":

> I believe that forms of institutional oppression ultimately devolve into individual relationships, specific concrete relationships between you and me. After all, institutions are not abstract objects; institutions are run by individuals, they are staffed by individuals, individuals make policy deci-

sions that determine the lives of others, and so ultimately individuals have to be held accountable for any form of social oppression. . . . [My work] concerns the immediate relationship in the indexical present—that is, the present of the here and now—between the art object and the viewer as a kind of medium for social relations.[13]

Fred Moten describes Piper's notion of the indexical present as "the deictic-confrontational field her art produces and within which it is to be beheld," which occasions "a kind of resistance to . . . aversion."[14] For Moten such "aversion" signifies both a fear of the "object" of otherness that marks everyday encounters with difference (a fear mapped and plumbed by Piper in such pieces as *Mythic Being* and the *Catalysis* performances)[15] and a tendency in art criticism to ignore or to lambaste the kinds of performance-centered interventions epitomized by her work. Moten writes, "For Piper, to be for the beholder is to be able to mess up or mess with the beholder. It is the potential of being catalytic. Beholding is *always* the entrance into a scene, into the context of the other, of the object."[16] Moten is writing against "antitheatrical" responses to midcentury minimalist art exemplified in Michael Fried's widely influential (and widely criticized) essay "Art and Objecthood." In that early essay Fried was responding to the minimalist (or, to use his word, "literalist") objects forged by the artists Richard Serra, Tony Smith, and Robert Morris. In particular Fried loathed the manner in which such works laid themselves open to encounters with the spectator and thus activated the role of that spectator as witness; he called such art "incurably theatrical," gesturing to its elicitation of a durational, spectatorial encounter. Fried recognized that the meaning of literalist sculpture, for example, alters radically as the position and proximity of the spectator changes. Such sculptures make sense as such only when apprehended, engaged as interactive (and interacting) works of art. Their meaning, indeed their very "presence" is durational, utterly reliant upon the viewing space and time of a given encounter. This quality of presence, as opposed to the complete, unalterable "presentness" of Fried's beloved modernist artworks, is precisely what characterized them as "theatrical." Alternately those modernist works—a twist from Anthony Caro, a stroke by Jackson Pollock—were structured to "defeat theater":[17] they stood "on their own," their meanings fully refined, and thus venerated both the individualized creative gesture and the recitation of the work's meaning by an observer as site and sign of the autonomous, authentic subject. To borrow Moten's description of Fried's idealized scene: "The beholder is never estranged, never lost or even dark to himself; rather he continually fulfills that self in the ascription of meaning to the beheld and, more fundamentally, in the ascription of greatness or not, authentic and autonomous aestheticity or not, to the artwork. The beholder becomes a subject again in this profoundly antitheatrical moment."[18]

For Fried "theatrical" encounters, eliciting durational, interactive articulations of subject and object in the scene of the spectacle, were deeply antithetical to the assertion of modernist artworks as sealed up in their own appraisability (and semiotic commodifiability) and of artists as beatified by their own relationship of mastery over the work. In more recent (1998) revisions of his early criticism Fried again insists on the "completeness" of such "great" art in "a single infinitely brief instant that would be long enough to see everything, to experience the work in all its depth and fullness, to be forever convinced by it."[19] His distinction between a "long enough" instant of seeing modernist art and the centrality of *duration* in seeing literalist art, which he names the difference between "presentness" and "presence," respectively, reveals what he calls the "corruption" of painting and sculpture by theatricality. His attribution of value to the former over the latter positions artworks as singular, closed, and insistently complete, that is, fully packaged, available for our consumption on the condition that we take them in the instant in which they are given.

Piper's work complicates both the time of such instants and the nature of their givenness; she reinvests objecthood itself with social and political presence. While Fried's criticism of literalist art poses, in Moten's words, "consciousness of art [as] nothing other than consciousness of self," Piper's embrace of the object and, crucially, its interiority demonstrates the acutely social imbrication of art and life, looking at and being-with, subjectivity and objecthood. But as Moten reminds us, "Just because we are all literalists most of our lives does not mean that we actually ever pay attention to or experience objects in their intensity."[20] It is on this precise point that Piper's work resounds as poetically urgent and performatively political: the object, she reminds us, is alive.

Similarly Piper's colleagues Ana Mendieta and Marina Abramović have worked to intervene in the consumption that defines conventional aesthetic exchange in the gallery, to deploy the artist's body as both subject and object in performance, to complicate the relationship between artist and audience that constitutes the economy of the spectatorial encounter, and to use documentation as an index for the relentlessly lost presence of the performance event. With these interventions in mind I use the term *self-starvation* principally as an allegory for the modes in which Mendieta and Abramović seize upon the power of performance as resistant to the economy of consumption organized around the commodity, that is, as the *live*. In this sense self-starvation signifies not the literal abstention from food, as in *Food for the Spirit*, although Abramović does undertake extended fasts in several performances, but rather as a complicated, at times paradoxical attempt to withdraw, in the interests of the live, from the most conventional understanding of aesthetic exchange enacted within the gallery. In embracing the effervescence of their performance work, whether staged in a well-attended exhibition or enacted privately in an uninhabited desert, Mendieta and Abramović demonstrate performance to be the site and the sign of the live, variously articulated by the artists as "energy," "presence," or "consciousness." As with Piper's supple and evocative work on objecthood, through Mendieta's and Abramović's haunting, at times overwhelmingly affective work "the gallery" becomes "the world."

I should stipulate, especially given Fried's criticism of theatricality, that while I consider the significance of Mendieta's and Abramović's work as performance, I do not mean to allegorize that work as *theater*. In drawing a distinction between performance and theater I intend not to drive an irascible wedge between those two modes of production, but rather to acknowledge the break from theatrical conventions signaled and emblematized by these artists' work. In its most recent conventional form theater represents both an architectural location set apart from other social spaces and a set of prescriptions founded upon the distinctions between actor and character, rehearsal and production, presentation and representation, onstage and off. Taken together these oppositions function to designate some spaces, but not others, as theatrical and to distinguish between the founding principles of theater and other genres of visual art; it is in this vein that Fried vilified literalist art as exceeding the genre-specific bounds of sculpture and painting by incorporating aspects of theatricality.[21]

Although the theater has been used metaphorically to describe other forms of cultural practice—for Erving Goffman, social interaction; for Victor Turner, rites and rituals[22]—and although contemporary playwrights have contested and redrawn the divisions that have historically defined theatrical production, conventional theater continues to depend ontologically on the difference between that which is generally recognized as the stage and that which is affirmed as the real world. To attribute or otherwise consign a given production to the theater is to designate its existence within a specific architectural and institutional domain; to distinguish between that domain and the materiality of cause and effect; to trust that whatever actions it demonstrates within the world of its narrative are not actually occurring; and to believe that the people we watch on stage have lives that extend well beyond and may in fact not resemble at all the passions and pleasures of the characters they portray. These represent the most classic conceptions of theatrical representation as a fabricated reality, no matter how biographical or journalistic its narratives may be, no matter how profoundly it may affect or sway the audiences that bear witness to it.

This is not to imply that theater is an ineffective mode of making art, or an insignificant cultural practice, or an apolitical custom whose impact is limited to the aesthetic domain. On the contrary: theater is a critical site for the production and contestation of social narratives that describe lived experience and historically has eventuated a broad range of social and political effects. In distinguishing between theater and performance I mean simply to direct attention away from the curatorial urge to place the work of Mendieta and Abramović in a genealogy of theatrical tradition. Similarly I do not mean to consign these artists' work strictly to the domain of body art, a designation that seems to embrace the human body as aesthetic object while simultaneously eschewing the language of performance. Instead I consider the works of Mendieta and Abramović precisely as performance, in the broadest possible sense of that word,[23] so as to attend to the following key qualities of those works' social, cultural, and political impact.

First, these works emphasize the duration of their enactment. Indeed duration is central to the meanings they produce as ephemeral works of art, with life spans that hinge on their eventual disappearance. For Mendieta the *Silueta* works in particular embraced their own materially temporal character as central to their consequence as subjects and objects of art; indeed precisely because of the flickering duration of their presence these works fused the subject and the object of art production into a single figure.[24] For Abramović, whose works are often staged over days, weeks, or months, duration becomes in part a question of durability and in part a question of intersubjective presence. Watching as she endures extended periods of stillness, minimal action, and abnegation, audiences become implicated in the practice of witnessing and simultaneously become subject to the "crescendo" of her work, through which is reflected "a glimpse of the threshold between form and formlessness, between knowing and unknowing, between life and death."[25] The durationality that so completely infects these works of art, disparaged by Fried, becomes foundational for Mendieta and Abramović, the most effusive articulation of mortality and productive finitude at the heart of their work.

Second, the works of Mendieta and Abramović are embodied spectacles whose meaning and effects are not bound to specularity. Their performances and installations are fully embodied acts, visually accessible but also productive through other modes of affect. As enacted embodiments these works explore, for example, the tactility of carving the shape of a body into the earth, the audible growls of hunger pangs, the stench of decay, the competing senses of connection and alienation produced in "energy exchanges" with artists embedded in live performance.[26] Such broad sensual and affective experiences are definitive, if not exclusive aspects of performance's distinction from many other modes of art production and display, which privilege the visual over all other forms of sensual access and in so doing produce the pretense of "a single infinitely brief instant that would be long enough to see everything."

Third, the works of Mendieta and Abramović are explicitly designated as aesthetic productions, but as performances they exceed that designation. This renders the pieces I explore both performance and performative, for just as they exist as aesthetic, embodied acts, they also reflect and produce shifts in the cultural and political contexts of which they are a part. This is not to say that the work of Mendieta and Abramović effects political changes immediately recognizable as such; there is no legislation being amended, no election, no explicitly named protest. Indeed Mendieta and Abramović have both insisted that their work is not political.[27] I propose that this negation functions not to deny the political resonance of their work, but to distinguish between them and the didactic style of what commonly goes under the heading of, for example, "political theater." I suggest that it is precisely the question of consumption and its connection to the artists' resistance to commodification and to their staging of the live that politicizes their work.

The question of consumption and its supple framing in these works thus extend far beyond the domain of aesthetics. It is obviously *the* question for alimentary concerns and for the domain of hunger. Since the 1950s the subject of food and the rituals of alimentary consumption have been taken up by artists as one mode of critiquing the consumptive drives that fuel capitalist exchange. These artists — the Living Theater, Karen

Finley, Eleanor Antin, and Carolee Schneeman, among others[28] — spotlighted the practices and artifacts of eating as art objects either by staging normalized scenes of dietary consumption or by radically subverting the anticipated functions of hunger, feeding, and food. Several of these artists, including Chris Burden, staged fasts as part of their work.

Here we see self-starvation in its most literal form: the regimented and sustained refusal to consume that requires a great deal of discipline and results in slow emaciation, among other effects. But the question of consumption, particularly in the second half of the twentieth century, simultaneously occupies the very heart of global politics, where certain superpower states literally starve less financially stable peoples and nations into submission. Here self-starvation becomes an allegory for the only possible strategies of resistance for those faced with embargos and sanctions, especially from the United States and increasingly since 11 September 2001. In other words, the work of Mendieta and Abramović, who themselves represent communities on the outskirts of Western imperialism, Cuba and the former Yugoslavia, pivot on the theme of consumption to speak both to the politics of aesthetic production and to the arts and sciences of domination that define the context and the condition of global political formations.

It is no accident that the primary medium represented by Mendieta and Abramović is a woman's body. The question of consumption is key for the inflection of gender differences and alliances in artistic production and global politics alike. The spectatorial consumption of women and women's bodies — laid bare, open to the spectator's gaze — extends throughout the history of art, and the figuring of maleness and men's bodies as the creative function, that which produces art objects but is itself hidden from view, is corollary in that history. In confounding expectations epitomized by Fried's insistence that art be bound up in its self-sufficiency, Mendieta and Abramović perform sophisticated critiques of such confining gendered conventions and offer new directions for a political, globally conscious, insistently feminist practice of performance and visual art. The key to this critique, surprisingly, is self-consumption.

Images of sand, of dirt and mud fill the screen. The film is old and bears signs of age: scratches that flicker and fade, spots where the celluloid has melted away, bleached-out hues that blend the borders of the landscape into one another, confusing the jagged hills with the surrounding sky. Shot by Ana Mendieta to document her most famous body of work, these images mirror the decay and sheer evaporation that define the *Silueta* series of environmental installations.[29]

In one of the most haunting pieces Mendieta has carved the shape of her body into the sand on a beach, filled it with gunpowder, and set it alight. The hallucinatory figure sparks and glows, seemingly burning its own afterimage into the surface of the film, before being slowly washed away in the surf. Its flames sizzle and fume; as the kindling becomes drenched the ghostly silhouette exhales billows of steam and smoke before finally being extinguished entirely. In another piece fireworks are hung on a scaffold in the shape of a body, set at a distance from the camera, and lit. The body burns brightly at first, so hot that its flames actually drip to the ground, and then falls into darkness. It takes longer than we might expect, and as the last fires die away our breathing slows in anticipation of that inevitable moment when darkness once again prevails, defining the image before us rather than simply emptying it out. This night is changed for the absence of the body that briefly blazed so insistently.

Both of these works are emblematic of Ana Mendieta's interest in the contours of the human form, set in stark relief against landscapes that will inevitably consume them. Their affect also functions through a kind of self-consumption that embraces rather than attempting to embalm the slowly vanishing, inexorably mortal body. The representational force of these *Siluetas* functions by highlighting the form of a disappearing body; they "save nothing," in the doubled verbal resonance of that phrase,[30] keeping nothing in reserve and simultaneously recuperating the abundance of disappearance as a generative force rather than a vector of simple erasure.

Mendieta was born to a politically and economically privileged family in Havana in 1948. When in 1961 the recently empowered Fidel Castro declared his intentions to adopt socialist policies in designing his post-Batista government, the Mendieta family, who had supported Castro during his revolution, made plans to send their two daughters to the United States. On 11 September 1961 (forty years to the day before that other fateful 11 September) Ana and Raquel Mendieta, along with many other Cuban children, were flown to Miami as part of the corporate- and Catholic-funded Operation Pedro Pan. Four years later the family patriarch, Ignacio Mendieta, was arrested on suspicion of assisting the United States during the Bay of Pigs invasion; he would spend nearly twenty years as a political prisoner in Cuba.[31] Ana and Raquel were settled in

Iowa, "shuffled between foster homes, orphanages, and juvenile correction facilities,"[32] where they would not be reunited with their mother until 1966 and with their father until 1979.[33]

Mendieta's forced move to the United States, as well as her "quest for a reconnection or reconciliation with her cultural heritage,"[34] would have a defining impact both on her daily experience during a tumultuous period in U.S. cultural politics and on her eventual work as an artist. At the University of Iowa in the late 1960s she began working as a painter but soon turned to film, installation, live performance, and especially the "earth-body works" for which she is best known.[35] She would write of her move to the United States:

> Pain of Cuba
> body I am
> my orphanhood I live. . . .
> As my whole body is filled with want of Cuba
> I go on to make my work upon the earth.[36]

Della Pollock cautions that Mendieta's continual, and continually fraught, reference to her simultaneous experience of abjection and belonging is "tied less to the nostalgic regimes of symbol-making than to the rigors of living in exile, on the edge of death."[37] That is, Mendieta's claim to the experience of exile operates in her work not as a cultural-nationalist nostalgia, but as an evocative, embodied articulation of the profoundly fraught and potentially fatal position of the refugee in the United States during the 1960s.[38] In this vein Kaira Cabañas describes Mendieta's work as "located in the gap between artist and culture . . . reinforc[ing] the dialogic character of this space in the production of meaning."[39]

Mendieta's earliest performances at the University of Iowa were conceived as "temporary art works outside the traditional gallery or museum . . . to incite public reaction and conversation about violence."[40] In *Rape Scene*, for example, she invited a small audience to her apartment, where they discovered her tied over a table with blood and other evidence of extreme brutality scattered around the room; she created similar tableaux for her subsequent works *Rape Performance* and *Bloody Mattresses*. As Petra Barreras del Rio and John Perreault remark, these stagings "allowed the young artist to develop a personal vocabulary in which her own body became the medium for ephemeral performances."[41] In Jane Blocker's words, such early works adapted and synthesized the artistic trends of the decade . . . to animate the territorial boundaries between artist and audience, male and female, body and spirit. . . . [But] by virtue of her identity and her politics, she exposed and troubled the assumptions that lie hidden behind those directives. Her work challenges the philosophers of dematerialization to imagine more complex and extensive models of authority, more diverse constituencies, and more sophisticated concepts of identity and subjectivity.[42]

Although she is chiefly responding to theories of dematerialization epitomized by the work of the art historian Lucy Lippard,[43] I take Blocker's invocation of this challenge as a call to reconsider the very premise of disappearance around which Mendieta's work is often framed. Mendieta's performance work, and the *Silueta* series in particular, was "time-based and ephemeral," supple in the modes through which it "documented erasure."[44] But its primary significance, its affective impact, derives not from its evaporation into nothingness, but from its augmentation of formal disappearance with a radically grounded and deeply materialized productive force. For Mendieta ephemerality marked both the time and the space of the live and, like Adrian Piper's complex embrace of objecthood, the production of cultural, political, *geographical* presence.

It was in the *Silueta* series that Mendieta most articulately and evocatively forged this claim. Carving the shapes of female figures out of mud, sand, soil, and other organic media, she would create the substance of bodily interiors with materials that would likewise decay or burn away into ash. These figures thus were given life spans: they exploded into existence, maintained a brief period of stability in form and content, and then slowly died away. They were markedly called the *silhouettes*, a nomenclature that gestures to an empty form, a shadow, a border defining the difference between *fort* and *da*, here and gone. The significance of that naming is in its simultaneous reference to that which has produced the silhouette, a foregrounded body that we cannot see, and that body's shadow. A silhouette thus functions by illuminating both a figure and a field that indicates that figure's absence. For Mendieta the paradox in the meaning of the word, a conundrum that both identifies a subject and indexes the erasure of that subject, is precisely the paradox of her own position, "torn from [her] homeland" but at home in the United States; belonging to both, belonging to neither.[45]

Amelia Jones writes of the significance of the *Siluetas*, "I experience the burning wound that links Mendieta's body to the earth as the same wound that marks the absence and loss of her body/self (as a Cuban immigrant woman trying to be an artist in the United States in the 1970s).... [She] produces subjectivity in absence rather than plentitude."[46] Mariana Ortega offers a slightly more complex rendering of this evocation: "When encountering or seeing these silhouettes, one can get a sense of this absence and of Mendieta's presence.... In the end, however, neither definite absence nor definite presence defines the space, only presence in absence and vice-versa."[47] The absence produced by the *Silueta* series, enacting the continuous disappearance of the live, simultaneously implicated itself within what Mendieta embraced as the "energy of existence" (or *ashé* in the Cuban Santería tradition: "the blood of living creatures, the moving wind, the growing plants, consuming fire, and flowing water all expend ashé"), which "magically animated her works with anger, pleasure, hunger, and longing."[48] With the simplest of gestures Mendieta thus connected her isolated, sculptural earth-body works, many of which were witnessed only by her and a camera, to broader philosophical and geopolitical incantations of the live: "She creates a space that leads us to question her very existence and place in the world and perhaps all of our existences."[49] Simultaneously, as Della Pollock writes, "[The *Siluetas*] perform the beauty and fragility of life as dying, as gaining its flickering beauty in the process of (always already) disappearing. Centered in that place where life and performance intersect as dying, as disappearance, they moreover tremble with the beauty of life as performance."[50]

In her study of the "explicit body in performance" Rebecca Schneider contends that Mendieta's *Siluetas* "both illustrate and disallow the service of her body to the infinite recession of the vanishing point, or the insatiability of desire, because they are so infinitely *finite* — shrouds of sand, mud, stone, tree, or the fertile grave-bed stuff of dirt." This description appears in Schneider's larger exploration of four functions of feminist performance art beginning in the 1960s: staging the historicity of gender and race at the scale of the female body; critically interrogating the role of specularity in contemporary art production; disclosing the role of desire in fueling and compelling capitalist exchange; and contesting the precedent of masculine "shock value" in art of the avant-garde.[51] For Schneider, Mendieta's earth-body works exemplify these functions, eloquently staging themes of dislocation and alienation in order to demonstrate the drama of racial and gender formations within the context of contemporary global economies of cultural and political exchange. The *Siluetas* staged Mendieta's erasure at the same time that they marked her presence; they traced with an inexorable fade the contingency and fragility of her national ties, and so expunged the political articulation of presence of its strictly personalistic, identificatory (read: neoliberal) tenor; and they withdrew from the conventions of production and display, the claims to ownership in any sense, that define aesthetic commodification and exchange.

By definition, an environmental installation, much like performance, "becomes itself through disappearance" in the slowly accelerating vanishing that corresponds with the erosion of time, gravity, and decay;[52] such installations literally consume themselves, much as a starving body will gradually turn to its own fluids and tissues for sustenance, shrinking and wasting away more and more. For Mendieta the iconography of the female body was defined in part by form, often the recognizable Venus figures of ancient art, and in part by this slow emaciation. The question of consumption is thus at the heart of her work: the consumption of art itself, so heavily contested during the era of her work; the consumption of women and women's bodies; the refusal to consume designated by traditions in performance art and by resistance to capitalist values of property and exchange; and the ideological consumption so prominent in the foreign policies of economically powerful nations who demand and enforce the subordination of others, whose place in global political formations becomes defined by exploitation. (It was this kind of international intervention that so dramatically informed Castro's Cuba and led directly to Mendieta's girlhood exile from her homeland.) Removed from the scene of the gallery and the museum, Mendieta's haunting figures fade from view due to weather, erosion, or decay, unownable, unreproducible (in the strict sense of mass production), defying all hope for simple commodification and claims to tenure.

As environmental installations the *Siluetas* fade with time, but what precisely fades are these already silhouetted figures, these marks of presence infused with absence. This double-erasure, the creation of a hollowed human form and its slow disappearance, embodies what Schneider highlights as the "pressure to disappear into disappearance": precisely the force of assimilation compelling Mendieta "to conform, to Americanize, . . . to erase and forget her cultural heritage, or to commodify it."[53] The self-consumption of the *Siluetas*, their erosion by the very elements used to forge them into existence, gracefully but insistently staged the drama of colonization and the exile from homeland and heritage that drama enforced.

Several works from the series, subtitled "La Venus Negra," suggested a connection between what I have allegorically described as self-consumption and literal self-starvation. The "Venus Negra" works were based on a legend in which the Spaniards who first landed on an island off the south coast of Cuba found a single inhabitant living there: a woman described as wearing nothing but jewelry of seeds and seashells, a woman who was "so lovely that the most demanding artist would have considered her an example of perfect feminine beauty."[54] The Spaniards chased her into the woods, eventually capturing and incarcerating her in the home of one of the colonists; he clothed and attempted to feed her, expecting physical and sexual devotion in return. The Spaniard was astonished and confused to find that she remained huddled in a corner, refusing to work, refusing to submit to him, and refusing to partake of his food. Frightened that she might die of starvation — leaving him with her blood on his hands — he returned her to her island. La Venus Negra began haunting those who had captured her, sneaking into their homes at night, repeatedly staging her refusals to eat, and disappearing again by morning. Mendieta described this legendary figure as "represent[ing] the affirmation of a free and natural being who . . . with her passive protests . . . refused to be colonized."[55]

With the *Silueta* series Mendieta sought to establish a fraught connection between her body and the land, one that had been denied her by her exile from Cuba. In the works based on the Venus Negra legend she explicitly politicized that connection by summoning the story of a woman whose stark refusal to participate in her own commodification coincided (narratively, if not precisely historically) with the beginning of colonial rule in Mendieta's homeland; she refined the haunting narrative of the legend by reclaiming it as theme and mode in her own work. Reinscribing her form on and within the landscapes of the United States and Cuba (to which she briefly returned in 1981),[56] Mendieta made explicit the protest, graceful if not passive, of her own aesthetic work. She staged gender, race, and ethnicity as overlapping registers of difference and belonging, or, as in the legend of La Venus Negra, the refusal to accept a belonging that insists upon denying all other ties and affiliations. For Mendieta it was the staging of La Venus Negra's protests — huddled in a corner, refusing to work or to eat — that most clearly articulated that refusal. In the images that document the "Venus Negra" works we once again see absence engraved in silhouette: the simultaneous assertion and denial of a figure whose place in the history and mythology of colonialism is defined by a repudiation of the modes of consumption imposed through and upon her.

In the closely related *Tree of Life* series of environmental installations Mendieta moved on to erase the clear distinction between the silhouettes and their ample geographical surroundings. Covered in mud and standing with arms raised in supplication against the trunk of an enormous tree, Mendieta insistently becomes a part of the terrain that surrounds her; while maintaining the integrity of her own form, she becomes the land. On 8 February 1985, shortly after their wedding, the minimalist sculptor Carl Andre wrote Mendieta a love letter: "Darling Ana: Your theme is the pregnant earth. My theme is the universe before the earth and after. Yours is the jewel, mine the setting."[57] These disturbing, though poetic lines represent the most lucid articulation of the masculinist drive that defines modern art: the divinity of males as universal, preexisting, and poised to survive the lush, maternal efficiency of the temporal, earthly feminine. Not coincidentally they also reproduce the drama between Mendieta's environmental performance and the neomodernist sculptural work with which it was in relentless dialogue. In a chilling irony—perhaps, in the end, not an irony at all—Mendieta died a few months after this letter was written after falling from the window of Andre's thirty-fourth-floor New York apartment.[58] The conditions of her fall were suspicious, and her friends and supporters clamored for an investigation of Andre and his troubled relationship with Mendieta. In 1992 the Guggenheim Museum in New York staged an exhibition of his work. Protestors picketed the museum, carrying signs that asked "Where is Ana Mendieta?"[59] This haunting query, unresolved by the courts that did not convict Andre,[60] unanswered even with posthumous retrospectives of her work, is precisely the one staged by her earth-body works and performances, given no final response by the elusive, ephemeral, and live figures at the heart of her work. As a critic wrote during the first posthumous retrospective in 1987, "It may be impossible to view her . . . [work] apart from her terrible death . . . [because] the political force of her art has a good deal to do with her effort to give negative space a positive presence and voice."[61]

Variously known as a masochistic, confrontational, or endurance artist, Marina Abramović has dramatically restaged the artistic encounter over her extended career, refusing to acknowledge that encounter as defined by its strict division between art and audience and by its treatment of the art object as hallowed and constant. Playing at the boundaries of life and death, of possibility and danger, Abramović's work opens up the prospect that even the artist's body, the last possible vestige of commodification in a medium where art objects cannot be bought or sold, may disappear, leaving absolutely nothing to be consumed. Exploring, like Mendieta, the profound productivity of disappearance, Abramović has sketched the contours of the live; her performances, like Mendieta's silhouettes, have infused disappearance with significance, with the personal and political resonance of alienation and connection, of abundance and abnegation, of subjectivity and objecthood.

The gallery is opened to the public; a sign at the door proclaims, "There are 72 objects on the table that one can use on me as desired. I am the object. During this period I take full responsibility." On the table lie a gun, a bullet, needles, scissors, knives, a rose, perfume, and other assorted implements. One man uses the scissors to slice open the artist's clothing. Another uses a marker to scrawl "End War" across her body. A third holds the gun to her forehead, frozen in a terrifying moment of unthinkable possibilities. After six hours the artist has been cut and is bleeding, and stunned audience members put an end to the performance.[62]

In another room, at another time, a film begins in close-up. We see the head and shoulders of a young woman holding a metal brush in one hand and a comb in the other. She begins speaking: "Art must be beautiful. Artist must be beautiful." She repeats these lines again and again, accelerating and decelerating the pace of her voice at various intervals. As she does so she pulls the brush and comb roughly through her hair and across the skin of her face, increasing the ferocity of these gestures as time passes. Her hair becomes a tangled mess, her face red, scratched, and bleeding.

Marina Abramović has developed an astonishingly refined body of performance work that foregrounds the gendering of subjects within the context of aesthetic, cultural, and political domains, structured around the opposition between ideological and material domination and submission. Her performances have been called "exercises in passive aggression,"[63] a phrase that gestures both to the intricate relationship she develops with her audiences and to her nuanced critique of the simplistic distinction between subject and object. Using her body alongside iconic objects and minimal actions she operates at the limits of performed passivity, mobilizing that position as an eloquent and supple critique of consumption in many of its forms: the consumption of art by audiences and spectators, the consumption of women's bodies by men and masculinist modes of exchange, and the consumption that drives capitalist expansionism and structural oppression. *Aggression* may be the least useful word one might deploy to describe Abramović's work, although many of her performances are certainly designed in response to aggressive enactments of violence on individual, interpersonal, local, and global scales. Her performances do not simply reenact the antagonistic relationship between performance artists and audiences or between works of art and their political contexts; they also open up the possibility of live performance as a medium that defies aesthetic commodification and thus exemplifies what Peggy Phelan has called "representation with reproduction."[64]

For *Nightsea Crossing*, staged more than a dozen times during the 1980s,[65] Abramović and her partner Ulay sat opposite one another, silent and still, at an unadorned table. The performance lasted for anywhere from one to sixteen days, during which time the two artists did not speak or eat, attempting to maintain eye contact for as long as possible. *Nightsea Crossing* staged, as RoseLee Goldberg remarks, the "fullness of emptiness" between the two lovers and collaborators.[66] That emptiness was resplendent in the physical pain of sitting still for days on end, in the growing exhaustion that accompanies any fast, and in the intense eye contact maintained over excruciating stretches of time. Abramović retrospectively described the piece:

> Presence.
> Being present, over long stretches of time,
> Until presence rises and falls, from
> Material to immaterial, from
> Form to formless, from
> Instrumental to mental, from
> Time to timeless.[67]

Abramović and Ulay consumed nothing, no food, except the sight of one another and the time of the staging's duration. This psychological and emotional devouring, simultaneous with a silent asceticism, staged both the consumptive economy of the spectacle and the morbid consumption of time; in short, *Nightsea Crossing* staged the live.

During the period when Abramović and Ulay collaborated, most of their performances were similarly structured around the dynamic of heterosexual relationality; often, as in *Rest Energy*, the "fullness of emptiness" between the two was filled up with the tension of threat of imminent death. For *Rest Energy* they stood facing one another in a gallery space, leaning away from one another at opposite ends of a taut bow; Abramović held its staff while Ulay extended the string.[68] Poised in precarious balance was a single sharp arrow aimed at Abramović's chest. As audience members stood watching, the artists' heartbeats were amplified and projected through microphones taped to their chests and speakers hung on the walls. As the performance proceeded the rhythm of Abramović's pulse would increase, seeming to reveal her recognition that at any moment Ulay could lose his balance and fall and the arrow shoot her through her heart. *Rest Energy* designated the space between the lovers and the marked distinction in their positions as a site of mortal danger, of morbid possibilities, but not equally for the two: Ulay controlled whatever agency the bow could be said to possess, while Abramović claimed the position of its potential victim.

In what was perhaps their most famous joint work, *The Lovers*, Abramović and Ulay traveled to opposite ends of the Great Wall of China and then followed its trail for weeks before finally meeting in the middle. Here the space between the two was filled with the tread and time of a long and arduous journey, ending with a rendezvous that was itself a goodbye: Abramović and Ulay separated personally and professionally at the conclusion of their Great Wall walk. In many ways *The Lovers* defined the character of Abramović's future solo work: its duration confounded any possible continuous spectatorship; it measured heartbreak in slow, deliberate steps; and it leaped scales between the personal and the national by tracing (and ending) an interpersonal relationship along the architecture of a wall originally constructed to delineate and protect a unified China against invaders from the north.

In the years after the Great Wall walk Abramović created solo performances that dealt explicitly with the question of the national body. Born in the former Yugoslavia, she had previously developed with Ulay works that contended with the imperialist regimes that had divided the European continent after the Second World War. On her own Abramović created *Cleaning the Mirror*, for one part of which she sat with a skeleton, peeling and scrubbing the grit and grime from its surfaces.[69] Such performances were intended to speak to the ethnic cleansing sanctioned in various parts of Eastern Europe and elsewhere during the cold war; the image of scouring a skeleton, perhaps the definitive marker of extreme emaciation, mirrored her earlier performance of *Art Must Be Beautiful, Artist Must Be Beautiful*. In this work Abramović was clearly offering a critique of expectations that women in particular maintain a specific standard of beauty, so dramatically and perversely undone in the staging of the piece. But the performance also called upon its audience to bear witness to an extended choreography of preening, staged as brutal gestures that wound. ("I find that beauty hurts," she commented in a later interview with Laurie Anderson.)[70] Abramović confounded the desire to see beauty emerge from that choreography, and thus refused to present herself at the performance's conclusion as an appreciably (and commodifiably) beautiful façade. Likewise in *Cleaning the Mirror* the audience was summoned to bear witness to the *aesthetics* and the *effects* of genocide. In the context of her broader body of work these two functions are correlative: the human body, Abramović's primary medium, is fully infused with the world outside itself; the effects of political, cultural, and aesthetic violence upon the body are both a function of and akin to the systems and ideologies of violence performed to define and enact broader coalitions and concentrations of power.

Just as it was not by chance that the particular body deployed in these performances was a woman's body, it was not inconsequential that Abramović chose the particular gestures of *grooming* and *cleaning*, labor that is classically gendered female. Confronting the ethnic cleansing associated with genocide, Abramović took on the cultural work so often asked of women, who are expected to clean up the messes that men make. In the case of her homeland, the former Yugoslavia, that mess was a domestic warfare that aimed itself to cleanse the *body politic* of difference. That Abramović performed cleaning upon a skeleton, which the piece named a "mirror," further concentrated the meaning of the performance. That is, the mirror cleaned was representative of the organization of identification enforced within a genocidal political regime; the cleaning was emblematic of the cultural work of nurturing and mourning gendered as female and relegated to women. Of course a mirror is also a surface that allows one to see oneself; for Abramović this skeletal looking-glass initiates our power to witness the communion, the compliance, between modes and registers of personal, national, and global enactments of violence.

In a more recent performance, *The House with the Ocean View*, Abramović built upon her previous work to deploy the artist's body as a site with which to deny aesthetic commodification, to demonstrate the affect and the effects of silent abnegation, and, in Phelan's words, to "illuminate the mutual and repeated attempt to grasp, if not fully apprehend, consciousness as simultaneously intensely personal and immensely vast and impersonal."[71] Staged in the Sean Kelly Gallery in New York City, *The House with the Ocean View* was performed on "a striking design object that leaves the minimally accessorized performances of the 70s far behind":[72] three connected, raised platforms, fixed to the rear wall of the gallery, modestly furnished to represent particular areas of a domestic space (living room, bedroom, bathroom). The decor was exceedingly sparse, consisting of simple, iconic furniture pieces (table, chair, cot) and fully functioning toilet, shower, and sink. For twelve days in November 2002 Abramović complemented her spare setting by moving deliberately in slow, regimented, meditative steps, "like a person on a tightrope,"[73] or sitting for hours at a time gazing back at the audience. During those twelve days, reminiscent of the lengthier versions of *Nightsea Crossing* staged in the 1980s, Abramović lived on the platforms, sitting to rest, lying on the wooden bed, taking small sips of water, using the toilet, and showering. Nothing she did was hidden from view; indeed in the directive posted outside the gallery audience members were instructed to use a large telescope installed at the rear of the gallery to inspect every inch of her body. Those in attendance during any part of the performance were also asked to engage in an "energy exchange" with the artist by returning and holding her gaze.[74]

Propped against the platforms were the only possible means by which Abramović might have exited the scene: ladders built with upturned butcher knives as rungs. In his review of *The House with the Ocean View* the performance critic Steven Henry Madoff suggested that the "22½-inch butcher knives, blades turned up, . . . [made] the point that she's not going anywhere."[75] Several years earlier, discussing another of her performances, Abramović had described a scene from her work with South American indigenous groups: "If you put this ladder with knives in front of a shaman in Brazil, he will walk on it. It's our problem that we can't."[76] This suggests that the ladders were intended not precisely to enforce her remaining on the platforms, but rather to demonstrate the limitations of fear. Indeed after ending the performance Abramović apologized to her audience for not having had the courage to descend.[77]

The gallery's owner, Sean Kelly, and members of his staff signed contracts with Abramović vowing not to remove her from the platforms under any circumstance, medical or otherwise.[78] These contracts, reminiscent of Abramović's "I take full responsibility" declaration for *Rhythm 0*, also stipulated that she would not be force-fed; for twelve days she starved, living alone in her miniature house though witnessed by thousands of visitors; she was silent except for occasional singing, crying, and laughing; she followed a strict regimen of three showers per day and seven hours of sleep per night; she moved in the rhythm of a metronome that ticked away the seconds and hours of her stark life in *The House with the Ocean View*. Madoff remembers, "No talking. No reading. No writing. No eating. During gallery hours, she will stare at us and we will stare back, or peer, if we want to, through a telescope specially set out, every inch of her privacy stripped."[79] Another critic recalled:

> The masochism of her earlier work, or her explicit confrontation of violence against bodies, . . . has shifted from the symbolic to a highly reduced, minimalist existentialism which, to some, may be infuriatingly close to an uncritical and unreflective new age spiritism. The asceticism of fasting and silence now belong to her strategies of creating works which ritualize very basic actions of everyday life.[80]

The performance replicated the extended duration of her earlier work, especially *Nightsea Crossing*, but with the public taking Ulay's place across the table, and summoned *The Lovers* as Abramović wore the boots she had used to walk the Great Wall. Abramović herself spoke of the piece not as a protest, but as a "gift" for New York City after 11 September 2001; to use a more Maussian notion, it was perhaps the economy of a gift supplanting the commodity.[81] But *The House with the Ocean View* was not, in Abramović's words, a "political act,"[82] and yet it was in this performance that the direct political commentary of *Cleaning the Mirror* became fully refined. In its sparse aesthetics and regimented ascetics the performance was both a demonstration of and a response to the grief and loss experienced by New Yorkers on and after 11 September 2001, a reminder that although that day seemed exceptional in the lives of U.S. citizens, it is an "everyday occurrence" in other parts of the world.[83] But *The House with the Ocean View* also reflected the United States back to itself, locked in its insular geography and its failure to see or reach past immense bodies of water to a world its policies attempt to contain and control. Abramović's performance staged a decidedly nonaggressive mode of confrontation, a mode deeply unlike the swift and relentless response of the United States in the Middle East and elsewhere after 11 September 2001. That is, Abramović issued a cry antithetical to the one proclaimed by George W. Bush: "If you're not with us, you're against us."[84] *The House with the Ocean View* was thus a response of the most generous, rigorous, and difficult sort: it was a gift, a demonstration of mournful, meditative abnegation that evenly met the gaze of those who arrived to behold it. It called upon its U.S. audience to see, in perhaps a new light, the dangers of failing to see the world beyond those oceans as anything other than resources for our wildly consumptive policies and drives, to consider how the fields of energy might shift if, when looking out the window of this isolationist house, we might see past the ocean that surrounds us.

In fasting, in limiting her daily routines to the most base and austere gestures and activities, in building and inhabiting such a sparse and unadorned space that nonetheless met all of her needs, Abramović demonstrated how affiliations across the gallery lines—affiliation, not aggression, as a mode of encounter after the event of a tragedy—might compel the most intense, striking, and evocative conditions for communication. In starving herself—her fast (expectedly) became one of the most talked-about qualities of the performance—Abramović did not, like Kafka's hunger artist, shore herself up as a spectacle (where the desperation to be seen and recognized for the feat of self-immolation might trump any possibility for exchange across the bars), but eloquently articulated and dramatically refined the intersubjectivity made possible by her gift. "There was no object," Phelan recalls; "there was a kind of fused subjectivity."[85] Abramović created "voids made of darkness and hunger, which the viewer is called on to fill," wrote Roberta Smith.[86] For Abramović, who embraced the risks associated with self-consumption as a kind of personal and communal purification, seeing became an aesthetic, worldly, political form of compassion. The refusal to consume or be consumed was embraced as a turning away from both the conventional politics of art production and reception and the destructive modes of political violence that respond to tragedy with brute force and unforgiving terror. The suffering of *The House with the Ocean View* becomes *our* suffering, but its grace also becomes our grace, its life our *live*.

The performance with which I opened this chapter, *Food for the Spirit*, represented Adrian Piper's attempts to work through the logic of Kant's notion of the transcendental self. In her philosophical writing Piper has similarly contended with the individualist concepts of identity developed by Hume and Hegel,[87] in part by considering *action* as a fundamental model for the self, as opposed to Hume's rationality of desire and Hegel's defense of personal property. In particular she has argued for "responsible and morally committed action" as the venue for the ethical subject.[88] In other words, for Piper the subject is recognized and accountable as such according to how she or he performs in and of the world. In all of her work audiences have been called upon to witness scenes invoking embodied objecthood and were compelled to respond—some gracefully, others with repulsion.[89] This production of what Piper calls "the indexical present" makes it impossible when viewing her work to escape or otherwise ignore its summons to action, however passive those actions may seem. As Moten argues, we are summoned "into the context of the other, of the object." In *Food for the Spirit* alimentary and visual self-consumption stage the "indexical present" as fusion of subject and object: the relentlessly mortal body stares evenly at its own gradual disappearance, objectified by the reflection of an unforgiving mirror, simultaneously subjectified by its spoken and unspoken desire to find itself wholly there.

Likewise for Ana Mendieta and Marina Abramović the labor of tracing and embodying the ephemerality of presence in ghostly silhouettes that insistently imprint themselves upon the land, even as they gradually vanish, in the painstaking hours and days of an intersubjective fast, represented not only a method for recircuiting aesthetic exchange, but also of positioning themselves, subjects and objects of the gaze, within political geographies of abjection and belonging. Their evocations of self-consumption in these haunting (and haunted) works of art plumb the deepest cultural currents that, first, demand that we consume all that we can and, second, call us to ask at every turn, with every glance and uttered phrase, "What can I devour next?" The refusal to respond affirmatively to such incantations, to suggest "I will absent myself from that consumptive exchange," has in other places and at other times been a strategy of resistance for those who similarly labor at the boundaries between the active and the passive, between the twin poles of the subject named by Althusser, Foucault, and Butler. These remarkably moving performances manage to show us, without explication or apology, the imbrication of subjectivity and objecthood, presence and absence, here and gone. Their power is forged in the constant, flickering oscillation between the individual body of the artist and the social body of the *we*. Their mastery, in contradistinction to Fried's desired "see[ing] everything," is in the generosity with which they intertwine these axes of concern, the supplication with which they interrogate self- and other-directed violence, and the rigor with which they summon us, as still breathing but slowly expiring bodies, to encounter them.

CHAPTER FOUR

to lie down to death for days

•

Appetite is the chaos which makes discipline so necessary.

— Morag MacSween, *Anorexic Bodies*

The prison must be an exhaustive disciplinary apparatus.

— Michel Foucault, *Discipline and Punish*

O, yes, fasting is as full of specters as a field of battle.

— Edward Bulwer-Lytton, *Zanoni*

Ebru Dinçer sits at a flimsy table, wearing a nondescript beige uniform in front of a nondescript concrete-block wall. As the filmmaker Metin Yeğin interviews her, she stares back at him with the intensity of one who has a short time to live. Her face is sunken, worn thin from months of starvation, and scarred from the many surgeries required to heal her chemically burned skin. Her eyes are large, and when they occasionally gaze at the floor or the ceiling they are filled with a despair that will never find its way into language; she is despondent but intense. Speaking softly and clearly she responds to Yeğin's questions with impressionistic precision in describing the time since her recent release from prison: "Life now is like a dream. Like a fantasy. It's like a non-existent thing. . . . It has lost its reality. Nothing to add. No, there is nothing else I want to add."[1]

Dinçer was one of 816 Turkish political prisoners who, on 20 October 2000, began the longest and deadliest hunger strike in modern history.[2]

Of the strikers' original demands the most fundamental was the termination of all construction on and transfer of prisoners to so-called F-type prisons, based on Euro-American designs intended to isolate prisoners, to limit (and largely to deny) their rights to interact with one another, and ultimately to facilitate unrecorded, unchecked, and unpunished torture. During the duration of the strike more than two thousand people participated for various intervals; by the middle of 2003 107 strikers had died.[3]

The staging of the hunger strike coincides with two larger-scale affairs that have dominated domestic and foreign policy in Turkey for at least the past decade: continuing attempts to obtain member status in the European Union and renewed Western (imperialist) interest in the Middle East, especially after 11 September 2001. Turkey was officially named a candidate for EU membership in 1999 despite promises from several nations to veto any final accession.[4] This step renewed the Turkish government's interest in continuing to adapt official policy to European standards—particularly policies concerning capital punishment, prison conditions, human rights protections, and economic development—and simultaneously renewed critics' charges against Turkey. As Turkey continues to attempt to color itself European, those unquestionably inside the EU (e.g., Greece, Germany, France) continue to position Turks as other and Turkey as outside. At the same time Turkey represents a pivotal ally for U.S. and U.K. military forces (and others) who have sought easy access to Iraq, Iran, Syria, and other majority-Muslim nations. At once solicited by Western superpowers for right of entry to its land between Europe and the Middle East and maligned by European Union officials who criticize its policy and sneer at its agrarian culture, Turkey is uniquely situated, or rather imagined, as ally-other.

Of course the dynamics that go by the name *inside/outside* and that so vividly mark Turkey's role in contemporary world politics are hardly as simplistic as such a characterization may make them seem. Typically figured (as the subtitle for a recent book puts it) "between two worlds,"[5] a positioning that will forever refuse to recognize Turkey as its own world, Turkey is generally treated as the *effect* of a staid borderland geography. In the logic of imperialism and unionization Turkey marks that place where the potential for European identification (the referent of EU membership) is unsettled by the proximity of a disparate set of states (Iraq, Iran, Syria, et al.) generally imagined as the other against which Europe defines itself. Against this geographical background—conceived, as geography often is, as stable, natural, or fixed[6]—Turkey represents both the promise of Western expansion and the ultimate threat to the integrity of Western identification. In the words of Valéry Giscard d'Estaing, former French president and former chair of the EU Constitutional Convention, Turkey's membership would "open the door" to West Asian and North African Arab states and would thus "be the end of the European Union."[7]

Given this context, in which Turkey is asked to perform the role of ally when it comes to colonizing the Middle East and other when it comes to identification with Europe, this hunger strike articulates on a domestic scale the anxieties and the violence associated with the production of a state whose global affiliations are in flux. I argue that the hunger strike reframes that question of affiliation in terms of political subjectivity, staging a challenge to more conventional relationships between state and subject. Indeed the Turkish hunger strike, itself bound up in a complicated reversal of violence performed on individual subjects by the state, demonstrates that the political subjectivity (which we might recognize as a consortium of freedoms: of representation, of expression, of association) so desperately sought by the strike's constituency is underpinned by subjugation to more dire forms of institutional and ideological power.

In this chapter I explore both the role of the F-type prison in contemporary Turkish politics and the conditions of the prisoners' hunger strike: its aims and demands, the experiences of its practitioners and casualties, its representation in state-sanctioned and other media, and its effects. I trace the context of the strike's beginnings and the history of the demands named by its constituency. I explore the progression of the strike and the implications of its various main events. I ask how and why this strike stages and interrogates the relationship between political subjectivity and the integrity of the Turkish state. Finally I consider the potential of hunger striking as a viable, sustainable form of political action and the production of political subjects through the performance of the hunger strike.

The contours of my argument follow four specific suggestions for how the Turkish hunger strike functions *as performance* to refigure the relationship between state and subject, to facilitate the deployment of new kinds of political subjectivity, and to redraw the meaning of Turkey as a borderland state. First, at its height, the strike expanded in constituency to include not only political prisoners in a number of prisons throughout Turkey, but also activists outside the prison altogether, particularly those in the Kuçuk Armutlu neighborhood of Istanbul. The manner in which the strike was staged *across prison walls* resymbolizes the significance of the boundary represented materially and discursively by those walls, as a producer of political alliance rather than a block to it. This is not to say, of course, that the techniques of surveillance, discipline, and containment performed within Turkish prisons are empty of the meanings and effects that distinguish them as specifically carceral; rather this particular strike opened up the possibility for identification and alliance, questioning what precisely "Turkishness" means in the context of state penal policy, across the very walls that are traditionally conceived as intense divisions between those who are held within and those who are able to move outside penal institutions.

Second, in part because such intense lines of affiliation developed across prison walls, the hunger strike effected the signification of the prison, and in particular the F-type prison, as the context and the condition for contemporary Turkish state-production. Due largely to the specific performance of this hunger strike (and the rhetoric surrounding its performance) the prison became both a specific site for the production of Turkishness and a metaphor for the production of state power in Turkey more generally. This metaphor takes the form of, for example, specific statements aimed to solicit support for the strike ("The entire Turkey is like the F-Type prisons," wrote Turkish human rights workers after military attacks on Kuçuk Armutlu were reported)[8] and of sophisticated attempts by prisoners and activists alike to show that the effects of the prison crisis extend well beyond any penal policy that may be linguistically amended or erased. The hunger strike, devoted explicitly to a list of demands, is not simply a question of prison design, of increasingly restrictive legislation, or of the impunity afforded to the practitioners of prison torture. At question is the very nature of Turkish political subjectivity as defined, delimited, and compelled by the state.

Third, and in part as a result of efforts to force into crisis the difference between being inside and being outside the prison, the hunger strike effected a mode of resistance for which *coalition* was the primary unit of political action and signification. This is exceptional in the history of hunger striking, which traditionally promotes the names, and not the numbers, of hunger strikers as the standout representatives of the strikers' struggles. Bobby Sands, Mahatma Gandhi, César Chávez: these names do not merely denote oft-cited events in the history of hunger striking; as symbols they embody those events, and so bear the burdens of both representing the issues at the heart of past strikes and commemorating those strikes. In Turkey, though press releases named those strikers who died, there was no single figurehead whose image or name signified the movement as a whole. More significant for this strike were the immense numbers of those who were on strike and those who died; this shift in attention repositions the effects of resistance and the desired outcome of the strikes in terms of a political subjectivity squarely situated within the context of group affiliation. Rather than striving for a kind of martyrdom in individualization, for the recognition of the individual subject as the principal unit and site of political signification, the multiple solidarities epitomized by the Turkish strikers produced and reflected subjects deeply connected to their political community despite the potential for what is essentially a highly individualized consequence of striking: death.

Finally, and also exceptionally, the Turkish strike redefined the practice of hunger striking, from what is traditionally conceived as a necessarily short-term, last-ditch effort to effect change, to a budding sustainable mode of political action whose organizing center is the potential death of individual subjects. That is, the Turkish hunger strike was not merely *notable* for its unusual duration; it recast hunger striking itself as a form of protest whose extended performance could alter both the meaning of the protest itself and the notions of success and failure that often limit how the protest's larger impacts may be understood. Attempts to read the effects of the Turkish hunger strike strictly in terms of whether or not its specific demands were met ignore its many implications not only for the conditions of prisons themselves, but for the very heart of the production of Turkish subjects.

To call 20 October 2000 the *beginning* of the current Turkish hunger strike is, though technically accurate, a misnomer. First, the strike itself followed several previous hunger strikes in Turkish prisons, in particular one in 1996 that claimed twelve lives.[9] Rhetoric used both to announce the strike and to name its demands not only referred back to these previous strikes, but named their participants as part of its own constituency, especially those killed in military operations intended to break up the strikes and those suffering from medical problems as a result of the strikes:

> Our friends named below were imprisoned alive at different times. The state was responsible for the security of these friends' lives. As is well known, the acceptability and legality of the prisoners' status [as imprisoned] is based on the state's guarantee of the security of their lives. These friends were massacred by the state. We want our friends back.
>
> . . .

All our friends who have suffered from permanent illness, whose health problems have continued since the 1996 Death Fast, who were injured during state operations and denied medical treatment, must be immediately released.[10]

Second, the strikers' demands circulated within a larger set of concerns about the relationship between the Turkish state and its many marginalized subjects: Kurds, Islamists, dissident writers and journalists, human rights workers, and members of outlawed leftist political parties.[11] Since the inception of the Turkish state in the 1920s this relationship has been contentious at best, and warlike at worst. Thousands of Kurds, for example, have been incarcerated after being charged — many fewer have actually been convicted[12] — with membership in one of the country's many leftist political groups, several of which have historically fought for an independent Kurdish state. Islamists have struggled to find a way in to Turkey's political scene, reformed as strictly secular by Kemal Atatürk's government in the 1920s, and are often imprisoned because of those struggles. Writers and journalists are regularly sentenced for publishing texts critical of the Turkish government or explicitly covering the "Kurdish problem" or any of a number of other restricted journalistic and literary activities.[13] While in recent years the election of representatives from moderate Islamist and Kurdish political parties have altered the context somewhat,[14] these struggles have defined and continue to define the context and the conditions of political resistance in Turkey since its establishment as a republic in 1923.

In this context the commencement of the hunger strike was announced in a manifesto released to the press on 18 October 2000 by the Devrimci Halk Kurtuluş Partisi-Cephesi (Revolutionary People's Liberation Party/Front) and the Türkiye Komünist Partisi/Marksist-Leninist (Turkish Communist Party/Marxist-Leninist), and on 20 December strikers began their fasts. The most immediate concern of the prisoners was the government's plans to move political prisoners (who made up ten thousand to twelve thousand of the seventy-two thousand people incarcerated in Turkish prisons) into the new F-type prisons.[15] Traditional Turkish prisons were built in the style of dormitories, consisting of large bunkrooms (holding up to one hundred people) in which prisoners were able to interact with one another regularly.[16] Concerned that certain political groups use these prisons as "indoctrination and recruitment centers," and as part of its intense push for EU membership, the Turkish government decided to reform its penal system by adopting a U.S.- and European-based design for the F-type prison in order to hold incarcerated people in isolated cells and to limit (and often to deny outright) time allotted for interaction with others.[17] This decision followed attempts in the 1980s to develop what was then called a "special type prison," most notoriously Istanbul's Kartal Prison, which has served more or less as an immense holding cell for political prisoners *awaiting trial* for offenses under the draconian Anti-Terrorism Laws enacted in 1991. Kartal represented a jarring shift in the penal system, from the old-style dormitory prisons to a large institution broken up into single or small-group cells where prisoners are being held (according to most reports) all day, every day with little to no interaction (or even visual contact) with other human beings. By 1999 of the roughly three hundred prisoners held at Kartal only one had been convicted of any crime. The Kartal special type prison and its conditions of incarceration both rehearsed and set the stage for the implementation of the F-type prison regime.[18]

The F-type prisons subject political prisoners to isolation and to vulnerability to ill treatment and torture. The prisons are divided into 109 cells holding up to three prisoners each and fifty-nine solitary cells. Typically cells in F-type prisons are windowless, are relatively small, and include the most basic furnishings: a bed, a shower, a toilet, and often a desk. Each cell opens into a small high-walled courtyard of sixteen to fifty square meters. Prisoners have reported that those doors, as well as the doors leading to the wards' corridors, remain locked for most of the day, typically the entire day. According to the Ministry of Justice, the prisons also include "lawyers' reception rooms, a library and an extensive reading room for personnel and prisoners, and indoor multipurpose area for social, cultural, and sports activities, . . . and working sites for various purposes (so prisoners can learn a trade)."[19] These spaces, compulsory for meeting the Minimum Prison Requirements of the United Nations and Council of Europe, are, however, typically closed to prisoners, who report that their access to libraries, education, and socialization programs is random and sparse to nonexistent. These conditions render the F-type prison an isolationist prison *regime* as well as the specific architectural space in which that regime may assert itself. In other words, the prisons represent both an ideological force that restricts contact and communication between political prisoners and the most intense site of that ideological constraint.

Plans to develop the F-type prisons were announced in 1989. Following that announcement, and throughout the 1990s, several strikes were staged to oppose the transfer of political prisoners to the new prisons.[20] The transfers were explicitly justified in Article 16 of the Anti-Terrorism Law; this article, which was repealed in 2006, served as the legal basis for discriminating between political prisoners and other prisoners, for isolating political prisoners in small cells, and for thoroughly restricting communication among prisoners and between prisoners and their families. The article begins:

> Sentences of those convicted of offences within the scope of the provisions of this law [i.e., the Anti-Terrorism Law] shall be served in special penal establishments, constructed according to a system of one-person and three-person cells. No open visits shall be permitted in such establishments. Communication between inmates and with other convicts shall be prevented.[21]

Discriminating between "acts of terror" and other crimes and (more important) between terrorists and other criminals has been a major project for Turkish legislators since the early 1980s. In 1983 the new Official Prison Regulations were adopted; Articles 78/3 and 78/4 of those regulations defined the categories of "political prisoner," "terrorist," and "anarchist" and rendered legal the confinement of prisoners designated as such in special prisons.[22] Strikes against such legislation intensified after the adoption of the antiterrorism legislation in 1991; the strike in 1996 was the first to specify the F-type prison as its central complaint. Despite an official announcement that all plans to build the new prisons would be put on hold to allow time for reconsideration, construction continued, and by mid-2000 four F-type prisons had been opened.[23] Further the Turkish government undertook military operations in the prisons in 1995, 1996, 1999, and 2000 in order to end the strikes and forcibly to extract selected prisoners from the large wards and relocate them in the new prisons.[24] Under the Anti-Terrorism Law political prisoners were classified as terrorists, enabling the government to exact even more specialized discipline and punishment, including solitary confinement and the restriction of many, if not all, daily activities (including socialization, exercise, and formal education).

The terms of the Anti-Terrorism Law gathered in their expansive sweep a range of activities that together construct an idiom of terrorism synonymous with dissent, with discourse, and indeed with difference. Article 8, which was repealed late in 2003, stated, "No one shall, by any means or with any intention or idea, make written and oral propaganda or hold assemblies, demonstrations and manifestations against the indivisible integrity of the state of the Turkish Republic with its land and nation."[25] In addition to outlawing a wide (and vague) range of activities, this article drew attention to the fundamental relationship between the state and its various geographies: the land it occupies or aims to occupy; social service infrastructures and the territories they transverse; and the architecture of the government's many institutions, including the prison. Article 8 was not merely a crackdown on resistance propaganda or protest; it rendered many oppositional voices terrorist simply by virtue of their dissenting political claims. If officials have been centrally concerned with attempts by Kurdish political groups in the East attempting to develop and enforce independent rule (an immediately recognizable assembly aimed to divide the land Turkey claims as its own),[26] they have also been fully aware that prisons built to house such dissidents are themselves vital architectures of the "indivisible integrity of the state." Legislation such as Article 8 enables the official classification of hunger strikers, whose demands include massive prison reform, as terrorists simply by virtue of their demonstrating against state penal policies. As I commented earlier, this legislation has a genealogy, including, for example, the Turkish Constitution, the most recent version of which was written during three years after a military coup in 1980 to restore democratic control of the government. The preamble to the Constitution specifies:

> No protection shall be given to thoughts or opinions that run counter to Turkish national interests, the fundamental principle of the existence of the indivisibility of the Turkish state and territory, the historical and moral values of Turkishness, or the nationalism, principles, reforms, and modernism of Atatürk, and that as required by the principle of secularism there shall be absolutely no interference of sacred religious feeling in the affairs of state and politics.[27]

Kemal Atatürk was the first president appointed after the fall of the Ottoman Empire in the early 1920s. Deeply invested in "dragging Turkey into the West," his government initiated a series of policies in the 1920s aimed at outlawing traditional practices associated with former notions of Ottoman identity, including such everyday actions as wearing the fez and such abstract practices as organizing as a minority group. By restricting citizens' travel and controlling communications and mass media, these policies had the effect of isolating Turkey from neighboring states and closing Turkey's national borders. At the same time Atatürk's government opened the door to Western imperialism by welcoming, and in some ways legally enforcing, influence from Western nations, including the United States. Sweeping changes mesmerized the national populace, which was nonetheless suspicious of the rapidly changing Turkish scene. This modernism, however, made Atatürk something of a national hero, not merely a president whose leadership was pronounced in its sweeping reform of the former Ottoman Empire, but himself an intensely loaded metaphor for bold economic and cultural progress. To this day Atatürk's name appears throughout national legislation as a sign of Turkey's desire to implement many Western policies, to open the door to identification with the West, and to deny the more pluralist nature of Ottoman culture; that is, the principles of Atatürk, typically called Kemalism, are based on the coherence of a congealed, conventional Turkish national identity based on the denial of difference.[28]

In what is perhaps the most remarkable example of this kind of legislated denial, the Political Parties Law includes an article "preventing the creation of minorities": "Political parties cannot put forward that minorities exist in the Turkish Republic based on national, religious, confessional, racial, or language differences."[29] This third piece of legislation is not simply an institutional denial of difference among the Turkish populace, but the ideological arm of a nationalist project of racial and ethnic cleansing; as many of those incarcerated in Turkey's prisons have learned, it has the force not only to designate certain activities as terrorist, but to activate various state-sanctioned techniques of punishment. (Although attempts to reform the Political Parties Law continue, many doubt that any consensus on changes to the law will be reached in the near future.)[30] Kevin Robins artfully and compellingly dispatches cultural theory to this scene of nationalized homogeneity, suggesting that the denial of internal difference is a kind of "repression of identity." The repressed, he argues, is "returning": "There is still iron in the soul of the [Turkish] state; seemingly devoid of political imagination of nuance, it continues to pursue the uncompromisingly adamantine principles. . . . The 'Other' Turkey is making its declaration of independence, making its reality felt, manifesting the complexity of its social being."[31]

During the 1990s, in the context of these articles of legislation, the "other Turkey" had little to hope for in political recognition or representation. The forced patterns of identification initiated by such legislation, and the widespread arrest and incarceration of political prisoners that it sanctioned, are suggestive of Foucault's argument in *Discipline and Pun-*

ish: that the juridical is subordinate to the punitive in the service of the state and that the prison is not merely a disciplinary edifice that houses criminal offenders, but a "penitentiary *technique*" that produces marginalized subjects.[32] He writes:

> The penitentiary technique bears not on the relation between author and crime, but on the criminal's *affinity* with his crime. . . . The correlative of penal justice may well be the offender, but the correlative of the penitentiary apparatus is someone other; this is the delinquent, a biographical unity, a kernel of danger, representing a type of anomaly. . . . The penitentiary technique and the delinquent are in a sense twin brothers. . . . It is now this delinquency, this anomaly, this deviation, this potential danger, this illness, this form of existence, that must be taken into account when the codes are rewritten. Delinquency is the vengeance of the prison on justice.[33]

Political prisoners are delinquents par excellence; they represent the most dangerous threat against, and their incarceration is the sine qua non of the integrity of, the state. Through its many forms of discipline incarceration enables the production of "docile bodies" whose political subjectivities are defined and determined by their subservience to the state.[34] The ultimate aim of the penitentiary technique includes not simply the rehabilitation or reform of the incarcerated, but the specific production of delinquents whose subjugation becomes the condition of their very existence. Such subjugation is likewise the condition of state integrity. Foucault argues:

> The carceral network does not cast the unassimilable into a confused hell; there is no outside. It takes back with one hand what it seems to exclude with the other. It saves everything, including what it punishes. It is unwilling to waste even what it has decided to disqualify. . . . The delinquent is not outside the law; he is, from the very outset, in the law, at the very heart of the law.[35]

The state defines itself with these delinquents at its very core; it asserts itself in designating delinquents as such; it produces itself precisely through the exclusion by incarceration exemplified by the F-type regime. *Rehabilitated* comes to mean *docile*.

Later I focus more directly on the hunger strike's gendered makeup and implications; however, it is important to take notice here of Foucault's complicated omission of gender from his analysis. This omission is represented linguistically by his constant referral to prisoners as "he," narratively by his exclusive use of historical examples of imprisoned men, and generally by the lack of any legible recognition that his theory may be differently inflected across lines of gender identifications. And yet it seems that gender, though unexplored by Foucault, is at the heart of his argument: *docility*, after all, is not so far from *domesticity*, both of which are hallmarks of patriarchal ideological frameworks that situate feminized subjects, spaces, and behaviors on the far right side of the pairing active/passive. This pairing, often treated as synonymous with the binaries male/female and masculine/feminine, also describes the performance and the anticipated effects of the hunger strike, variously portrayed as political *action*, *passive* resistance, or an *act* of terror. Foucault's insistent concentration on male subjects is thus deeply infused with gendered implications: his docile bodies are essentially feminized bodies; his law is essentially a masculine regime whose power is derived in part from its highly specialized and specifically gendered tactics of discipline and constraint.

Foucault's focus on *affinity* suggests that in the logic of the prison a crime is not, as conventionally conceived, simply an act in a moment in which a person chooses badly; prisoners are delinquents insofar as their crimes become a part of them, an extension of their characters, indeed central to their characters. Imprisoned, a criminal *is* her or his crime. This logic becomes an articulation of state-sanctioned racism in the case of Turkey, where the legislation worked to marginalize, if not to prohibit outright, political activity as traditionally practiced by most Turkish Kurds (who maintain that sharp racial and ethnic differences divide them from non-Kurdish Turks), Islamists (for whom "no interference of sacred religious feeling" has little practical meaning), and others. Turkey's attempts at various points in its seventy-five-year national history to prohibit public use (in education, publication, and radio transmission) of the Kurdish and Arabic languages only extend this agenda of erasing difference in the interest of protecting a streamlined, purified Turkish national identity.[36] If, in Foucault's theory of the penitentiary technique, the criminal *becomes* her or his crime, many Turkish political prisoners become delinquents precisely when and where they identify as (racially, ethnically, religiously) different.

The articles of legislation described earlier, along with various portions of the Penal Code similarly intended to suppress political dissidence,[37] have been the courts' main legal justification for handing down sentences for the great majority of Turkey's political prisoners. They represent core values of the systems of political representation and domestic policymaking, systems that have historically reproduced and institutionalized the "vengeance of the prison on justice," against which the prison hunger strike was organized. The construction of F-type prisons is the central issue behind which the hunger strikers organized. But it was not the only issue. For if the prison *qua* prison is a material *function* of the state's attempts to expel certain groups from its populace, it is also (to use Foucault's word) a *tactic* used to *produce* state power in immediate acts of ideological and material violence. The prison may be the most concentrated architecture of that production, the site and the sign of the state becoming itself in discrete enactments of violence and in the institutionalization of violence-as-law.

This renders the construction of F-type prisons the most coherent rallying point for the hunger strikers. Resplendent in its own very real dangers (extended solitary confinement, torture), the F-type prison is also emblematic of the state's reproduction and defense of its veracity and of its power; as such, it sets the terms, if not the limits, of resistance. As the hunger strikers know all too well, these two operations are correlative. Implicitly drawing attention to the prison-as-tactic, the strikers listed eight other demands in their manifesto. These included the immediate and unconditional repeal of the Anti-Terror Law, independent monitoring of prisons and treatment of prisoners, release of prisoners suffering from permanent injury or illness as a result of previous hunger strikes, and trials for prison staff and others accused of torturing incarcerated people during the past several decades.[38] Couched in the language of an astonishingly violent genealogy of carceral practice and juridical policy, these demands clarified the meaning of the prison in terms of an experiential economy not just of subordination and resistance, but of nationalism, state making, and the production of docile *and* resistant political subjectivities.

The meaning of resistance within that economy becomes especially potent when the terms of its performance potentially occasion the death of its practitioners. Hunger striking explicitly increases the stakes of political action. In his intensely intimate ethnography of political violence in Northern Ireland, Allen Feldman pays special attention to the Blanketmen hunger strike in Belfast in 1981. Probably the most famous strike of its kind in modern history, the Blanketmen hunger strike lasted for 217 days and resulted in the deaths of ten incarcerated members of the IRA (including MP Bobby Sands).[39] Feldman says of the strike:

The performance of the hunger strike would stage the abuse and violence of the Other in the eviscerated flesh of the dying protester. The penal imperative to incorporate the panoptic presence of the Other as a form of compliance and subjugation would itself be subjected to deflating mimesis and a final ironic reversal. . . . No other action more eloquently demonstrated the condition and image of the human body infested with the state apparatus.[40]

The eloquence of hunger striking lies in its potential to throw into crisis the binary passive / active in terms of violence performed and to undermine the conception (suggested, for example, in Ankara's official responses to the strike) of individual and state as absolutely discrete entities at odds with one another, a conception that facilitates the dumbing-down of questions about political terror into the language of cause and effect. In other words, hunger striking rebuffs a particular notion of domination and resistance that positions subjects simply as the *victims* of state power and simultaneously stages the seizure, resymbolization, and enactment — one might say the *ingestion* — of modes of violence typically performed by the state. This is the "condition and image of the human body infested with the state apparatus," the function of the hunger striker as representative of, deeply entrenched in, and radically resistant to the complicated machinery of state violence. The body of the hunger striker, in other words, asserts itself as a body, as a visceral representative for state-produced delinquency, by performing its own gradual decline, through self-consumption, to death. And so that body becomes not only the object of state punishment and torture, but simultaneously an agent imminently responsible for performing violence upon itself. In the case of the Turkish hunger strikers, embodiment became not only a mode of resistance, but also a seizure of state power, especially the state's power to enact violence upon its subjects. This kind of embodiment represented the dying symbol, ever larger in its political and cultural effects, of what has otherwise been denied to the incarcerated: political agency. Hence "starvation of the flesh in the hunger striker was the inverting and bitter interiorization of the power of the state. Hunger striking to the death used the body of the prisoner to recodify and to transfer state power from one topos to another."[41]

The most dramatic example of the state's attempt to interrupt such a transfer of power in Turkey took the form of an intense military operation on 19 December 2000, two months after prisoners began their strike.

Government officials were no doubt concerned that the rhetoric of the strikers' demands, and the inevitable images of dead strikers' bodies being carried out of Turkish prisons, would be a PR disaster for a country attempting to mend its reputation as backward, premodern, and barbaric. And so Operation Return to Life, perhaps the most ironically named military exercise in modern history, was staged in twenty prisons across the country. Narratives of what exactly happened on that day, including the few official statements from Ankara, confirm that at 4:30 A.M., as people in those twenty prisons were sleeping, military commandos dressed in fatigues and carrying automatic weapons, semiautomatic weapons, tear gas, flame throwers, and various chemical agents broke through the prisons' roofs. Prisoners were terrified as they were torn from their slumber, herded or chased through different sections of the prisons, gassed, set afire, shot, or chemically burned. Thirty were killed; many more were seriously wounded.[42] And more than a thousand were dragged out of the prisons and transferred to cells in the four completed F-type prisons.[43]

Reports about the operation from different sources tell radically different stories about conditions inside the prisons and about those responsible for the thirty deaths and the many more serious injuries. Government sources argued that they were regaining control of certain parts of the dormitory prisons to which they had had no access for nearly a decade.[44] These sources also claimed that the prisoners set themselves and their comrades on fire and used small arms to fire on soldiers, prison staff, and their fellow prisoners. Investigations after the operation and statements from various prisoners have suggested that these claims were mostly fabricated.[45] But because many of the prisoners were transferred to F-type isolation cells, where they are not permitted to communicate with one another, with legal advocates, and in many cases with their families, very few narratives from prisoners have been publicized. All of those that have been released indicate that the soldiers' attack on the prisoners was direct and relentless:

> Before we put our clothes on, they opened fire at us and we took cover. We soaked all the towels we could find. Then they started to dig into the ceiling from various places. . . . "We came here to kill you," they were saying. . . . After opening several holes in the ceiling, the bombardment with gas bombs began. We were choking and trying to gasp for air.[46]

> They told us that they wanted us to capitulate. But we said no. Our friends brought those of us who were on hunger strike to death to the back of the

dormitory in an effort to save [us]. The soldiers sprayed a chemical agent that we couldn't recognize on [some of us]. Six of our friends were burned in front of us. I was also on hunger strike to death. Ozlem, one of my friends who was not on hunger strike to death lay on my body in order to save me. But they sprayed that chemical agent on her and burned her. She died as a result.[47]

The bombardment continued non-stop for 9 hours. And we could not leave the dormitory. Because we had no place to go. We could not even raise our heads. We could not stand. . . . Most of those who survived, except for a couple of our friends, have been burnt. 6 of us were burnt completely and even their corpses could not be identified.[48]

These narratives illustrate one of the most central and complicated rules of hunger striking: that hunger strikers must not die directly at the hands of police, military, or prison officials, and yet that their deaths stand as representative of the terror of the state. This rule symbolizes the hunger-striking subject's seizure of one of the mechanisms of state power: discrete acts of violence performed on the bodies of prisoners by state and prison officials. In the case of Turkey it was imperative that every striker, and every striker's death, should stand as equally significant representatives of the strike's mission; no single striker (or category of strikers or type of striker) exceeded the significance of the group as a whole. Feldman says of the Blanketmen strike, "The individual hunger striker was a representative of their collective condition. He would sacrifice his individuality at the same time that he committed the most individual of acts."[49]

Feldman's argument is that hunger striking positions "the most individual of acts," dying, as representative not of the individual striker's needs and desires, but of the group as a whole. In such an economy of representation, an economy some might call martyrdom but that in the Turkish case more closely resembles intersubjectivity, a single hunger striker infuses her or his rapidly disappearing, eviscerated flesh with meanings that renounce the individual as the basic unit of political action and signification; the body of the dying hunger striker becomes fully saturated with significance, particularly at the moment when the sacrifice is complete. Feldman continues:

At the moment of the striking Blanketman's disappearance, he was to attain his highest condition of visibility. But despite this parasitic swarming over his body, the hunger striker became an isolate, dominated by the solitary ordeal of his dying body, witnessing the submersion of his politically constructed self by the decimations of biological process. . . . In reaching the edge, death, pain, blindness, and coma moved the body beyond all cultural/political constructs. As he entered into the time of his death, the hunger striker realized the politics of silence as the termination of his long passage through the joined labyrinths of the prison and his body.[50]

In the case of Northern Ireland the bodies of the dying hunger strikers were "swarmed over" with their representation of both their fellow prisoners and the republican movement more generally; similarly the Turkish hunger strikers stood out as political symbols for both the country's many political prisoners and the maligned communities outside the prisons, the "other Turkey." But whereas in Northern Ireland the postmortem unit of signification became the names of the strikers themselves — Bobby Sands as a figure became an almost literary production of the strike's eschatological function[51] — in Turkey the isolate defied any expectation of being the most eminent (and most cited) unit of political significance. This was no doubt a strategic use of the hunger strikers' capacity to embody the demands of the larger movement; it mirrored the strikers' opposition to isolation in the penitentiaries. Conscious of the extreme significance of the strikers and in particular of their strong lines of affiliation, government officials knew that they needed to bring an end to the strike in order to seize control of the prisoners' evocative productions of political meaning. The violence performed on 19 December 2000, staged after the strikes had been in process for several months, was to be the definitive end to the hunger strike, and (through the transfer of political prisoners to isolation cells) the containment of any potential future action. Individualizing the prisoners' experience in the prisons — "breaking up" the communities that had formed, disallowing "contact and communication" between individual prisoners — was the method by which the government hoped to confound the prisoners so fully that political action, if it were able to continue at all, would have to be radically reconfigured.

Operation Return to Life further asserted the government's active role in weeding out political prisoners and squelching the dissent so powerfully articulated by the hunger strikes. This process of isolation and elimination was explicitly demonstrated with transfers of strikers from prison to prison, the violent, rushed transport of prisoners from the dormitory cells to the solitary confinement of F-type prisons. These transfers were themselves discrete performances. Scenes from Metin Yeğin's films show prisoners, many of whom are covered in scars, wounds, and burns, being moved in and out of police cars, vans, and ambulances. As the prison officials exerted the power to confine, to silence, and to convey the inmates between spaces, the inmates themselves seized the opportunity to shout their testimonials during every exposure to the outside world: "Dozens were killed! . . . Look at my burns! . . . Six of my friends are dead!"[52]

Given these increasingly intense conditions of isolation, how did the strikers' lines of affiliation develop, and what traditional lines of division and difference did they transgress? First, the strikers went to great lengths to show that the effects of the F-type regime extend to all prisoners, including women, who were not immediately transferred to the F-type prisons. The excerpts of narratives about Operation Return to Life I selected for inclusion are drawn from interviews with incarcerated women, typically underemphasized in literature and critical theory about prison torture. In her compelling ethnography of women's prisons Jill McCorkel argues, "The history of the prison is almost exclusively the history of men's institutions."

> The omission of gender [in the vast majority of prison literature] is particularly troubling in the case of Foucault, whose historical analyses of a variety of eighteenth-century disciplinary institutions have earned a prominent place in contemporary discussions of punishment and modern power. . . . Bodies are not only gendered by specific practices and regimes intended to code them as masculine or feminine. Bodies are actively gendered within institutions whose stated mission is directed to other goals.[53]

McCorkel's argument is useful for considering the case of the Turkish penal system, which (like all penal systems purporting to conform to the UN's international prison standards) distinguishes between men's and women's institutions and men's and women's wards within a single prison. Women transferred from the dormitory-style prisons during operations such as Return to Life were moved to remand prisons, many of which were specifically restructured to divide large groups into smaller, often solitary cells resembling those in the Kartal special prison. According to Turkey's Human Rights Association, initially there were no women housed in F-type prisons.[54] What does it mean that many women joined a strike explicitly oriented against the construction of prisons then holding men? How were their lines of affiliation drawn and maintained? Is women's self-starvation a different kind of political activity than men's, with different forms, meanings, and effects? Does the death of a striking woman have political currency distinct from that of a striking man?

Reports from both men and women suggest that the amount of brutality used to transfer prisoners to the F-type prisons was extreme: verbal abuse, beatings, rape. Images from the operation, along with prisoners' narratives and autopsy reports, show that many men and women suffered burns (from chemical agents dropped through the roofs) over large portions of their bodies, along with many other injuries and abuses. In both the men's wards and the women's wards prisoners described mobilizing themselves and their comrades strategically in order to save, at all costs, the lives of the hunger strikers among them.[55] Men and women strikers were similarly resilient after the operation, recommitting themselves to the strike and its demands. The coalition of strikers seems to have strengthened after 19 December 2000, becoming larger, more resolute, and more refined.

If these similarities suggest that the Turkish government was indiscriminate in terms of gender in its extreme use of violent techniques to attempt to bring an end to the hunger strike, they also imply that the solidarity of the strikers was developed by organizing *across* gendered differences between men's and women's experiences of the prison system specifically and of the political climate in Turkey more generally. Simply put, in order to justify their demands and in order to organize effectively around those demands, the strikers stressed the great similarities among experiences within the penitentiary system; for its part, the government exacted similar forms of violence among both women's and men's prison communities. That is, in order to strengthen the community participating in the strikes, hunger strikers developed intense lines of identification and affiliation *across* gender differences. Indeed what is remarkable about the Turkish hunger strike is its development of a large base of strikers and supporters across several traditional divisions (between many Kurds and Islamists, for example, and between working-class or peasant populations and strikers whose backgrounds indicate greater degrees of privilege).[56]

At the same time gendered differences between strikers were not fully unremarked by reporters and others interested in the cultural and political ramifications of this unprecedented protest. Among many medical professionals asked to investigate the physical effects of the extended hunger strike and to develop methods of intervention to force an end to its enactment, the clinical psychiatrist Sahika Huksel suggested that there was "an anorectic aspect to [the strike], especially among the women. They have this morbid fascination with watching their bodies deteriorate. And just as with normal anorexics, they reach a point where they cannot think straight, where they literally cannot see how bad off they are."[57]

In her fusion of two different practices Huksel implies that the fasting woman is a recognizable form (the anorectic) within a larger representational domain, and that her function as such affects the meaning of her rearticulation in the context of a hunger strike. For Huksel anorexia nervosa seems to be the prior term against which women on hunger strike are defined, specifying the meaning of the self-starving woman in terms of a historically articulated vernacular of diminished mental capacities, hysteria, and a "morbid fascination with watching" her gradual emaciation. Cast as genealogically and symbolically linked to anorectics, in Huksel's observation women on hunger strike symbolize the particular terms of their specific strike and simultaneously gesture toward more general concerns surrounding gender inequality and the oppression of women.

Similarly in her study of the meaning of self-starvation in various kinds of literary texts Maud Ellmann argues that self-starvation has become a "symptom of the discontents of womankind." She writes of "the" self-starving woman, "Her emaciated form belongs to a collective economy of images, symbolizing not only her own malaise but that of the community at large."[58] For Ellmann images of women on hunger strike are always already marked in relation to the "malaise" associated with patriarchal oppression, signifying not only the individual striker, but also the larger community (women) of which she is a part. Huksel's comment on the "anorectic aspect" of hunger striking directs our attention to a community she calls "normal anorexics," which we may take to mean those starving women whose political aims may be implied in their self-starvation, but who remain silent on the explicit expression of their political discontent. Hunger strikers, in Huksel's imaginary, are "normal" only in terms of the physical effects of long-term self-starvation — emaciation, dementia, blindness — and presumably "abnormal" in terms not only of the context of their fasts, but also in their explicit acknowledgment of the concerns that have driven them to strike. In Ellmann's terms Huksel's comment suggests that the striking women are "symptomatic" in the same ways that anorectics are, but deviant in their use of self-starvation as an explicitly political practice, perhaps even more deviant for their affiliation with striking men.

If these arguments seem to emphasize a critical distinction between men and women on strike, they are also specific to observations made by or on behalf of audiences of the strike, especially *Western* audiences. These arguments were not, that is, explicitly articulated meanings produced locally by the strikers themselves, whose protests were defined by the lines of identification drawn across traditional boundaries. This is not to say that gender differences had no relevance for the hunger strikers; it does suggest, conceivably, a mode of conceptualizing gender differences as a bridge to identification rather than a barrier to it. Indeed difference emerged as a key register for affiliation more generally for the strikers and their supporters. Perhaps most significant, lines of identification were consciously fostered and intensified across prison boundaries, from the prison cells to areas outside the prison altogether. Within weeks of 19 December 2000 more than two thousand people joined the strike, which had spread outside the bounds of the prison and into Kuçuk Armutlu, a so-called shantytown on the northern (European) edge of Istanbul. Kuçuk Armutlu was primarily populated by members and sympathizers of the Revolutionary People's Liberation Party/Front; many of its residents were former political prisoners or relatives of current prisoners, but many were not.[59] The strike's expansion beyond the walls of the prisons was significant not only because it meant that more people were striking, but also because the lines of political affiliation transgressed the otherwise impenetrable steel-and-stone walls of penal institutions and the specific penitentiary technique of the F-type regime. The mode and the manner of containing delinquency were suddenly thrown into crisis, and the government responded with several military operations outside the prisons similar to the one staged inside. Rather than ending the strike, it seems that Operation Return to Life galvanized a movement that had been characterized (in national and international media and by Turkish government officials) as hovering on the brink of failure.

By October 2001, one year and forty deaths after the beginning of the strike, four houses in Kuçuk Armutlu had been designated "houses of resistance." Together the houses held nineteen strikers, eleven of whom were women; twenty-nine strikers had already died in the town.[60] These strikers, along with the prisoners, adopted a meticulous set of distinctions between what I mark as the hunger strike and the death fast. While the death fasts were intended to quickly advance through the late stages of self-starvation, hunger strikes were to be sustained over lengthy periods of time. Those on hunger strike kept themselves alive as long as possible, relying on the political currency of gradual emaciation and increasing physical weakness. Those on death fast moved speedily and relentlessly toward the inevitable, relying for political effect on the moment of death and the steady transfer of corpses from bed to grave.

In practice the difference between being on hunger strike and being on death fast came down to a drink. Most strikers prepared their bodies for extended hunger strikes with a feast-and-famine regimen (eating huge quantities of food and then starving for days at a time) for weeks or months before the strike began. Death fasters drank only salt water for the duration of their strike. In contrast Onder Ozkalipci, a forensic doctor at the Human Rights Foundation of Turkey, describes the drink used by hunger strikers:

> They take a lot of liquids because that slows down the muscular atrophy. They've discovered that potassium chloride is better than sodium chloride and that crude sugar is better than refined. In 1996, the strikers took only one spoonful of salt and sugar a day, and their daily weight loss was about 400 grams. This group, by taking a lot more salt and sugar, has brought that way down.[61]

The strikers designed, tested, and implemented a regimented mode of self-starvation that both short-circuited the government's attempts to paint them as violent terrorists and transformed them into highly charged political subjects who managed, at the scale of the individual body, the physical effects of state violence. As I discussed earlier, hunger striking represents a reformulation of the binary active/passive in terms of political action and, more generally, political subjectivity. Colloquially understood as practitioners of *passive* resistance, as peaceful protesters vividly performing the domination of the individual subject by the state, hunger strikers have also been depicted (by the Turkish government during the prison strike, as by the British government in 1981) as terrorists, actively engaged in discrete acts of political terror and rabidly invested in dismantling state apparatuses. Recognizing the dynamic tension between these two interpretations, Feldman argues that hunger striking presents such a conundrum for the state precisely because it "fus[es] the subject and object of violent enactment into a single body."[62]

Moreover in honing the performance — we could almost call it a *skill*, and certainly a *tactic* — of hunger striking, prisoners and Kuçuk Armutlu residents aimed to develop a sustainable mode of resistance based on the practice of self-starvation. This is a radical turn in the history of hunger strikes, which typically have a relatively short life span precisely because

strikers die after no more than six months or mediators broker a resolution to the crisis that eventuated the hunger strike in the first place.
Indeed before the prison strike in Turkey the very idea of a hunger strike
was predicated on its unsustainability as political practice. The inevitable
death of its practitioners is fantasized at the core of the hunger strike; each
death of a hunger striker marks the end of a hunger strike. It is this death
that has historically given hunger striking its power as political protest
and its force in effecting change. But in the Turkish case government
officials made it painstakingly clear that they would not capitulate on the
question of the F-type prisons; strike leaders similarly refused to call off
the strike until demands were met.

The events of 19 December were the government's attempt to declare
the hunger strike a failure, both in terms of its original demands and in
terms of its sustainability as political action. The government hoped on
that day to *end* the hunger strike, to place a final and definitive stamp of
refusal on the list of its demands, and to dissuade prisoners from planning
any future strikes. This was to be accomplished first by terrorizing prisoners into compliance, and second by transferring many prisoners to
isolation cells, where they would have no further contact with their comrades. The fact that the operation occasioned both the *expansion* of the
strike and the *refinement* of the strike's regimen befuddled government
officials, who had been holding out hope that the strike would simply
fade away into a productive amnesia that would reinstall the strikers into
a collective vernacular of terrorism. Officials had also hoped to force strikers into their roles as compliant prisoners ("docile bodies"); if it is ever to
become European, Turkey needs its prisons and its delinquents — and it
needs them quiet, clean, and orderly, in Foucault's words, "at the heart of
the law." In beginning their own arm of the hunger strike the residents of
Kuçuk Armutlu radically unsettled the state's attempts to contain and
defuse the strike and shortchanged governmental attempts to equate hunger striking with terrorist activity.

Despite all of this, however, the rhetoric of failure underlies most
mainstream media representations of the strike and governmental responses to the strikers' demands. Consider, for example, the following
selection from Scott Anderson's exposé on the strike featured in the *New
York Times Magazine*:

> [The hunger strike seems like] an act of desperation, a weapon of last
> resort for the powerless, but the reality is a bit more complex. Politically

motivated hunger strikes tend to occur in a very specific kind of society and at a very specific time: namely, in places with a long history of official repression, but where that repression has gradually begun to loosen. If it is the institutionalized nature of abuse that fuels the strikers to such extreme action, it is the cracks of liberalization that lead them to believe that such a course might shame the government into change — and often they are right. . . . What is remarkable about the Turkish hunger strike, by contrast, is both the apparent smallness of the issue that sparked it and that it continues despite all evidence that it is and will remain a failure.[63]

Anderson's article was published just a few weeks after 11 September 2001 in an issue of the *New York Times Magazine* whose other lead article, "Jihad's Women," spectacularized and demonized anti-American sentiment among Middle Eastern Muslim women. The article on the hunger strike was centered on Anderson's obsession with Fatma Şener, "an extraordinarily beautiful woman, with an infectious smile and penetrating brown eyes," who was striking in one of the houses of resistance in Kuçuk Armutlu. At the end of the piece Anderson reveals that during his research he was working with Şener's father to convince her to stop striking. He confesses, moreover, his desire to "proselytize" the entire group of Kuçuk Armutlu strikers: "I will do this by bluntly telling them what the justice minister so bluntly told me: that there will be no concessions, that there is no hope," a confession that reveals his conflation of "hope" with governmental concessions, that delimits "success" to legislative change, and that exposes his fundamental disregard for the strike's potential to foster and to produce on its own terms a new kind of political subject and coalition. He is of course unable to convince any of the strikers to quit; one responds "by looking at [Anderson] with a slight tilt of the head, the way a mother does when consoling a child. 'You shouldn't take this so hard,' she says softly. 'This is a war, and there is nothing you can do about it.' She gives [him] a smile that at one time must have been very pretty. 'Be calm,' she whispers."[64]

Note that in writing about the strike Anderson focuses on the women involved: "extraordinarily beautiful," "infectious," "penetrating," "a mother," as if he, the Westerner who has arrived to clarify the strike for the participants, to make its dangers and its meanings known to those who are performing it, is being overtaken — sexually, maternally — by the women he interviews. This distinctly gendered approach to the strike mirrors in many ways Western colonial encounters with what becomes, in representation and in colonization, the "feminized East." Anderson argues in the quotation above that hunger striking is made possible by "cracks of liberalization" in an institutional history of violence, as if hunger striking were a symptom of premodern, primitive statehood. Even more astonishing is his reference to the "smallness of the issue" of prison torture and a long history of political violence. But most disturbing is his notion that the strike "is and will remain a failure," a statement that implies that success can be read only in terms of the government's agreement to the strikers' demands. Such a claim is reminiscent of the capitalist telos of consumption against which performance artists of the avant-garde positioned themselves; like the artists explored in chapters 2 and 3, the Turkish strikers deployed self-starvation especially to resist such a limited conceptualization of political action.

The Turkish hunger strike had little hope of provoking officials to reform Turkey's penal system; as I have argued throughout this chapter, however, the strike is significant in other ways, for example, in the reversals it staged in the production and representation of political violence. I would suggest further that in its production of nontraditional coalitions inside the prisons and in its expansion to areas outside the prisons, the Turkish hunger strike performed a sophisticated iteration of Foucault's critique of the penitentiary technique. For the strikers the space of the prison-as-tactic extends far beyond any single prison's walls, just as the reality of prison conditions intensifies within the carceral buildings themselves. In short, the Turkish hunger strike embodies Foucault's charge: "The political, ethical, social, philosophical problem of our day is not to try to liberate the individual from the state, and from the state's institutions, but to liberate us both from the state and from the type of individualization which is linked to the state."[65]

Certainly the strikers did not eventuate radical shifts in Turkey's penal policies and in the production and enforcement of a naturalized, Europeanized sense and state of Turkishness. Certainly too the Turkish government succeeded neither in fully subjugating strikers to the bounds of that nationalist identity nor in silencing the isolated strikers or their protests. In performing and sustaining such an unresolved, agonistic struggle between state and subject the hunger strikers insisted upon the recognition and articulation of the intricate complexities both of subject production within a nationalist context that has worked to erase difference and to discipline patterns of identification that diverge from anticipated norms, and of state production within a world that continues to situate Turkey at and as the border of the West.

During six days in October 1927 the Turkish president and national hero Kemal Atatürk gave an extended address to representatives of his Republican Party. That address, which outlined the manner in which Turkey had gained independence in 1923 and presented a roadmap for the secularization and modernization of Turkey in the following several decades, has since become an official nationalist text as important to Turkish policymakers as the country's constantly changing constitution. On 20 October 1927 Atatürk ended his address with an appeal to young Turkish citizens:

> Turkish Youth! Your first duty is ever to preserve and defend National Independence, the Turkish Republic. That is the only basis of your existence and your future. This basis contains your most precious treasure. . . . If one day you are compelled to defend your independence and the Republic, then, in order to fulfill your duty, you will have to look beyond the possibilities and conditions in which you might find yourself. It may be that these conditions and possibilities are altogether unfavorable. . . . Assuming, in order to look still darker possibilities in the face, that those who hold the power of Government within the country have fallen into error, that they are fools or traitors, yes, even that these leading persons may identify their personal interests with the enemy's political goals, it might happen that the nation came into complete privation, into the most extreme distress; that it found itself in a condition of ruin and complete exhaustion. Even under those circumstances, O Turkish child of future generations! It is your duty to save the independence, the Turkish Republic. The strength that you will need for this is mighty in the noble blood which flows in your veins.[66]

Fusing the "only basis of your existence" with the preservation and maintenance of the Turkish state, Atatürk suggested that Turkish citizenship was not merely one of the many productions of the state, but the very site of its ontology. The rhetorical force of his declaration of youth's "first duty" was to link, essentially, state formation and political subjectivity, to argue that the very political subjectivity that was the condition for independence was itself subordinate to the broader charge of defending the integrity of the state. The force of that charge moreover was tied directly to the bodies of Turkish subjects, those expendable sites in which "noble blood," the stuff and sign of an ascendant national kinship binding contemporary Turk to ancient Ottoman king to the project of nationalist passion, would forever flow. If not a particularly unusual articulation of republican citizenship, it does remind us that modern Turkey was formed out of a desire to deny what Kevin Robins has called the "cosmopolitanism [and] pluralism of identity" represented by the Ottoman Empire and to replace it with a homogeneous, Westernized "nation without minorities."[67]

In the context of Turkey's current attempts — so similar to the Kemalists' work in the 1920s — to accede to the European Union, to prove beyond the shadow of many other nations' doubts that it is essentially Western, modern, democratic, and sound, might not the hunger strikers have fully (and ironically) taken up Atatürk's charge to lay their bodies on the line for the larger cause of global independence? Or is the meaning of *independence* too bound up with the notion of the active, self-determining individual so precious to Western liberalism? In rebutting human rights organizations' critiques of the F-type prison, Justice Minister Hikmet Sami Türk explained that "the old prisons with communal dormitories had become 'training camps' for the left-wing groups; that the new prisons conformed with UN and Council of Europe guidelines; and that, far from crushing the prisoners, the F-Types would allow them to develop their identity away from the ideological constraints of their colleagues."[68] In the same interview Türk suggested that the F-type prisons "are state policy, and that [will] not change." Fusing state policy with the prisons and arguing that it is through the function of the prison that prisoners "develop their identity," Türk implied that the isolationist tactics practiced and policed by the F-type prisons were intended to produce a particular type of political subject, one who submits to enactments of state power and eschews association with the "ideological constraints" of resistance. The Justice Ministry aimed to eventuate that production with both a penitentiary regime of isolation and through the specific architecture of the F-type prison.

With the development of the F-type prisons the Turkish state strove to cleave group opposition into fragments and then incarcerate those fragments in rehabilitation (read: torture) cells that function not to restore prisoners into a social order, but to desocialize them entirely. In other words, there's nothing rehabilitating about solitary confinement. Indeed the isolation cells of the F-type prisons exemplify what Orlando Patterson has called "social death": alienation from all other human attachments, subjection to random and unrecorded acts of torture, and general dishonor as inhuman.[69] Social death is registered on the level of personal interaction and experience, and also institutionally, as a systemic function. The F-type prisons represent the site and the sign of that function, providing not merely the space for its most explicit enactment, but the model for its dispersal over space and time.

I have refrained from writing about any of the 107 deaths resulting from the hunger strike in part because death implies a sort of completion, an end to one individual's participation in the strikes, an instance of resolution. To focus too closely on actual deaths would imply some closure to the meaning and the effects of a hunger strike that refused to allow death to diminish its resolve. Such resilience — not in spite of the many deaths, but because of them — represents a direct challenge to the social death described in Patterson's study and ratified by a prison system designed to terrorize through direct and indirect performances of violence and through systemic processes of isolation and torture. Against all hope of traditional success the Turkish hunger strike staged a refusal to submit to that system, just as it effected the demise of more than a hundred strikers, a seeming paradox reflected in the declaration at the end of the original manifesto: "LONG LIVE OUR DEATH FAST RESISTANCE!" Such a complicated declaration, which situates death as the theme and the mode of a resistance that can live over an extended period of time, epitomizes the Turkish hunger striker's attempts and varied, underemphasized successes to build a coalition aimed explicitly at confounding nationalist attempts to produce docile subjects whose relationship to the state is defined by subjugation, streamlined identification, and unwavering participation in the project of purification that such a relationship requires.

the ends of hunger

•

He who hath learned to die, hath unlearned to serve. . . . To know
how to die, doth free us from all subjection and constraint.

— Montaigne, "That To Philosophise is to Learn How to Die"

The stomach is a place almost as private as the grave.

— Maud Ellmann, *The Hunger Artists*

But what is your life? Can you see it? It vanishes at its own appearance. Moment by moment. Until it vanishes to appear no more.

— Cormac McCarthy, *Cities of the Plain*

In the recovery house, the rituals of daily life are decidedly rote. Recently
released from prison, the residents seem despairingly to cling to these all-
too-fleeting enactments of presence: grooming themselves before broken
mirrors, preparing their meals, circling the space of a small living room to
share tea and partial remembrances. Melek Tokur, who starved for 205
days while incarcerated, calls this place "a symbol of our ties with life.
Because who can have such an indirect connection with life when [par-
ticipating in] an action which may result in death?" Tokur remembers her
friends and comrades, also striking in Usak Prison, clarifying the profound significance of their morbid, indelibly mortal resistance with the
simple gesture of "planting": "[They] plant the seeds of the last apple
they ate before the strike to a soil they gather from rubbish or leftover tea.
[While] their own cells are dying, they are watching the apple grow."[1]

These are the human remains of the Turkish strike, those who, like the late-stage anorectics described in chapter 1, have developed the fractured relationship to memory symptomatic of Wernicke-Korsakoff syndrome. As Tokur relates, they are here no less alive than they were before; indeed their relationship to the live, at once endangered and fortified by the death fasts, has been multiplied by loss, triply textured by the vicissitudes of time and flesh, by the spaces between bodies starving and fed, by the bidirectional transitions between here and gone. Ömar Ünal fasted for more than a hundred days; his memories are few and weave themselves seamlessly into his experience of now: "[When I arrived here] I did not know I was out of jail. It seemed like a dream to me. . . . I was seeing myself with a third eye. It is like, for instance, *you* are *here*. *I* was seeing myself from a different angle, such as *behind* you and *this* way. I was seeing you and myself. It was like that."[2] These radically unsettled contexts of presence, so fraught with their own failures, so infused with the *knowing* those failures afford, are simultaneously the conditions for what Heidegger called *being-with*. As Cülnaz Kuruçay explains, "We live the days, and the daily dissolving, together. Our bodies are being dissolved, [we are] walking to death together."[3] This is the choreography of the *live*, of what Rainer Maria Rilke called the "great death each of us has within us."[4]

But that "great death," as Giorgio Agamben has so powerfully demonstrated,[5] is increasingly expunged as a possibility for *being* by what we may recognize generally in the relentlessly disingenuous rallying cry "the culture of life" and more specifically in the institutional and ideological domains that provide the context for that cry's enforcement. Throughout this book I have traced scenes in which that cry is resisted with the seemingly paradoxical staging of self-starvation. In each of the studies in this book—in and between clinic, gallery, and prison—the ghost of hunger persists, restlessly unsated and relentless in its calls. And in each of those domains—as refusal, fast, and strike—performance has both mediated and embodied hunger's determined summons; as form *and* practice, as representation *and* ontology, as presence *and* disappearance, performance has forged from hunger's undying demands a ghostly premise (if not promise) of hope.

If, as Freud proposed, hunger describes the primordial experience of being, then it is also the paradigm for all somatic, psychic, and social need. Hunger models and rehearses desire in all of its forms: the unfulfilled in dreams, the *objet-a* of love,[6] the utopia of hope. And hunger's calls are simultaneously the seed of the social: a pleading, from the deepest bodily core, for something or someone else. To dwell in the space of hunger means to dwell in this place of need, to confess a search for *being-with*, to acknowledge the intersubjective character of the fading, mortal *live*. Capital—and its current political twin, the neoliberal—dwells in a converse space: the space of *satisfaction*. In each of the studies that compose this book the politics of morbidity have organized against such proprietary structures of capture. For better or worse, as sickness and health, these performances of self-starvation have resisted life-as-compensation, and in so doing have embraced the flickering, morbid, "maniacally charged" possibilities of the live.

In this afterword I reflect briefly on how ideological and institutional domains collide and collude both as structures in which contestations at the rheostatic threshold of state sovereignty and political subjectivity are staged and as interpretive frames through which those contestations are anticipated and read. I locate the concentration of such contests within the figure of the feeding tube, used in Camp X-Ray at Guantánamo Bay to force-feed detainees, and its role in the political economy of life, as distinguished from the live, in the early years of the twentieth-first century. I turn briefly to other uses of the tube and suggest that the feeding facilitated in those uses is contiguous with the force-feeding at Camp X-Ray. I close with Agamben and Kafka, a long, winding return to the politics of morbidity with which I opened this book.

On 29 April 2002 Camp X-Ray in Guantánamo Bay was officially closed. The camp was first used as a temporary facility to house migrants from Haiti as part of Operation Sea Signal before its more recent history of incarcerating foreign nationals with suspected affiliations with anti-American political groups during the U.S. occupations of Afghanistan and Iraq, an architectural genealogy that demonstrates the proximity of *refugees* and *terrorists* in the narrative of state integrity. As a signifier of wartime spatial coordinates Camp X-Ray now signifies all of the incarceration facilities at Guantánamo, imaged as chicken-wire cells open to the elements, imagined as a simultaneous staging of penitentiary hypervisibility and imminent political disappearance. Just as significantly the name Camp X-Ray borrows rhetoric from the medical sciences, suggesting in its translation that the borders so passionately produced and policed by the state become more secure as the boundaries of the human body become more available for transgression by the oculotechnics of state power. By the end of March 2002 around three hundred detainees representing thirty-three countries were being housed at the camp. When the camp was closed, all detainees, along with the military personnel who supervised them, lodged at the neighboring Freedom Heights area, were transferred to Camp Delta on the southern end of the base.

Camp X-Ray represents a political architecture quite distinct from the penal institutions whose numbers seem continually to multiply across the U.S. landscape. Those other institutions — we may designate them as *prisons* — are purportedly (and arguably) designed as architectural and ideological regimes deployed by the state both to rehabilitate abject subjects into normative, docile citizens and to put that rehabilitation on display. These sites provide the backdrop for juridical and legislative enactments that determine what precisely the citizen should and should not be, represent the stage on which the state demonstrates its considerable power to test the limits of enforced conformity, and act as the mechanical arm with which the state concretizes what Dwight Conquergood called its "monopoly on violence."[7] Although these sites represent neither the essence nor the limit of state power — not even its ultimate degree — they are simultaneously iconic for and the most banal instantiations of that power, the sine qua non of both the state and its analogue, the citizen. Indeed the citizen *is* the citizen only insofar as she or he may be detained, and the state *is* the state only for as long as it has the power to arrest.

To be clear: my distinction between the detention center at Camp X-Ray and other carceral institutions is not founded upon any belief, intellectually or otherwise, in the mythology of penal rehabilitation, but is intended to mark the absence at X-Ray of any similar premise. That is, the justification for the cells at X-Ray was remarkably, purely and simply, couched as and within the rhetoric of arrest. This arrest is twofold, indicating both the power of the state to seize, to hold, and to confine according to its own specific will and the power of the state to fix in time, to name, and to define the ideological borders outside of which the normative citizen is not permitted to venture without penalty. At the same time that Camp X-Ray acts as a holding cell for those incarcerated within, it also functions by soliciting in the nonincarcerated public a common faith in the distinctly moral merit of upright citizenship, in the identifiable differences between normalcy and delinquency, and in the power of the state to police those differences not only within its own considerable terrain, but also in a terrifyingly broad "elsewhere." Further this gap between the prison and Camp X-Ray both resembles and is founded upon a second distinction of profound significance for contemporary U.S. politics: that fatal linguistic loophole between *prisoner of war* and *enemy combatant*.

Just before the closure of the camp more than one-third of the detainees began a hunger strike, sparked when two U.S. soldiers forcibly removed one man's turban as he was praying. At its height, more than 230 men were simultaneously participating in the strike. Within days of the strike's commencement medical professionals at the camp were enlisted to use intravenous drips and feeding tubes to force-feed the detainees; in the words of the camp commander, Brigadier General Michael Lehnert, "Nobody is going to die," or as the *Daily Telegraph* put it, "There will be no Bobby Sands . . . at Camp X-Ray."[8] In the context of their institutional domain such responses to the strike reveal how the clinic and the prison function together in attempts to fix the incarcerated firmly within the pressing momentum of war time, where feeding becomes an act of war contiguous with more recognizable tactics of occupation.

In an attempt to foreclose whatever potential the strike may bear the state becomes more regimented in its prophylactic and reactionary responses. Masked as a liberal humanist discourse of protection, what Wendy Brown might call "the man in the clinic in the prison of the state,"[9] alimentary normativity becomes political normativity as the clinic and the prison function together in one of the most dramatic stagings of state intervention: force-feeding. Deemed unethical by virtually every professional medical association, force-feeding hunger strikers at Guantánamo Bay is not simply an ad hoc response to any given striker, but a tactic central to the work of the base's clinic, that is, a clinical "state of exception." As the camp's medical commander recently revealed, physicians are screened for ethical objections to force-feeding before being deployed to the base.[10]

It should come as no surprise that Guantánamo detainees are not allowed to speak to the press; as a result few reports documenting the conditions in the camp or testifying to the detainees' experiences have been published by sources other than the Department of Defense or the International Red Cross. But in a radio report for the BBC on 3 March 2006 the journalist John Manel circumvented the restrictions on detainee-journalist meetings by dispatching to the camp an attorney, Tom Wilmer, to speak with Fawzi al-Odah, a Kuwaiti man incarcerated at Guantánamo since 2002 and a key participant in the hunger strikes. Manel sent questions to al-Odah through Wilmer, who then returned with his transcribed responses. In the BBC broadcast Manel reads his questions, and a hired actor responds in al-Odah's words:

They told me, "if you continue to hunger strike, you will be punished." First they took my comfort items away from me one-by-one: you know, my blanket, my towel, my long pants, then my shoes. I was put in isolation for ten days. Then an officer came in and read me an order from [Major General Jay W.] Hood. It said, "if you refuse to eat, we will put you in the chair"—these are special new metal chairs they have brought to Guantánamo—that "you will be strapped up and down very tightly in the chair," and that liquid food would be forced into me using a thicker tube with a metal edge. The tube would no longer be left in all the time, but would be forced in and pulled out at each feeding and that this would happen three times a day. I told him, "this is torture." He said to me, "call it whatever you like, this is the way it's going to be. We're going to break this hunger strike."

Manel continues by reading a response from the Department of Defense to al-Odah's narrative: "The focus has never been on breaking the hunger strike, but on a policy of humane treatment and on the preservation of life."[11]

The astonishing implication in al-Odah's report that blankets, towels, clothing, and shoes are "comfort items" that the Department of Defense can strip from noncompliant detainees directly contradicts the Bush administration's own military order on detentions: "All individuals subject to this order shall be . . . afforded adequate food, drinking water, shelter, clothing, and medical treatment,"[12] and the likening of force-feeding, particularly in the manner described by al-Odah, as "humane treatment" runs directly counter to the disposition of most medical associations and human rights organizations against the use of medical technologies without the consent of patients, whether or not they are incarcerated. Indeed here the practice of force-feeding emerges, as I suggested, more as a military maneuver staged on the theater of war than as an enactment of the humane choreographed as medical treatment. But what is most telling about the Department of Defense's response to al-Odah's statement is its justification of this treatment simply as "the preservation of life." I will not rehearse the many critiques that have been made of the modes through which life, in all of its presumed splendor, is summoned and dispatched in the rhetoric of state protectionism, except to note that it does often seem to be cast about aggressively whenever a controversial feeding tube appears.

One tube in particular comes to mind. During the early spring of 2005 debates in the United States about the right to die concentrated around a single figure in a Florida hospice, Terri Schiavo, and the contentious struggle between her husband and her parents to decide her fate. Schiavo had collapsed in 1990 from a potassium imbalance that her doctors believe resulted from an eating disorder; she lost consciousness, and blood flow to her brain was severely diminished for around five minutes. When she was revived doctors found that she had become significantly brain damaged and declared her to be in a permanent vegetative state. Over the next fifteen years Schiavo's husband and parents became involved in a bitter debate about whether or not she should be allowed to die. After numerous attempts to adjudicate continuing life support, in March 2005 Schiavo's parents finally lost their appeals to the U.S. Supreme Court. Within days the feeding tube that provided water and nourishment to her was removed, and around nine o'clock on the morning of 31 March Terri Schiavo "died."

In the period between the removal of Schiavo's feeding tube and the signing of her death certificate the Florida hospice where she was housed became the geographical center of clashes between pro-life activists and right-to-die advocates. The scene was highly publicized in the national media, and the space outside the hospice was quickly converted into a stage: an area was set for press releases and statements from family members and doctors; small tents were constructed where religious activists could publicly sing and pray; and an array of picket signs and enlarged photographs created by representatives from both camps circulated slogans and images pleading either for the reinsertion of the tube or for support of her husband's decision to remove it. Hundreds of cameras captured the scene and reproduced it in newspapers and television broadcasts nationwide. The rhetoric of morbidity was transposed onto the body of Terri Schiavo, translated through the various images of her released to the public, and transfixed on the question of what it could possibly mean, in her case, to choose to die.

The Schiavo case represents a concentrated example of the complicated nature of hunger at the very heart of mortality, or in Freud's words, of the drive "to die in one's own way."[13] The concentration of hunger is especially strong at the site of the alternately lionized and demonized medical apparatus at the center of the controversy: the feeding tube. In standard medical practice the feeding tube is used both as a short-term prosthetic esophagus for those who have temporarily lost the ability to swallow and as a long-term form of life support for those who require permanent assistance with eating. But as the narrative from Fawzi al-Odah demonstrates, the broader history of the feeding tube includes other applications too, including the practice of force-feeding hunger strikers and anorectics who, despite their gastronomic competencies, refuse to eat. In this light the feeding tube represents and facilitates the enforcement of normative alimentary exchange by the institutional apparatuses, such as the prison and the clinic, of the state.

But in these cases the feeding tube also represents the struggle between the enactment of individual will and the force of state intervention. Just as it seems to provide an intuitively simple solution to the problem of malnourishment, the feeding tube stands in as a metaphor for Foucault's subjectivation: the simultaneous production of subjectivity and subordination to state power.

In the case of Terri Schiavo and anorectics and hunger strikers, the feeding tube aims to mediate between the demands and the denials of hunger, a material symbol of the discomfort that surrounds the morbidity of hunger, its potential to cast the question of care in the language of life and death. The "voicelessness" in Enzo Cozzi's graphism for hunger cited in the introduction to this book is also intensely reminiscent of Schiavo's place in the performances surrounding her death. As described by several journalists and commentators, the scene in and around her hospice was a "circus," but what is most telling about the Schiavo case and its eventual resolution is not the specular scene but the manner in which Schiavo herself was compelled to appear and disappear from the systems of representation that surrounded her. In the 1 April airing of his weekly talk show on HBO, Bill Maher invited Cornel West, Alec Baldwin, and Whoopi Goldberg, "three godless liberals," in Maher's words, to discuss the political implications of Schiavo's death. Their conversation focused on the judicial decisions and congressional actions that corresponded with the case. But at one point during the show Goldberg interrupted Maher to say:

> You know what's bothering me more than anything, more than anything that I've seen, is the fact that she has ceased being a person and become a cause. No one has said "A woman died today." A woman, a person died today, you know? And I'm sorry, goodbye, Terri Schiavo, whenever you went, go in peace, girl, go in peace. I just wanted to say that.[14]

Goldberg could almost explicitly be summoning Lacan here. Speaking sharply to those who claimed the grainy images of Schiavo's head seem-

ingly leaning into her mother's kiss, Goldberg keenly criticizes the anticipated function of those images, of their circulation within the "circus"
outside the hospice and in the media blitz, and of the force with which
they occlude their referential subject, Terri Schiavo. The promiscuous
reproduction of those images, and their proposed pronouncement of her
mental state, paradoxically but effectively killed off Schiavo long before
her feeding tube was removed.

This is not merely a philosophical argument; indeed the confusion of
life and *to live* in Schiavo's case was further complicated as her husband
was accused of fabricating stories about her ad hoc living will. Those who
claimed that she was not so severely brain-damaged as to be permanently
vegetative simultaneously stripped her of the ability to decide for herself if
she should continue to be kept alive. This is an example of those terribly
disturbing moments when the rhetoric of the Right seems to echo the
language of the Left: in claiming disability rights for Schiavo, in suggesting that she required the protection of a larger contingency of (in George
Bush's words) the "culture of life," the advocates of reinserting Schiavo's
feeding tube effectively made her a "voiceless person with disabilities . . .
living at the mercy of others."[15]

The function of the feeding tube as an agent of the "culture of life"
took on especially vibrant significance with the concurrent convalescence
of the pope, who died soon after Schiavo. Just as news of Schiavo's death
broke, the Vatican announced that Pope John Paul II had collapsed from
an infection, was suffering an extremely high-grade fever, and had had a
feeding tube inserted to provide him with liquids and nutrients. This
rendered the figure of the feeding tube holy and, by association, Schiavo's
death the work of the devil. Responding to one of Schiavo's doctors
explaining the difference between her death and the pope's condition, the
conservative commentator Nancy Grace succinctly summarized this exal-
tation by saying, "A feeding tube is a feeding tube is a feeding tube."[16]

Grace's broadcast all but canonized Schiavo as a martyr for the culture
of life that so desperately wanted to feed her; her extracted feeding tube
became the icon of that culture, occluding the discrepancies between
Schiavo and the pope. At one point in the broadcast Grace asked Patrick
Mahoney, director of the Christian Defense Coalition, to speak to the
significance of the pope's illness for the Schiavo case. Mahoney commented, "She was not a vegetable. She was not being kept on life support.
Terri Schiavo was not sick. She was not terminal. . . . She died a barbaric
death, a painful death, a horrible death."[17]

Mahoney's claims contradict the expert opinions from her doctors about her mental state, deny the nature of the feeding tube as life support, and ignore medical evidence that she became absolutely unconscious before experiencing a painless death. But more important, his comments were not staged to uncover any underlying truth of Schiavo's premorbid condition or to expose the experience of dying from starvation; rather they reproduce the *figure* of Terri Schiavo as the symbol of victimization and ultimately resonate with Whoopi Goldberg's reminder that Schiavo had "ceased to be a person" long before she finally died. Even more chillingly, Mahoney's comments about Schiavo, who collapsed from complications attending an eating disorder, resemble remarks made in other contexts to justify force-feeding anorectics and hunger strikers. In these other contexts institutional officials will often name force-feeding as the only possible humane state intervention in practices typically considered deviant or disordered. Mahoney's suggestion that in Schiavo's case the tube does not constitute life support similarly suggests that the feeding tube should be considered a kind of treatment for her affliction, but not the single treatment on which her life depends. In other words, for Mahoney the feeding tube does not *provide* Schiavo *with* life; this would confirm the doctors' declaration of her persistent vegetative state. Rather in Mahoney's logic the feeding tube allows Schiavo to continue experiencing her life, and its removal *literally* takes her life from her.

Also on Bill Maher's show Cornel West highlighted "the difference between biological life and biographical life": "[If] my biological life has persisted [but] my biographical life is over, if you find me in that state, honey, please pull the plug!" West's invocation of this scene of pleading, his recognition that the life of the subject exceeds and is not defined by the life of the body, returns the figure of Terri Schiavo to the scene of her death, embracing her mortality not as a loss, but as the venue of her subjectivity. That is, for West the choice to end a biological life when its biographical period has passed paradoxically produces a moment of agential determination, *subjectivation* for Schiavo precisely at the moment when she acknowledges and assumes her own finitude rather than succumbing to her role in the representational field of the culture of life.

We might thus find in the case of Terri Schiavo an example of how the rhetoric of the life that so insistently performs itself in contemporary U.S. politics in effect promotes the death of the subject. In the mythology of this culture that stages itself in every possible political venue, from abortion to marriage to euthanasia, life is terrorized by mortality and lives are defined in relative value by their dismissal of death in the future perfect. The *will have been* of subjectivity, its dependence upon finitude in constituting meaning of and for itself, is expunged by the increasingly restrictive culture of life that demands, in spite of its own impending demise, the denial of Heidegger's *being-toward-death*. The culture of life that so desperately clings to its messianic hope for immortality forecloses the possibility for the kind of agency that Silverman finds in Heidegger's notion of *Dasein*. This is the lesson in feeding tubes, in their melancholic potential to nourish and in the mournful rehearsal of their removal.

To return to Guantánamo Bay, I would like to consider in closing the invocation of life as that which the military clinic of the state aims violently to preserve precisely through the juridical suspension of the law itself. In his haunting study of Auschwitz Giorgio Agamben highlights Foucault's figuring of sovereignty:

> The ancient right to kill and to let live gives way to an inverse model, which defines modern biopolitics, and which can be expressed by the formula *to make live and to let die*. . . . Hence the progressive disqualification of death, which strips it of its character as a public rite in which not only individuals and families but the whole people participate; hence the transformation of death into something to be hidden, a kind of private shame.[18]

It is this paradoxical function of modern sovereignty, a calculus in which biopolitics coincides with thanatopolitics, that Agamben eventually locates within the state of exception, a "no-man's-land between public law and political fact":

> If exceptional measures are the result of periods of political crisis and, as such, must be understood on political and not juridico-constitutional grounds, then they find themselves in the paradoxical position of being juridical measures that cannot be understood in legal terms. . . . On the other hand, if the law employs the exception — that is the suspension of law itself — as its original means of referring to and encompassing life, then a theory of the state of exception is the preliminary condition for any definition of the relation that binds and, at the same time, abandons the living being to law.[19]

Oriented against this "bind[ing] and, at the same time, abandon[ing]" that redefines politics as "contaminated by law . . . reduced to merely the power to negotiate with the law,"[20] the hunger strikes in Guantánamo Bay are thus intricately involved in war *against* the practice of war, just as they are, at least in Agamben's terms, necessarily outside the realm of the political. The terrible truth in that *Daily Telegraph* line, that there will be no Bobby Sands at Guantánamo Bay, pivots on this point: what distinguishes these strikes from the long history of hunger striking in anticolonial political movements elsewhere is precisely the state of exception that defines the context of their occurrence, that attempts both to foreclose and to eclipse life as a matter of law, that deploys the state's bio- and thanatopolitical power at the site of the starving body in the disguise of a beneficent tube.

Indeed as demonstrated in the following case the hunger strike's profound central function is to "show law in its nonrelation to life and life in its nonrelation to law,"[21] to reveal the terror of the state of exception itself. Though they are unlikely to eventuate the kind of large-scale shifts in U.S. policy that would cease or reverse the damage done in the current war on terror, remarkably the practice of force-feeding hunger strikers has occasioned the first challenge, in March 2006, to the Detention of Enemy Combatants Act and the Detainee Treatment Act. Both of these acts ban torture, empower the secretary of defense to define torture, and forbid legal challenge in any federal, state, or international court or tribunal, a triptych of symptoms that seems summarily to diagnose the United States as a state of exception. In 2006, following military officials' response to his hunger strike in Camp Delta, Mohammad Bawazir filed suit against the Department of Defense, citing his force-feeding as a form of torture.[22] Though federal attorneys argued that the protections against torture provided by recent legislation expressly exclude those incarcerated as enemy combatants — here again the lethal linguistic swivel — U.S. District Judge Gladys Kessler responded to the camp commanders and military physicians, "I know it's a sad day when a federal judge has to ask a [Department of Justice] attorney this, but I'm asking you — why should I believe them?"[23]

Put another way, as the detainee Sami al-Haj brilliantly figures, "Architecture is not justice."[24] In practice the hunger strikes at Guantánamo Bay subvert at the most visceral level the insistent reproduction of sovereignty in contemporary U.S. politics and reveal the desperation with which that state deploys and intertwines its institutions to stage and seize "bare life." The strike may see little chance of traditional success in closing that loophole between enemy combatant and prisoner of war. But to cite the Turkish strikers, "LONG LIVE OUR DEATH FAST RESISTANCE!" — such a radical embrace of the political possibilities of necropolitical subject formations,[25] of coalitions sustained in and by the embrace of mortality pitted against the juridico-political insistence on life-at-all-costs, of the fragile but resilient project of hope.

Hope: a fragile but resilient project. Why is it that so many books end spiritedly, but almost in spite of themselves, with notes on hope? Perhaps because their authors feel, as I feel now, so deeply, overwhelmingly driven to concern themselves with that which seems most dire, most desperate, most restlessly and relentlessly hopeless. Could it be that hope's implied optimism is too arrogant to bear the weight or plumb the depths of its own unconscious premonitions of a terrible, terror-filled future? Could it be that what hope names is in part a promise of failure?

In the dying light of a tiny cage the hunger artist disappears, embittered by the fading, passing notice he receives from those who deign to stop and see. We live in a different world now, but once:

> The children stood open-mouthed, holding each other's hands for greater security, marveling at him as he sat there pallid in black tights, with his ribs sticking out so prominently, not even on a seat but down among straw on the ground, sometimes giving a courteous nod, answering questions with a constrained smile, or perhaps stretching an arm through the bars so that one might feel how thin it was, and then again withdrawing deep into himself, paying no attention to anyone or anything, not even to the all-important striking of the clock that was the only piece of furniture in his cage, but merely staring into vacancy with half-shut eyes.[26]

That all-important clock, the only furniture that matters, strikes away in the time of war. "The secret is out," Marya Hornbacher calls, "you're dying."[27] And when he, our hunger artist, fades forever into the straw that lines his cage, he is replaced with, of all things, a vicious feline beast, whose sleek muscularity is matched only by the ferocity of his desire to consume. Kafka mourns:

> He seemed not even to miss his freedom; his noble body, furnished almost to the bursting point with all that it needed, seemed to carry freedom around with it too; somewhere in his jaws it seemed to lurk; and the joy of life streamed with such ardent passion from his throat that for the onlookers it was not easy to stand the shock of it. But they braced themselves, crowded round the cage, and did not want ever to move away.[28]

Could this be what we call hope: the ungenerously consumptive thrill of amnesia, the imagined proximity of ardent passion and the joy of life, freedom lurking in the jaws of greed? Against hope, but hopeful still, "[the hunger artist's] performances are not spectacles for the amusement of others, but the unraveling of a private despair that he has permitted others to watch."[29] And in that moment of bearing witness a tiny space is made for something more rigorous than hope, something that remembers: it was not that they *could* not, but that they did not yet *want* to move away.

notes

•

1. Studies of self-starvation, both in individual forms and as a taxonomy of eating practices, have proliferated especially in the second half of the twentieth century. See, for example, Bell, *Holy Anorexia*; Brumberg, *Fasting Girls*; Bynum, *Holy Feast and Holy Fast*; Ellmann, *The Hunger Artists*; Heywood, *Dedication to Hunger*; Orbach, *Hunger Strike*; Vandereycken and van Deth, *From Fasting Saints to Anorexic Girls*.

2. Freud, *Beyond the Pleasure Principle*, 12–17.

3. See Foucault, "The Subject and Power"; Heidegger, *Being and Time*. I discuss these texts at greater length below.

4. I am gesturing here to Freud's use of the "aim" in theorizing the nature of instincts, which he describes as based on a model of hunger; for example: "Hunger could be taken to represent the instincts which aim at preserving the individual." *Civilization and Its Discontents*, 76.

5. This simple starting point is intended to evoke self-starvation in its broadest strokes, and so to include in its sweep a range of differentiated practices, including anorexia nervosa, hunger striking, dietary and religious fasting, staged performances of alimentary abstention, and others. I use this broad definition to consider larger political and philosophical questions about hunger and subjectivity and amend it in each of the chapters that follow. I do not, in other words, attempt to produce or argue for a universal taxonomy of self-starvation, and not all of the specific forms of self-starvation listed above appear in this book. For readers interested in a more expansive taxonomy of self-starvation, I recommend Walter Vandereycken and Ron van Deth's *From Fasting Saints to Anorexic Girls*, a historiographical genealogy of self-starvation from the Middle Ages to the contemporary era.

6. As should become clear in the course of this introduction, by *perform* I do not mean *pretend*.

7. See Freud, *Beyond the Pleasure Principle*; Heidegger, *Being and Time*.

8. Foucault, "The Subject and Power," 212.

9. Althusser, "Ideology and Ideological State Apparatuses," 182.

10. Ibid., 174.

11. See Foucault, *Discipline and Punish, The History of Sexuality, Vol. 1* and *Vol. 3*, and *Power/Knowledge*, especially 78–133.

12. Austin originally delivered his lectures on performativity for the William James Lecture Series at Harvard in 1955. These lectures were subsequently published in manuscript form as *How to Do Things with Words*.

13. Butler, *Gender Trouble*, 127.

14. Ibid., 137.

15. One of the most exquisite articulations of this distinction, between performativity and theatricality, appears in the introduction to Davis and Postlewait, *Theatricality*.

16. Butler, *Bodies That Matter*, 2, 7, 15.

17. Butler, *The Psychic Life of Power*, 3.

18. See Butler, *Bodies That Matter*, 11, 139–40, 210–18.

19. Butler, *Gender Trouble*, 135 (emphasis added).

20. Brecht, "The Street Scene," 122, 121, 122.

21. Austin, *How To Do Things with Words*, 13.

22. Althusser, "Ideology and Ideological State Apparatuses," 179.

23. Fanon, "The Fact of Blackness," 109.

24. Feldman, *Formations of Violence*, 264.

25. Phelan, *Unmarked*, 146.

26. Judith Halberstam's work similarly engages questions of masculinity and its discontents, especially as performed (and performatively embodied) by subjects whose relationship to "male" cannot be adequately described as "are." See *Female Masculinity*, especially 1–43.

27. Lacan, *Écrits*; Althusser quoted in Silverman, *Male Subjectivity at the Margins*, 24.

28. Althusser, "Ideology and Ideological State Apparatuses," 181.

29. Althusser leaves room in his treatise on interpellation for what he calls "bad" subjects, "who on occasion provoke the intervention of one of the detachments of the (repressive) State apparatus" (ibid.).

30. Heidegger, *Being and Time*, 232, emphasis added.

31. Ibid., 234.

32. Ibid.

33. Silverman, *World Spectators*, 33, 34.

34. Ibid., 35.

35. Heidegger, *Being and Time*, 233.

36. Lacan, *Écrits*, 65, 151, 153, emphasis added.

37. Cozzi, "Hunger and the Future of Performance," 121–22.

38. In this paragraph, I use the word *anorexia* in its most general and nondiag-

nostic sense, as the loss of appetite. The transposition of this word into the clinical category of anorexia nervosa is in this regard misleading; anorexia nervosa is defined diagnostically not as the *loss* of appetite, but as the refusal to satisfy the body's craving for food. In later stages of self-starvation, including anorexia nervosa, medical professionals have noted that the appetite generally wanes, a condition on which an initial diagnosis does not depend.

39. Oxford English Dictionary.

40. My use of this phrase is indebted to the work of Giorgio Agamben (*State of Exception*) and Achille Mbembe ("Necropolitics"), both of whom have extended our notion of state sovereignty, especially after the Second World War and even more especially after 11 September 2001, and its relationship to the death of political subjects. For Agamben contemporary state formation is characterized by what he calls a "state of exception," defined by "its close relationship to civil war, insurrection, and resistance" and as a "structure in which law encompasses living beings by means of its own suspension" (*State of Exception*, 2–3). I take up the state of exception, and its production of state sovereignty through the control of life and death, in chapter 4.

41. I am gesturing here to the model of intersectionality proposed by Kimberlé Williams Crenshaw in "Mapping the Margins."

42. Sedgwick and Parker, *Performativity and Performance*, 5.

43. Freud, *Three Essays on the Theory of Sexuality*, 1.

44. Laplanche, *Life and Death in Psychoanalysis*, 14.

45. Ibid., 14, 60.

46. Ibid., 48. For Freud, Laplanche, and Lacan "that milk" signifies the "originary lost object of desire," the milk fed to a newborn child. It is "that milk" that the growing child forever seeks and the warmth felt after drinking it that she or he wants (but is unable) again and again to feel. It is also "that milk" that is forever lost and that can be substituted for only by future objects of love. It is important to recall that Freud situates the moment of losing the original object of desire and satisfaction "just at the time, perhaps, when the child is able to form a total idea of the person to whom the organ that is giving him satisfaction belongs" (*Three Essays on the Theory of Sexuality*, 88).

47. Laplanche, *Life and Death in Psychoanalysis*, 48.

48. Freud, *Three Essays on the Theory of Sexuality*, 88.

49. Ibid., 31, 97–98, 104. See also A. Green, "Opening Remarks to a Discussion of Sexuality in Contemporary Psychoanalysis"; Sachs, "On the Genesis of Perversions."

50. Blau, "Universals of Performance"; Phelan, *Unmarked*; Schneider, "Performance Remains"; D. Taylor, *The Archive and the Repertoire*. See also Jane Blocker's discussion of several of the complexities in these arguments in *What the Body Cost*, 105–7.

51. Althusser, "Ideology and Ideological State Apparatuses," 184. I am im-

plicitly disagreeing with Althusser's claim that class marks the primary register of difference through which ideology functions: "The State and its Apparatuses only have meaning from the point of view of the class struggle, as an apparatus of class struggle ensuring class oppression and guaranteeing the conditions of exploitation and its reproduction" (184). Instead I deploy Kimberlé Crenshaw's model of "intersectionality" in "Mapping the Margins" to understand how various forms of difference function together within these domains.

52. Foucault, *Discipline and Punish*; Foucault, *History of Sexuality, Vol. 3*; Althusser, "Ideology and Ideological State Apparatuses"; Adorno, "Valéry Proust Museum"; Cohen, *The Boundaries of Blackness*; Crenshaw, "Mapping the Margins"; Crimp, *On the Museum's Ruins*; Gilmore, *The Golden Gulag*; Hartman, *Scenes of Subjection*; Miles, *Oath Betrayed*; Pécoil, "The Museum as Prison."

53. Blau, "Universals of Performance."

54. The phrase "trying ordeals" is in "Tanner Happy: The Fasting Doctor Rapidly Growing Stronger," *New York Times*, 9 August 1880, 4.

55. Mulvey, "Visual Pleasure and Narrative Cinema."

56. Agamben, *Homo Sacer*.

ONE The Archive of Anorexia

1. *Tom's Flesh*, directed by Jane Wagner and Tom DiMaria, Naked Eye Productions, 1995.

2. I have used *Tom's Flesh* in several university courses, including lecture classes on the history of eating disorders, seminars on masculinity, and studio classes on contemporary performance. In each of these contexts several students have made the comment that the mouth "looks like a woman" while the voice "sounds like a man."

3. Caruth, *Unclaimed Experience*.

4. Nietzsche, "On the Uses and Disadvantages of History for Life," 111.

5. Connerton, *How Societies Remember*.

6. Jack Schermerhorn and Michael Shain, "Karen Carpenter Found Nude in Closet: Star's Mystery Death Follows Starvation Diet," *New York Post*, 5 February 1983. See also "Karen Carpenter, 32, Is Dead: Singer Teamed with Brother," *New York Times*, 5 February 1983, 32.

7. Brumberg, *Fasting Girls*, 17–18.

8. Austin, *How to Do Things with Words*.

9. See, for example, Bruch, *The Golden Cage*; Ellmann, *The Hunger Artists*; Heywood, *Dedication to Hunger*.

10. Sours, *Starving to Death in a Sea of Objects*.

11. Chernin, *The Obsession*.

12. Spignesi, *Starving Women*, 5, 7.

13. Ellmann, *The Hunger Artists*, 23.

14. Sours, *Starving to Death in a Sea of Objects*, 205.

15. Heywood, *Dedication to Hunger*, 8.

16. Spignesi, *Starving Women*, 7.

17. Rosenberg, *The Cholera Years*, 5; also quoted in Brumberg, *Fasting Girls*, 9.

18. Vandereycken and van Deth, *From Fasting Saints to Anorexic Girls*, 5.

19. Ibid., 13.

20. Bordo, *Unbearable Weight*, 141.

21. Ellmann, *The Hunger Artists*, 2.

22. See *Killing Us Softly*, directed by Jean Kilbourne, Cambridge Documentary Films, 1978; Wolf, *The Beauty Myth*.

23. Orbach, *Hunger Strike*, 63.

24. Wang, *Aching for Beauty*.

25. Bordo, *Unbearable Weight*, 159.

26. "This does not mean that individuals do not *consciously* pursue goals that in fact advance their own position. But it does deny that in doing so they are consciously directing the overall movement of power relations or engineering their shape. They may not even know what that shape is" (ibid., 144).

27. Ibid., 159; Foucault, *Discipline and Punish*, 25. The citation of Foucault is included as part of a longer epigraph for Bordo's chapter on anorexia in *Unbearable Weight*, 139. I borrow the elegant incantation of the power of a propositional "if" from Peggy Phelan, *Mourning Sex*, 22.

28. Orbach, *Hunger Strike*, 107.

29. Ibid.

30. Ibid., 97.

31. Ibid.

32. Ibid., 98, 97.

33. Ibid., 97–98.

34. Probyn, "The Taste of Power."

35. See Krasnow, *My Life as a Male Anorexic*.

36. See Biddick, "Genders, Bodies, Borders"; Cartwright, *Screening the Body*; Spitzack, "The Spectacle of Anorexia Nervosa"; Didi-Huberman, *Invention of Hysteria*; Evans, *Fits and Starts*; Treichler, Cartwright, and Penley, *The Visible Woman*.

37. Biddick, "Genders, Bodies, Borders," 389.

38. Pollock, *Exceptional Spaces*, 6.

39. Kim Hubbard, Anne-Marie O'Neill, and Christina Cheakalos, "Out of Control," *People Weekly* 51, no. 13 (1999), 1.

40. Spitzack, "The Spectacle of Anorexia Nervosa," 2.

41. Austin, *How to Do Things with Words*. Austin and Butler focus primarily on performativity as a *discursive* function; others have worked to reacquaint the performative with representational forms, including a variety of performance genres. Diana Taylor proposes the adoption of the word *performático* to describe

performances—including political actions, theater, and other embodied forms of representation—that, like Austin's "I do," have demonstrable social impact (*The Archive and the Repertoire*, especially 5–14). Although I have chosen, for the sake of simplicity, to retain the word *performative* in the body of this book, I do so with Taylor's directive at heart; I am deeply indebted to her for articulating our need to deploy performativity more explicitly in considering the social force of embodied performance.

42. Butler, *Gender Trouble*, 137.

43. Spitzack also identifies this as a central assumption in writing about anorexia: "The sickness of the anorexic is informed by a more general equation between illness and femininity. The principal 'ailment' in both cases is a presumed inability to establish and enact a clear and fixed identity that is separate from the expectations of observers; yet, transgressing the boundaries of culturally acceptable articulations of the body is also seen as pathology" ("The Spectacle of Anorexia Nervosa," 3).

44. Probyn, "The Taste of Power."

45. Although Morton's text is often historicized as an early record of anorexia nervosa, it was written centuries before that diagnostic category was named or theorized. For a discussion of such problematic, presentist historiography, see MacSween, *Anorexic Bodies*, 18–19.

46. Morton, *Phthisiologia*, 2, 4.

47. Ibid., 10.

48. See Didi-Huberman, *Invention of Hysteria*; Evans, *Fits and Starts*; David-Ménard, *Hysteria from Freud to Lacan*.

49. Breuer and Freud, *Studies on Hysteria*.

50. See Hammond, *Fasting Girls*; Brumberg, *Fasting Girls*; Vandereycken and van Deth, *From Fasting Saints to Anorexic Girls*.

51. Breuer and Freud, *Studies on Hysteria*.

52. Ibid, 7.

53. Kaufman and Heiman, *Evolution of Psychosomatic Concepts*, 3.

54. Evans, *Fits and Starts*, 12.

55. Pope, Phillips, and Olivardia, *The Adonis Complex*; Silverman, *Male Subjectivity at the Margins*.

56. Flugel, *The Psychology of Clothes*.

57. Spignesi, *Starving Women*, 15.

58. American Psychiatric Association, DSM-IV-TR, 307.10.

59. I am gesturing here to Heidegger's notion of the *they*, as discussed in the introduction to this book. See Heidegger, *Being and Time*.

60. Althusser, "Ideology and Ideological State Apparatuses."

61. Spitzack, "The Spectacle of Anorexia Nervosa," 8.

62. Lacan, *Écrits*, 1–7; Althusser, "Ideology and Ideological State Apparatuses." In a previous version of the DSM (DSM-III-R) the final sentence of sec-

tion C read: "[She or he] believes that one area of the body is 'too fat' even if *obviously* underweight" (my emphasis). American Psychiatric Association, DSM-III-R, 307.10.

63. Heywood, *Dedication to Hunger*, 9.

64. Phelan, *Unmarked*, 146.

65. Phelan, *Mourning Sex*, 5.

66. American Psychiatric Association, DSM-IV-TR; Herzog, Bradburn, and Newman, "Sexuality in Men with Eating Disorders."

67. Herzog, Bradburn, and Newman, "Sexuality in Men with Eating Disorders," 40; Hasan and Tibbetts, "Primary Anorexia Nervosa (Weight Phobia) in Males," 151.

68. Silverman, *Male Subjectivity at the Margins*, especially 15–51; Chasseguet-Smirgel, *The Ego-Ideal*; Freud, "On Narcissism"; Laplanche and Pontalis, *The Language of Psycho-Analysis*, 144–45.

69. Spitzer, "The Diagnostic Status of Homosexuality in DSM-III."

70. Carlat, Camargo, and Herzog. "Eating Disorders in Males," 1127. See also Hasan and Tibbetts, "Primary Anorexia Nervosa (Weight Phobia) in Males."

71. Wabitsch et al., "Serum Leptin, Gonadotropin, and Testosterone Concentrations in Male Patients with Anorexia Nervosa," 2986; see also Andersen, "Eating Disorders in Males"; Tomova and Kumanov, "Sex Differences and Similarities of Hormonal Alterations in Patients with Anorexia Nervosa."

72. For a complicated meditation on the relationship between amenorrhea and subjectivity, see *Period: The End of Menstruation*, directed by Giovanna Chesler, g6 Productions, 2006.

73. Fortunati, *The Arcane of Reproduction*, 13.

74. Brown, *States of Injury*, 166–96.

75. Ibid., 169.

76. *Thin*, directed by Lauren Greenfield, HBO Documentary Pictures, 2006.

77. Feldman, *Formations of Violence*, 236.

78. I borrow this phrase from Guinn Batten's study of the "orphaned imagination" of the romantic poets and its relationship to industrialization: See *The Orphaned Imagination*, 19.

79. Derrida, *Archive Fever*

80. Ibid., 91.

81. Ibid., 7.

82. Freud, *Beyond the Pleasure Principle*, 48.

83. Derrida, *Archive Fever*, 10–11.

84. Ibid., 12.

85. Ibid., 94.

86. See Becker et al., "Characteristics of the Memory Loss of a Patient with Wernicke-Korsakoff's Syndrome without Alcoholism"; Handler and Perkin, "Anorexia Nervosa and Wernicke's Encephalopathy"; Parkin et al., "Wernicke-

Korsakoff Syndrome of Nonalcoholic Origin"; "Wernicke-Korsakoff Syndrome"; "Wernicke's Preventable Encephalopathy."

87. Becker et al., "Characteristics of the Memory Loss of a Patient with Wernicke-Korsakoff's Syndrome without Alcoholism," 171.

88. Gropman et al., "Wernicke's Encephalopathy Due to Self Starvation in a Child," 1704.

89. Blau, "Universals of Performance," 140.

TWO Enduring Performance

1. Kafka, "A Hunger Artist," 243–55.

2. Ritter, *Art as Spectacle*, 68.

3. Hammond, *Fasting Girls*.

4. Hazzard, *Scientific Fasting*, 20.

5. Sinclair, *The Book of Life*, 169.

6. Mitchell, "Franz Kafka and the Hunger Artists," 238; Gooldin, "Fasting Women, Living Skeletons, and Hunger Artists," 46; Robertson, *Kafka*, 57–58; "Fasting for Hire," *Scots Observer*, 3 May 1890, 652–53; Vandereycken and van Deth, *From Fasting Saints to Anorexic Girls*, 87–88.

7. Mitchell, "Franz Kafka and the Hunger Artists"; Goolding, "Fasting Women, Living Skeletons, and Hunger Artists"; Vandereycken and van Deth, *From Fasting Saints to Anorexic Girls*.

8. See "Searching for Symptoms: Visiting Doctors Poking Over the Faster's Body," *New York Times*, 27 July 1880, 5; "The Thirty-Day Faster," *New York Times*, 19 January 1880, 5.

9. "Tanner Happy: The Fasting Doctor Rapidly Growing Stronger," *New York Times*, 9 August 1880, 4.

10. Cheng, *In Other Los Angeleses*, 54.

11. Caruth, *Unclaimed Experience*, 5.

12. Reik, *Masochism in Sex and Society*.

13. Jones, "Dis/playing the Phallus," 567. Apparently conscious of this concern, Jones revises the citation in a later version of the same essay; in its more recent form the sentence reads, "Masochism in their case is most often metaphoric rather than clinical" (Jones, *Body Art/Performing the Subject*, 129). Although the same division between metaphor and clinic remains in this incantation, here Jones suggests that the performance of masochism in the cases of Chris Burden and others may share some characteristics with patients diagnosed as masochistic.

14. See Russo, *The Female Grotesque* 17–52.

15. "Starvation of Children: How It Was Practiced in the Shepherd's Fold," *New York Times*, 18 January 1880, 2.

16. "Revival of Monasticism," *New York Times*, 18 January 1880, 4.

17. "Fasting and Living Death: Dr. Tanner Replies to Dr. Hammond," *New York Times*, 18 January 1880, 4.

18. "A Remarkable Case," *Brooklyn Daily Eagle*, 7 June 1866, 2; Dailey, *Mollie Fancher*; Stacey, *The Fasting Girl*.

19. These descriptions and much of the information included here come from *Mollie Fancher, the Brooklyn Enigma*, a biography of Fancher written by her physician, Abram Dailey, in 1894, from years of experience treating her and the "unimpeachable testimony of many witnesses."

20. Dailey, *Mollie Fancher*, 11.

21. Ibid., 16.

22. Ibid., 19.

23. "Fasting and Living Death," 4; Dailey, *Mollie Fancher*, 19.

24. Dailey, *Mollie Fancher*, 21–25.

25. Ibid., 28; "A Remarkable Case," 2.

26. Quoted in Hammond, *Fasting Girls*, 54.

27. "Life without Food," *New York Herald*, 20 October 1878.

28. Hammond, *Fasting Girls*, 56, 59–60.

29. Ibid., 60–61.

30. Ibid., 28, 40, 75.

31. These challenges, originally published in local newspapers, were reprinted by Hammond in the appendix to *Fasting Girls*, 76–77.

32. Spignesi, *Starving Women*, 5–6.

33. "Fasting and Living Death," 4.

34. Wilder, "Dr. Tanner and the Forty Days' Fast," 458.

35. "Fasting and Living Death," 4; personal correspondence with Linda Burfield Hazzard, quoted in Hazzard, *Scientific Fasting*, 20.

36. Gunn, *Forty Days without Food*, 13.

37. "Fasting and Living Death," 4.

38. Gunn, *Forty Days without Food*, 18.

39. "The Long Fast Finished," *Brooklyn Daily Eagle*, 17 July 1880, 4; "Tanner's Fast," 27.

40. "Trying to Live on Air," *New York Times*, 21 June 1880, 1; "Dr. Tanner's Wife," *Brooklyn Daily Eagle*, 19 August 1880, 4.

41. Gunn, *Forty Days without Food*, 12.

42. Hazzard, *Scientific Fasting*, 16.

43. Gunn, *Forty Days without Food*, 13–14.

44. Ibid., 14–15.

45. Ibid., 16–18.

46. Ibid., 18.

47. Ibid., 18–19.

48. Ibid., 19.

49. "A Protest against Starving Matches," *New York Times*, 14 July 1880, 2.

50. "Jarring Tanner's Nerves," *New York Times*, 9 July 1880, 5.

51. Wilson and Geppert, *The Medical Advance*, 158.

52. Gunn, *Forty Days without Food*, 43.

53. "Wanted to Marry Tanner," *Brooklyn Daily Eagle*, 8 August 1880, 1.

54. "Tanner's Fast," 27.

55. "Inanition at Bellevue Hospital," *Medical Record*, 4 September 1880, 280.

56. "The Theologians Settle Down on Dr. Tanner," *Brooklyn Daily Eagle*, 30 July 1880, 2.

57. "Dr. Tanner's Fast—Cui Bono?," *Scribner's Monthly* 20 (May–October 1880), 936.

58. "Tanner's Fast," *New York Times*, 31 July 1880, 4.

59. These measurements were widely published; I am quoting from the extremely detailed daily accounts collated from the attendants' notes in Gunn, *Forty Days without Food*, 43.

60. Ibid., 42–79; "The Faster in a Bad Way," *New York Times*, 2 August 1880, 5; "The Long Fast Finished," 4; "Tanner Perseveres," *Brooklyn Daily Eagle*, 17 July 1880, 4; "Tanner Wins," *Brooklyn Daily Eagle*, 7 August 1880, 4.

61. "Tanner Perseveres," 4.

62. "Tanner," *Brooklyn Daily Eagle*, 5 August 1880, 4; "The Faster in a Bad Way," 5; "Still Fasting," *Brooklyn Daily Eagle*, 4 August 1880, 4; "Tanner Perseveres," 4.

63. "Jarring Tanner's Nerves," 5.

64. Wilder, "Dr. Tanner and the Forty Days' Fast," 458.

65. "Conclusions Drawn from Dr. Tanner's Fast," *Brooklyn Daily Eagle*, 6 August 1880, 2; "The Fortieth Day at Hand," *New York Times*, 6 August 1880, 5.

66. "Conclusions Drawn from Dr. Tanner's Fast," 2.

67. "The Theologians Settle Down on Dr. Tanner," 2.

68. Richardson, "The Philosophy of Fasting," 358–59.

69. Phelan, *Unmarked*, 148.

70. Evetsky, "On the Relation of Food to Life," 139, emphasis added.

71. "The Starving Doctor," *Brooklyn Daily Eagle*, 11 July 1880, 4, emphasis added; "The Social Lessons of Not Eating," *Brooklyn Daily Eagle*, 1 August 1880, 2.

72. Cockin, "Dr. Tanner's Fast," 49.

73. Schjeldahl, "Chris Burden and the Limits of Art," 132.

74. Quoted in Peter Plagens, "He Got Shot—For His Art," *New York Times*, 2 September 1973, 87.

75. Quoted in Horvitz, "Chris Burden," 26.

76. Ibid., 27.

77. Chalupecky, "Art and Sacrifice," 34.

78. Horvitz, "Chris Burden," 27.

79. Ward, "Gray Zone," 114.

80. Horvitz, "Chris Burden," 27.

81. Burden and Butterfield, "Through the Night Softly," 223.

82. Ibid., 227.

83. Rugoff, "Touched by Your Presence," 84–89.

84. Such laws were enacted to respond to Vietnam War–era protests, many of which included bomb threats called in to government buildings.

85. Burden and Ayers, *Chris Burden*, 58.

86. Morgan, "Survival Kit," 52–55.

87. Burden and Ayers, *Chris Burden*, 48.

88. Horvitz, "Chris Burden," 30.

89. Ibid., 27.

90. Ibid.

91. Ibid., 24–25.

92. Ibid., 25.

93. Kuspit, "Chris Burden," 42.

94. Ibid., emphasis added.

95. Ibid.; Silverman, *Male Subjectivity at the Margins*.

96. Kuspit, "Chris Burden," 42.

97. See Hobbes, *The Leviathan*.

98. Horvitz, "Chris Burden," 25.

99. Ibid., 24.

100. Ibid.

101. Schjeldahl, "Chris Burden and the Limits of Art," 133.

102. Burden and Ayres, *Chris Burden*, 74.

103. Alan Merridew and Frank Zehour, "This Body Artist Ain't Got Nobody," *Chicago Tribune*, 13 April 1975, 12.

104. Ibid.

105. O'Dell, *Contract with the Skin*, 67.

106. Burden and Ayers, *Chris Burden*, 74.

107. Roger Ebert, "Chris Burden: 'My God, are they going to leave me here to die?,'" *Chicago Sun-Times*, 25 May 1975.

108. Carr, *On Edge*, 24.

109. O'Dell, *Contract with the Skin*, 67.

110. Silverman, *World Spectators*, 73, 3.

111. Phelan, *Unmarked*, 148.

THREE How to Stage Self-Consumption

1. Piper, *Out of Order, Out of Sight*, 55.

2. See Kant, *Critique of Pure Reason*.

3. Piper, *Out of Order, Out of Sight*, 40. This paragraph is also cited in Peggy Phelan's review of *The House with the Ocean View*, "Marina Abramović," 570.

4. Perreault, "Earth and Fire," 10.

5. Blocker, *Where Is Ana Mendieta?*, 10. See also Popper, *Art—Action and Participation*, 11.

6. Goldberg, *Performance Art*.

7. B. Taylor, *Avant-Garde and After*, 9.

8. See Kirby, *Happenings*.

9. See Wagner, *Three Artists (Three Women)*.

10. Burden has displayed the lock, along with artifacts from other performances, as relics in retrospective exhibitions. See Burden and Ayres, *Chris Burden*, 48, 167.

11. In a survey essay written for Chris Burden's twenty-year retrospective Donald Kuspit echoed some of these questions by suggesting that Burden's performances might represent "a means of making his name 'a commodity'" and that he was thus engaged in "self-commodification—the final ironical form of self-mystification" ("Chris Burden," 37).

12. Phelan, *Unmarked*, 148; see also Pollock, "Performing Writing."

13. Piper, *Out of Order, Out of Sight*, 89, 257.

14. Moten, *In the Break*, 233.

15. Piper, *Out of Order, Out of Sight*, 91–139, 157–92.

16. Moten, *In the Break*, 235.

17. Fried, *Art and Objecthood*, 163, 167–68, 163.

18. Moten, *In the Break*, 236

19. Fried, *Art and Objecthood*, 163.

20. Moten, *In the Break*, 237, 239.

21. I am greatly indebted to the deeply historiographical tracing of theatricality provided by Tracy Davis and Thomas Postlewait in the introduction to *Theatricality*.

22. See Goffman, *Interaction Ritual*; Turner, *Ritual Process*.

23. See, for example, Diana Taylor's discussion of the many possible meanings of the word *performance* in *The Archive and the Repertoire*, 3–4.

24. I am borrowing this phrase from Allen Feldman, as quoted in the introduction to his book *Formations of Violence*, 264.

25. Societas Raffaello Sanzio, "What the Body Can Do," 141; Phelan, "Marina Abramović," 572.

26. See Blocker, *Where Is Ana Mendieta?*, 18; Kelly, "Notes from the Edge," 5.

27. These insistences have taken various forms over the years; see, for example, Tucker, preface and acknowledgements, 6; Kosmidou, "Transitory Objects," 30; Steven Henry Madoff, "A Viewable Fast, Enforced by Knives," *New York Times*, 10 November 2002, A37.

28. For examples of performances about feeding and food, see Carr, *On Edge*; Goldberg, *Performance Art*; Gough, *On Cooking*; Lindenfeld and Langellier, *Food in Performance/Food as Performance*; Montano, *Performance Artists Talking in the Eighties*, especially 143–223.

29. See *Ana Mendieta: Fuego De Tierra*, directed by Nereyda Garcia-Ferraz, Kate Horsfield, and Branda Miller, Women Make Movies, 1987; *Selected Filmworks*, directed by Ana Mendieta, Electronic Arts Intermix, 1997.

30. Phelan, *Unmarked*, 148.

31. Cruz, "Ana Mendieta's Art," 226–27.

32. Blocker, *Where Is Ana Mendieta?*, 52.

33. Ibid., 54.

34. Cruz, "Ana Mendieta's Art," 228.

35. Viso, *Unseen Mendieta*, 21, 77.

36. Quoted in Spero, "Tracing Ana Mendieta," 75.

37. Pollock, "Performing Writing," 85.

38. For a detailed and evocative description of this period in Mendieta's life, see Blocker, *Where Is Ana Mendieta?*, 50–54.

39. Cabañas, "Pain of Cuba, Body I Am," 15.

40. Viso, *Unseen Mendieta*, 23.

41. Del Rio, "Ana Mendieta," 28.

42. Blocker, *Where Is Ana Mendieta?*, 10.

43. Lippard, *Six Years*.

44. Viso, *Unseen Mendieta*, 8; Schneider, *The Explicit Body in Performance*, 117.

45. Quoted in Moure, *Ana Mendieta*, 108.

46. Jones, "'Presence' in Absentia," 13

47. Ortega, "Exiled Space, in-between Space," 30.

48. De La Torre, *Santería*, 12 (see also Canizares, *Cuban Santería*); Blocker, *Where Is Ana Mendieta?*, 18.

49. Ortega, "Exiled Space, in-between Space," 30.

50. Pollock, "Performing Writing," 84.

51. Schneider, *The Explicit Body in Performance*, 119, 3.

52. Phelan, *Unmarked*, 146.

53. Schneider, *The Explicit Body in Performance*, 119.

54. Mendieta, "*La Venus Negra*, Based on a Cuban Legend," 22. Mendieta's description of the legend is reproduced in full in Blocker, "Ana Mendieta and the Politics of the *Venus Negra*," 32.

55. Mendieta, "*La Venus Negra*, Based on a Cuban Legend," 22.

56. Michael Brenson, "Works by Ana Mendieta in a Retrospective Exhibition," *New York Times*, 27 November 1987, C30.

57. Quoted in Roulet, "Ana Mendieta and Carl Andre," 81.

58. Leonard Buder, "Sculptor Accused of Pushing Wife out Window to Death," *New York Times*, 10 September 1985, B3; Douglas C. McGill, "Verdict Due Today in Death of Artist," *New York Times*, 11 February 1988, B1.

59. See Blocker, *Where Is Ana Mendieta?*, 1.

60. Ronald Sullivan, "Greenwich Village Sculptor Acquitted of Pushing Wife to Her Death," *New York Times*, 12 February 1988, B3.

61. Brenson, "Works by Ana Mendieta in a Retrospective Exhibition," C30.

62. Abramović, *Marina Abramović*, 80–93.

63. Ibid., 106–11.

64. Phelan, *Unmarked*, 146.

65. Abramović, *Marina Abramović*, 258–93.

66. Goldberg, "Here and Now," 15.

67. Abramović, *Marina Abramović*, 258.

68. Ibid., 226–27.

69. Ibid., 330–33.

70. Anderson, "Marina Abramović," 28.

71. Phelan, "Marina Abramović," 574.

72. Roberta Smith, "Where Seeing Is Not Only Believing, but Also Creating," *New York Times*, 22 February 2002, B29.

73. C. Carr, "Hunger Artist: The 12 Days of Marina Abramović," *Village Voice*, 47, no. 49 (2002), 57.

74. Kelly, "Notes from the Edge," 5.

75. Madoff, "A Viewable Fast, Enforced by Knives," A1.

76. Kaplan, "Deeper and Deeper," 10.

77. After descending from the platforms on her final day Abramović addressed the audience: "Dear artists, dear friends, dear public. I am sorry to disappoint you by not using the knife-ladder. I am not there yet, but hopefully one day I will be." Quoted in Wescott, "Marina Abramović's *The House with the Ocean View*," 136.

78. Smith, "Where Seeing Is Not Only Believing, but Also Creating," B29. Abramović has required contractual agreements for performances in the past, most notably for *In Between*, staged in 1996 and 1997, for which audience members were required to sign the following declaration before begin admitted: "I agree to commit myself to take an active part in the video installation *In Between*. I promise that I will stay for the entire duration of the work — 40 minutes — and that I will not interrupt the process with my early departure" (Abramović, *Marina Abramović*, 349).

79. Madoff, "A Viewable Fast, Enforced by Knives," A1.

80. Birringer, "Marina Abramović on the Ledge," 66.

81. Steven Henry Madoff, "Reflecting on an Ordeal That Was Also Art," *New York Times*, 28 November 2002, B5. See Appadurai, *The Social Life of Things*; Mauss, *The Gift*.

82. Madoff, "A Viewable Fast, Enforced by Knives," 37.

83. "My opinion about September 11 is that there is a September 11 every day somewhere else in the world, but because it was here, you think that that's the only truth." Quoted in Catherine Saint Louis, "The Way We Live Now: What Were They Thinking?," *New York Times Magazine*, 15 December 2002, 54.

84. This is the most commonly used citation of Bush's line, which was actually

"Either you are with us or you are with the terrorists" (Bush, "Address to Joint Session of Congress").

85. Phelan, "On Seeing the Invisible," 178.

86. Smith, "Where Seeing Is Not Only Believing, but Also Creating," B29.

87. See Piper, "Property and the Limits of the Self" and "Two Conceptions of the Self."

88. Piper, "Property and the Limits of the Self," 62.

89. This quality of Piper's work — her interrogation of the action of responsibility and "moral commitment" — is perhaps most apparent in the *Mythic Being* series, the *Vanilla Nightmares* series, the *Calling Cards*, and *Four Intruders Plus Alarm Systems* (Piper, *Out of Order, Out of Sight*, 91–139, 157–92, 253–54; 219–22, 181–86).

FOUR To Lie Down to Death for Days

1. *F: To Lie Down to Death for Days*, directed by Metin Yeğin, Yeğin Productions, 2001.

2. TAYAD Komite Nederland, *Documentation on the Death Fast in Turkey*, 2.

3. Öndül, "Isolation, Death Fasts, and Women Deaths"; Doğan Tiliç, "Turkish Hunger Strike Takes 107th Life," *EFE News Service*, 13 January 2003.

4. Chris Morris, "Analysis: Can Turkey Fit In?," *BBC News*, 26 January 2000; "EU Urges Turkey to Reform," *BBC News*, 9 March 2000. Greek, German, and French representatives, among others, have expressed strong resistance to Turkey's accession to the EU.

5. Stephen Kinzer's *Crescent and Star* explicitly represents Turkey as inescapably bound up in a borderlands geography that compromises the country's ability to develop a sustainable form of liberal democracy.

6. For a detailed articulation of this problem, see Smith and Katz, "Grounding Metaphor."

7. Batuk Gathani, "Giscard Warns against EU Membership for Turkey," *The Hindu*, 10 November 2002.

8. TAYAD Komite Nederland, *Documentation on the Death Fast in Turkey*, 12.

9. Beynon, "Hunger Strikes in Turkish Prisons," 737; P. Green, "Turkish Jails, Hunger Strikes, and the European Drive for Prison Reform," 97–101.

10. "Political Prisoners in Turkey to Begin Hunger Strike on October 20."

11. Cemile Çakir and Frank Neisser, "'Courage and Determination' Fuel Prison Hunger Strike," *Worker's World*, 21 December 2000, 2.

12. According to the International Centre for Prison Studies at King's College London, in late 2007 more than 60 percent of Turkey's prison population had not yet been convicted of any crime ("Prison Brief for Turkey," 1). See also Walmsley, "World Prison Brief."

13. See, for example, Kinzer, *Crescent and Star*; Robins, "Interrupting Identities"; Le Pennec and Eberhardt, "The F-type Prison Crisis and the Repression of Human Rights Defenders in Turkey."

14. In the past several years the moderately Islamist and currently presiding Adalet ve Kalkınma Partisi (Justice and Development Party) and the Kurdish Demokratik Toplum Partisi (Democratic Society Party) have enjoyed greater influence and representation in the Turkish national government.

15. Çakir and Neisser, "'Courage and Determination' Fuel Prison Hunger Strike," 2. After a conditional amnesty intended to relieve drastic overcrowding in Turkey's prisons, political prisoners made up roughly six thousand of the remaining sixty thousand prisoners; see Öndül, "Isolation, Death Fasts, and Women Deaths."

16. Le Pennec and Eberhardt, "The F-type Prison Crisis and the Repression of Human Rights Defenders in Turkey," 9–10.

17. Turkish penal officials are also regularly sent to the United States for training in techniques of prisoner discipline and punishment; see Çakir and Neisser, "'Courage and Determination' Fuel Prison Hunger Strike."

18. "Small Group Isolation in Turkish Prisons."

19. "High Security F-type Prisons."

20. Beynon, "Hunger Strikes in Turkish Prisons"; Cemile Çakir and Frank Neisser, "Massacre Can't Stop Resistance," *Worker's World*, 11 January 2001; Le Pennec and Eberhardt, "The F-type Prison Crisis and the Repression of Human Rights Defenders in Turkey"; "Small Group Isolation in Turkish Prisons."

21. "List of Turkish Laws Violating Human Rights."

22. Ibid.

23. Jonny Dymond, "No Compromise to Turkey Prisoners," *BBC News*, 3 April 2002.

24. Le Pennec and Eberhardt, "The F-type Prison Crisis and the Repression of Human Rights Defenders in Turkey."

25. "List of Turkish Laws Violating Human Rights."

26. See Kinzer, *Crescent and Star*; Robins, "Interrupting Identities."

27. Preamble to the Constitution of the Turkish Republic, paragraph 5.

28. Gorvett, "Ankara Seethes as Parliamentary Reforms Fail to Open Door to EU"; Kinzer, *Crescent and Star*; Robins, "Interrupting Identities."

29. "List of Turkish Laws Violating Human Rights."

30. Yavuz Baydar, "Seeking Consensus Possible, but Reaching It Rather Unlikely," *Today's Zaman*, 27 August 2008.

31. Robins, "Interrupting Identities," 72.

32. "Although it is true that prison punishes delinquency, delinquency is for the most part produced in and by an incarceration which, ultimately, prison perpetuates in its turn" (Foucault, *Discipline and Punish*, 301).

33. Ibid., 253–55.

34. Ibid., 135–69.

35. Ibid., 301.

36. "World Report 1989"; "Turkey Violates Rights of Free Expression." Many of these restrictions have been lifted, particularly with the recent rise to power of the moderately Islamist Adalet ve Kalkınma Partisi (Justice and Development Party) and the election of several officials representing the Kurdish Demokratik Toplum Partisi (Democratic Society Party).

37. The particularly offensive penal codes are number 159, which outlaws "insult[ing] or ridicul[ing] the moral personality of Turkishness," and number 312, which outlaws "openly prais[ing] an action considered criminal."

38. "Political Prisoners in Turkey to Begin Hunger Strike on October 20."

39. See O'Malley, *Biting at the Grave*; Beresford, *Ten Men Dead*.

40. Feldman, *Formations of Violence*, 236.

41. Ibid., 237.

42. The number of casualties reported ranged from twenty-eight to thirty-two, depending on the source. The BBC reported thirty prisoner casualties and two military casualties (Chris Morris, "Shadow Hangs over Turkish Jails," *BBC News*, 10 January 2001).

43. "Turkey Halts Prison Plans," *BBC News*, 15 July 2001.

44. Morris, "Shadow Hangs over Turkish Jails."

45. TAYAD Komite Nederland, *Documentation on the Death Fast in Turkey*; Çakir and Neisser, "Massacre Can't Stop Resistance."

46. TAYAD Komite Nederland, *Documentation on the Death Fast in Turkey*, 14.

47. Çakir and Neisser, "Massacre Can't Stop Resistance."

48. TAYAD Komite Nederland, *I Want My Past Back*, 8.

49. Feldman, *Formations of Violence*, 241.

50. Ibid., 251.

51. "Death in the Hunger Strike was conceived as both the literal termination of biological functions and 'the countdown,' the long drawn-out sociobiological death that the endurance of starvation dramatically stretched into an iconic act of historic mediation. . . . Military eschatology and biological eschatology were intertwined" (ibid., 225, 237).

52. *F: To Lie Down to Death for Days*.

53. McCorkel, "Embodied Surveillance and the Gendering of Punishment," 44–45.

54. Öndül, "Isolation, Death Fasts, and Women's Deaths." In the years since Operation Return to Life this has changed. As the International Centre for Prison Studies reported in 2008, F-type prisons have been and continue to be used to incarcerate women. See "International Profile of Women's Prisons," 139–40.

55. Le Pennec and Eberhardt, "The F-type Prison Crisis and the Repression of

Human Rights Defenders in Turkey"; TAYAD Komite Nederland, "Documentation on the Death Fast in Turkey"; TAYAD Komite Nederland, *I Want My Past Back*.

56. Scott Anderson, "The Hunger Warriors," *New York Times Magazine*, 21 October 2001.

57. Ibid., 47.

58. Ellmann, *The Hunger Artists*, 2.

59. Anderson, "The Hunger Warriors."

60. Ibid., 46.

61. Ibid.

62. Feldman, *Formations of Violence*, 264.

63. Anderson, "The Hunger Warriors," 44.

64. Ibid., 43, 124.

65. Foucault, "The Subject and Power," 216.

66. Various translations of this speech exist. I have chosen the one preferred by the official Kemal Atatürk Library.

67. Robins, "Interrupting Identities," 69.

68. Dymond, "No Compromise on Turkey Prisoners."

69. Patterson, *Slavery and Social Death*.

AFTERWORD

1. *After . . .*, directed by Metin Yeğin, Yeğin Productions, 2001.

2. Ibid.

3. *F: To Lie Down to Death for Days*, directed by Metin Yeğin, Yeğin Productions, 2001.

4. Rilke, *The Book of Hours*, 90.

5. See Agamben, *Remnants of Auschwitz*, especially 41–86.

6. Lacan tellingly describes the *object-a* as "the object that cannot be swallowed, as it were, which remains stuck in the gullet of the signifer." Lacan, *Four Fundamental Concepts of Psychoanalysis*, 270.

7. Conquergood, "Lethal Theatre," 342.

8. Charles Laurence, "Sweet Tea and Therapy for X-Ray Inmates," *Daily Telegraph*, 9 March 2002.

9. Brown, *States of Injury*.

10. Miles, *Oath Betrayed*, 110.

11. John Manel, "Guantanamo Man Tells of Torture," BBC World Service, BBC, KQED San Francisco, 3 March 2006.

12. Bush, "Detention, Treatment, and Trial of Certain Non-Citizens in the War against Terrorism."

13. See Freud, *Beyond the Pleasure Principle*.

14. *Real Time with Bill Maher*, episode 306, HBO, 1 April 2005.

15. *The Nancy Grace Show*, CNN, 31 March 2005.

16. Ibid.

17. Ibid.

18. Agamben, *Remnants of Auschwitz*, 42–43.

19. Agamben, *Homo Sacer*, 1.

20. Ibid., 88.

21. Ibid.

22. Josh White and Carol D. Leonnig, "U.S. Cites Exception in Torture Ban," *Washington Post*, 3 March 2006, A4.

23. Ibid.

24. Al-Haj, "Humiliated in the Shackles," 42.

25. See Mbembe, "Necropolitics."

26. Kafka, "A Hunger Artist," 243–44.

27. Hornbacher, *Wasted*, 2.

28. Kafka, "A Hunger Artist," 255–56.

29. Auster, *The Art of Hunger*, 19.

references

•

Abramović, Marina. *Marina Abramović: Artist Body (Performances 1969–1998)*. Milan: Charta, 1998.

Adorno, Theodor W. "Valéry Proust Museum." *Prisms*. Translated by Samuel Weber and Sherry Weber, 173–86. Cambridge, Mass.: MIT Press, 1981.

Agamben, Giorgio. *Homo Sacer: Sovereign Power and Bare Life*. Translated by Daniel Heller-Roazen. Stanford: Stanford University Press, 1998.

———. *Remnants of Auschwitz: The Witness and the Archive*. Translated by Daniel Heller-Roazen. New York: Zone, 1999.

———. *State of Exception*. Translated by Kevin Attell. Chicago: University of Chicago Press, 2005.

Al-Haj, Sami. "Humiliated in the Shackles." *Poems from Guantanamo*, edited by Marc Falkoff, 42. Iowa City: University of Iowa Press, 2007.

Al-Noaimi, Abdulla Majid. "My Heart Was Wounded by the Strangeness." *Poems from Guantanamo*, edited by Marc Falkoff, 61. Iowa City: University of Iowa Press, 2007.

Althusser, Louis. "Ideology and Ideological State Apparatuses." *Lenin and Philosophy and Other Essays*. Translated by Ben Brewster, 127–86. New York: Monthly Review Press, 1971.

American Psychiatric Association. *Diagnostic and Statistical Manual of Mental Disorders: DSM-III-R*. Washington: American Psychiatric Association, 1987.

———. *Diagnostic and Statistical Manual of Mental Disorders: DSM-IV-TR*. Washington: American Psychiatric Association, 2005.

Andersen, Arnold. "Eating Disorders in Males." *Eating Disorders and Obesity: A Comprehensive Handbook*, edited by Kelly D. Brownell and Christopher Fairburn, 177–87. New York: Guilford Press, 1995.

———, ed. *Males with Eating Disorders*. New York: Brunner/Mazel, 1990.

Andersen, Arnold, Leigh Cohn, and Thomas Holbrook. *Making Weight: Men's Conflicts with Food, Weight, Shape, and Appearance*. Carlsbad, Calif.: Gürze, 2000.

Anderson, Laurie. "Marina Abramović." *BOMB* 84 (summer 2003), 25–31.

Appadurai, Arjun, ed. *The Social Life of Things: Commodities in Cultural Perspective*. Cambridge: Cambridge University Press, 1988.

Aristotle. *On Youth and Old Age, On Life and Death, On Breathing*. Translated by G. R. T. Ross. Whitefish, Mont.: Kessinger, 2004.

Auster, Paul. *The Art of Hunger*. New York: Penguin, 1997.

Austin, J. L. *How to Do Things with Words*. Cambridge, Mass.: Harvard University Press, 1975.

Batten, Guinn. *The Orphaned Imagination: Melancholy and Commodity Culture in English Romanticism*. Durham, N.C.: Duke University Press, 1988.

Becker, James T., Joseph M. R. Furman, Michel Panisset, and Christine Smith. "Characteristics of the Memory Loss of a Patient with Wernicke-Korsakoff's Syndrome without Alcoholism." *Neuropsychologia* 28, no. 2 (1990), 171–79.

Bell, Rudolph M. *Holy Anorexia*. Chicago: University of Chicago Press, 1987.

Beresford, David. *Ten Men Dead: The Story of the 1981 Irish Hunger Strike*. New York: Atlantic Monthly Press, 1989.

Beynon, Joe. "Hunger Strikes in Turkish Prisons." *The Lancet* 348, no. 9029 (1996), 737.

Biddick, Kathleen. "Genders, Bodies, Borders: Technologies of the Visual." *Speculum* 68, no. 2 (1993), 389–418.

Birringer, Johannes. "Marina Abramović on the Ledge." *Performing Art Journal* 25, no. 2 (2003), 66–70.

Blau, Herbert. "Universals of Performance: Or, Amortizing Play." *SubStance* 11, no. 4 (1983), 140–61.

Blocker, Jane. "Ana Mendieta and the Politics of the *Venus Negra*." *Cultural Studies* 12, no. 1 (1998), 31–50.

——. *What the Body Cost: Desire, History, and Performance*. Minneapolis: University of Minnesota Press, 2004.

——. *Where Is Ana Mendieta? Identity, Performance, and Exile*. Durham, N.C.: Duke University Press, 1999.

Bordo, Susan. *Unbearable Weight: Feminism, Western Culture, and the Body*. Berkeley: University of California Press, 1993.

Brecht, Bertolt. "The Street Scene." *Brecht on Theatre*. Translated by John Willett, 121–29. New York: Hill and Wang, 1964.

Breuer, Josef, and Sigmund Freud. *Studies on Hysteria*. Translated by James Strachey. New York: Basic, 1957.

Brown, Wendy. *States of Injury: Power and Freedom in Late Modernity*. Princeton: Princeton University Press, 1995.

Bruch, Hilde. *The Golden Cage: The Enigma of Anorexia Nervosa*. Cambridge, Mass.: Harvard University Press, 1978.

Brumberg, Joan Jacobs. *Fasting Girls: The History of Anorexia Nervosa*. Cambridge, Mass.: Harvard University Press, 1988.

Bulwer-Lytton, Edward. *Zanoni*. New York: Harper and Brothers, 1842.

Burden, Chris, and Anne Ayres. *Chris Burden: A Twenty-Year Survey*. Newport Beach, Calif.: Newport Harbor Art Museum, 1988.

Burden, Chris, and Jan Butterfield. "Through the Night Softly." *The Art of Performance: A Critical Anthology*, edited by Gregory Battcock and Robert Nickas, 222–39. New York: Dutton, 1984.

Bush, George W. "Address to Joint Session of Congress." Chamber of the United States House of Representatives, Washington, 21 September 2001.

——. "Detention, Treatment, and Trial of Certain Non-Citizens in the War against Terrorism." White House Press Office Press Release, 13 November 2001.

Butler, Judith. *Bodies That Matter: On the Discursive Limits of "Sex."* New York: Routledge, 1993.

——. *Gender Trouble: Feminism and the Subversion of Identity*. New York: Routledge, 1990.

——. *The Psychic Life of Power*. Stanford: Stanford University Press, 1997.

Bynum, Catherine Walker. *Holy Feast and Holy Fast: The Religious Significance of Food to Medieval Women*. Berkeley: University of California Press, 1988.

Cabañas, Kaira M. "Pain of Cuba, Body I Am." *Woman's Art Journal* 20, no. 1 (1999), 12–17.

Canizares, Baba Raul. *Cuban Santería: Walking with the Night*. Rochester, Vt.: Destiny Books, 1999.

Carlat, Daniel, Carlos Camargo Jr., and David Herzog. "Eating Disorders in Males: A Report on 135 Patients." *American Journal of Psychiatry* 154, no. 8 (1997), 1127–32.

Carr, C. *On Edge: Performance at the End of the Twentieth Century*. Hanover, N.H.: Wesleyan University Press, 1993.

Cartwright, Lisa. *Screening the Body: Tracing Medicine's Visual Culture*. Minneapolis: University of Minnesota Press, 1995.

Caruth, Cathy. *Unclaimed Experience: Trauma, Narrative, and History*. Baltimore: Johns Hopkins University Press, 1996.

Chaikin, Joseph. *The Presence of the Actor*. New York: Theatre Communications Group, 1991.

Chalupecky, Jindrich. "Art and Sacrifice." Translated by Jan Mladejovsky. *Flash Art* 80/81 (February–April 1978), 33–35.

Chasseguet-Smirgel, Janine. *The Ego-Ideal: A Psychoanalytic Essay on the Malady of the Ideal*. Translated by Paul Barrows. New York: Norton, 1985.

Cheng, Meiling. *In Other Los Angeleses: Multicentric Performance Art*. Berkeley: University of California Press, 2002.

Chernin, Kim. *The Obsession: Reflections on the Tyranny of Slenderness*. New York: Harper and Row, 1981.

Cockin, Hereward K. "Dr. Tanner's Fast." *Gentleman Dick O' the Greys and Other Poems*, 49. Toronto: C. B. Robinson, 1889.

Cohen, Cathy. *The Boundaries of Blackness: AIDS and the Breakdown of Black Politics*. Chicago: University of Chicago Press, 1999.

Connerton, Paul. *How Societies Remember*. Cambridge: Cambridge University Press, 1989.

Conquergood, Dwight. "Lethal Theatre: Performance, Punishment, and the Death Penalty." *Theatre Journal* 54, no. 3 (2002), 339–67.

Cozzi, Enzo. "Hunger and the Future of Performance." *Performance Research* 4, no. 1 (1999), 121–29.

Crenshaw, Kimberlé Williams. "Mapping the Margins: Intersectionality, Identity Politics, and Violence against Women of Color." *Stanford Law Review* 43, no. 6 (1991), 1241–99.

Crimp, Douglas. *On the Museum's Ruins*. Cambridge, Mass.: MIT Press, 1993.

Cruz, Carlos A. "Ana Mendieta's Art: A Journey through Her Life." *Latina Legacies: Identity, Biography, and Community*, edited by Vicki L. Ruiz and Virginia Sánchez Korrol, 225–39. London: Oxford University Press, 2005.

Dailey, Abram H. *Mollie Fancher, the Brooklyn Enigma*. Brooklyn: Eagle, 1894.

David-Ménard, Monique. *Hysteria from Freud to Lacan: Body and Language in Psychoanalysis*. Translated by Catherine Porter. Ithaca: Cornell University Press, 1989.

Davis, Tracy C., and Thomas Postlewait, eds. *Theatricality*. Cambridge: Cambridge University Press, 2003.

De La Torre, Miguel A. *Santería: The Beliefs and Rituals of a Growing Religion in America*. Grand Rapids, Mich.: Eerdmans, 2004.

Del Rio, Petra Barreras. "Ana Mendieta: A Historical Overview." *Ana Mendieta: A Retrospective*, edited by Petra Barreras del Rio and John Perreault, 28–63. New York: New Museum of Contemporary Art, 1987.

Derrida, Jacques. *Archive Fever: A Freudian Impression*. Translated by Eric Prenowitz. Chicago: University of Chicago Press, 1998.

Didi-Huberman, Georges. *Invention of Hysteria: Charcot and the Photographic Iconography of the Salpêtrière*. Translated by Alisa Hartz. Cambridge, Mass.: MIT Press, 2003.

Ellmann, Maud. *The Hunger Artists: Starving, Writing, and Imprisonment*. Cambridge, Mass.: Harvard University Press, 1993.

Evans, Martha Noel. *Fits and Starts: A Genealogy of Hysteria in Modern France*. Ithaca: Cornell University Press, 1991.

Evetsky, Etienne. "On the Relation of Food to Life." *Medical Record*, 31 July 1880, 139–40.

Fanon, Frantz. "The Fact of Blackness." *Black Skin/White Masks*. Translated by Constance Farrington, 109–40. New York: Grove Press, 1994.

Feldman, Allen. *Formations of Violence: The Narrative of the Body and Political Terror in Northern Ireland*. New York: Columbia University Press, 1991.

Flugel, J. C. *The Psychology of Clothes*. London: Hogarth Press, 1930.

Fortunati, Leopoldina. *The Arcane of Reproduction: Housework, Prostitution, Labor and Capital*. Translated by Hilary Creek. New York: Autonomedia, 1995.

Foucault, Michel. *Discipline and Punish: The Birth of the Prison*. Translated by Alan Sheridan. New York: Vintage, 1995.

———. *The History of Sexuality, Vol. 1: An Introduction*. Translated by Robert Hurley. New York: Vintage, 1990.

———. *The History of Sexuality, Vol. 3: The Care of the Self*. Translated by Robert Hurley. New York: Vintage, 1988.

———. *Power/Knowledge: Selected Interviews and Other Writings 1972–1977*. Translated by Colin Gordon, Leo Marshall, John Mepham, and Kate Soper. New York: Pantheon, 1980.

———. "The Subject and Power." *Michel Foucault: Beyond Structuralism and Hermeneutics*, edited by H. L. Dreyfus and Paul Rabinow, 208–26. Chicago: University of Chicago Press, 1982.

Freud, Sigmund. *Beyond the Pleasure Principle*. Translated by James Strachey. New York: Norton, 1961.

———. *Civilization and Its Discontents*. Translated by James Strachey. New York: Norton, 1961.

———. "On Narcissism: An Introduction." *General Psychological Theory*. Translated by Cecil M. Baines, 56–82. New York: Touchstone, 1963.

———. *Three Essays on the Theory of Sexuality*. Translated by James Strachey. New York: Basic, 1975.

Fried, Michael. *Art and Objecthood: Essays and Reviews*. Chicago: University of Chicago Press, 1998.

Gilmore, Ruth Wilson. *The Golden Gulag: Prisons, Surplus, Crisis, and Opposition in Globalizing California*. Berkeley: University of California Press, 2007.

Goffman, Erving. *Interaction Ritual: Essays on Face-to-Face Behavior*. Garden City, N.Y.: Anchor Books, 1967.

Goldberg, RoseLee. "Here and Now." *Marina Abramović: Objects Performance Video Sound*, edited by Chrissie Iles, 11–19. Oxford: Museum of Modern Art, 1995.

———. *Performance Art: From Futurism to the Present*. London: Thames and Hudson, 2001.

Gooldin, Sigal. "Fasting Women, Living Skeletons, and Hunger Artists: Spectacles of Body and Miracles at the Turn of a Century." *Body and Society* 9, no. 2 (2003), 27–53.

Gorvett, Jon. "Ankara Seethes as Parliamentary Reforms Fail to Open Door to EU." *Washington Report on Middle Eastern Affairs* 21, no. 9 (2002), 31–32.

Gough, Richard, ed. *On Cooking*. Special issue of *Performance Research* 4, no. 1 (1999).

Green, André. "Opening Remarks to a Discussion of Sexuality in Contemporary Psychoanalysis." *International Journal of Psychoanalysis* 78 (1997), 345–50.

Green, Peggy. "Turkish Jails, Hunger Strikes, and the European Drive for Prison Reform." *Punishment and Society* 4, no. 1 (2002), 97–101.

Gropman, Andrea L., William D. Gaillard, Pamela Campbell, and Sampath V. Charya. "Wernicke's Encephalopathy Due to Self Starvation in a Child." *The Lancet* 351, no. 9117 (1998), 1704–5.

Gull, William W. "A Paper on Anorexia Hysterica (Apepsia Hysterica)." *Medical Times and Gazette* 2 (1873), 534–36.

Gunn, Robert A. *Forty Days without Food*. New York: Albert Metz, 1880.

Halberstam, Judith. *Female Masculinity*. Durham, N.C.: Duke University Press, 2000.

Hammond, William A. *Fasting Girls: Their Physiology and Pathology*. New York: G. P. Putnam's Sons, 1879.

Handler, Clive E., and G. D. Perkin. "Anorexia Nervosa and Wernicke's Encephalopathy: An Underdiagnosed Association." *The Lancet* 320, no. 8301 (1982), 771–72.

Hartman, Saidiya. *Scenes of Subjection: Terror, Slavery, and Self-Making in Nineteenth-Century America*. Oxford: Oxford University Press, 1997.

Hasan, M. K., and R. W. Tibbetts. "Primary Anorexia Nervosa (Weight Phobia) in Males." *Postgraduate Medical Journal* 53 (March 1977), 146–51.

Hazzard, Linda Burfield. *Scientific Fasting: The Ancient and Modern Key to Health*. New York: Grant Publications, 1927.

Heidegger, Martin. *Being and Time*. Translated by Joan Stambaugh. Albany: State University of New York Press, 1996.

Herzog, David B., Isabel S. Bradburn, and Kerry Newman. "Sexuality in Men with Eating Disorders." *Males with Eating Disorders*, edited by Arnold Andersen. New York: Brunner/Mazel, 1990.

Heywood, Leslie. *Dedication to Hunger: The Anorexic Aesthetic in Modern Culture*. Berkeley: University of California Press, 1996.

"High Security F-Type Prisons." Justice Ministry of Turkey Briefing Paper, 2003.

Hobbes, Thomas. *The Leviathan: Or, The Matter, Forme, and Power of a Common-Wealth Ecclesiasticall and Civill*. London: Andrew Crooke, 1651.

Hornbacher, Mayra. *Wasted: A Memoir of Anorexia and Bulimia*. New York: HarperCollins, 1998.

Horvitz, Robert. "Chris Burden." *Artforum* 14, no. 9 (1976), 24–31.

"International Profile of Women's Prisons." International Centre for Prison Studies (Kings College London) Report, 2008.

Jones, Amelia. *Body Art/Performing the Subject*. Minneapolis: University of Minnesota Press, 1998.

——. "Dis/playing the Phallus: Male Artists Perform Their Masculinities." *Art History* 17, no. 4 (1994), 536–84.

——. "'Presence' in Absentia: Experiencing Performance in Documentation." *Art Journal* 56, no. 4 (1997), 11–18.

Kafka, Franz. "A Hunger Artist." *The Penal Colony: Stories and Short Pieces*. Translated by Willa Muir and Edwin Muir, 231–77. New York: Schocken, 1961.

Kant, Immanuel. *Critique of Pure Reason*. Translated by J. M. D. Meiklejohn. London: J. M. Dent, 1991.

Kaplan, Janet A. "Deeper and Deeper: Interview with Marina Abramović." *Art Journal* 58, no. 2 (1999), 7–21.

Kaufman, M. Ralph, and Marcel Heiman, eds. *Evolution of Psychosomatic Concepts: Anorexia Nervosa, a Paradigm*. New York: International Universities Press, 1964.

Kelly, Sean. "Notes from the Edge." *Marina Abramović: The House with the Ocean View*, edited by Amy Gotzler, 4–5. Milan: Charta, 2003.

Kinzer, Stephen. *Crescent and Star: Turkey between Two Worlds*. New York: Farrar, Straus and Giroux, 2001.

Kirby, Michael. *Happenings: An Illustrated Anthology*. New York: Dutton, 1965.

Klein, Melanie. *Love, Guilt, and Reparation*. New York: Free Press, 1984.

Kosmidou, Zoe. "Transitory Objects: A Conversation with Marina Abramović." *Sculpture* 20, no. 9 (2001), 27–31.

Krasnow, Michael. *My Life as a Male Anorexic*. New York: Harrington Park, 1996.

Kuspit, Donald. "Chris Burden: A Sculptor's Sensibility — The Early Years." *Chris Burden: A Twenty-Year Survey*, edited by Chris Burden and Anne Ayres, 35–43. Newport Beach, Calif.: Newport Harbor Art Museum, 1988.

Lacan, Jacques. *Écrits: A Selection*. Translated by Alan Sheridan. New York: Norton, 1977.

——. *The Four Fundamental Concepts of Psychoanalysis*. Translated by Alan Sheridan. New York: Norton, 1973.

Laplanche, Jean. *Life and Death in Psychoanalysis*. Translated by Jeffrey Mehlman. Baltimore: Johns Hopkins University Press, 1976.

Laplanche, Jean, and J.-B. Pontalis. *The Language of Psycho-Analysis*. Translated by Daniel Nicholson-Smith. New York: Norton, 1973.

Le Pennec, Elsa, and Sally Eberhardt. 2001. "The F-Type Prison Crisis and the Repression of Human Rights Defenders in Turkey." Euro-Mediterranean Human Rights Network, Kurdish Human Rights Project, and World Organisation against Torture Report. Geneva: OMCT, 2001.

Lindenfeld, Laura A., and Kristin M. Langellier, eds. *Food in Performance/Food as Performance*. Special issue of *Text and Performance Quarterly* 29, no. 1 (2009).

Lippard, Lucy. *Six Years: The Dematerialization of the Art Object from 1966 to 1972*. New York: Praeger, 1973.

"List of Turkish Laws Violating Human Rights." Human Rights Watch Press Release. February 1998.

MacSween, Morag. *Anorexic Bodies: A Feminist and Sociological Perspective on Anorexia Nervosa*. New York: Routledge, 1993.

Mauss, Marcel. *The Gift: The Form and Reason for Exchange in Archaic Societies*. Translated by W. D. Halls. New York: Norton, 2000.

Mbembe, Achille. "Necropolitics." Translated by Libby Meintjes. *Public Culture* 15, no. 1 (2003), 11–40.

McCorkel, Jill A. "Embodied Surveillance and the Gendering of Punishment." *Journal of Contemporary Ethnography* 32, no. 1 (2003), 41–76.

Mendieta, Ana. "*La Venus Negra*, Based on a Cuban Legend." *Heresies* 4, no. 1 (1981), 22.

Miles, Steven H. *Oath Betrayed: Torture, Medical Complicity, and the War on Terror*. New York: Random House, 2006.

Mitchell, Breon. "Franz Kafka and the Hunger Artists." *Kafka and Contemporary Critical Performance*, edited by Alan Udoff, 236–55. Bloomington: Indiana University Press, 1987.

Montaigne, Michel de. "That To Philosophise is to Learn How to Die." Translated by John Florio. *The Essayes of Michael Lord of Montaigne, Volume 1*, 73–95. New York: G. Richards, 1908.

Montano, Linda, ed. *Performance Artists Talking in the Eighties: Sex, Food, Money/Fame, Ritual/Death*. Berkeley: University of California Press, 2000.

Morgan, Stuart. "Survival Kit." *Frieze* 28 (May 1996): 52–55.

Morton, Richard. *Phthisiologia, or a Treatise on Consumption*. London: Smith and Walford, 1689.

Moten, Fred. *In the Break: The Aesthetics of the Black Radical Tradition*. Minneapolis: University of Minnesota Press, 2003.

Moure, Gloria, ed. *Ana Mendieta*. Barcelona: Polígrafa Obra Gráfica, 1996.

Mulvey, Laura. "Visual Pleasure and Narrative Cinema." *Screen* 16, no. 3 (1975), 6–18.

Nietzsche, Friedrich Wilhelm. "On the Uses and Disadvantages of History for Life." Translated by R. J. Hollingdale. In *Untimely Meditations*, edited by Daniel Breazeale, 57–124. Cambridge: Cambridge University Press, 1997.

O'Dell, Kathy. *Contract with the Skin: Masochism, Performance Art, and the 1970s*. Minneapolis: University of Minnesota Press, 1998.

O'Malley, Padraig. *Biting at the Grave: The Irish Hunger Strikes and the Politics of Despair*. Boston: Beacon Press, 1990.

Öndül, Hüsnü. "Isolation, Death Fasts, and Women Deaths." Human Rights Association of Turkey Press Release, 26 August 2002.

Orbach Susie. *Hunger Strike: The Anorectic's Struggle as a Metaphor for Our Age*. New York: Norton, 1986.

Ortega, Mariana. "Exiled Space, in-between Space: Existential Spatiality in Ana Mendieta's *Siluetas* Series." *Philosophy and Geography* 7, no. 1 (2004), 25–41.

Parkin, Alan K., J. Blunden, J. E. Rees, and Nicola M. Hunkin. "Wernicke-Korsakoff Syndrome of Nonalcoholic Origin." *Brain and Cognition* 15 (1991), 69–82.

Patterson, Orlando. *Slavery and Social Death*. Cambridge, Mass.: Harvard University Press, 1982.

Pécoil, Vincent. "The Museum as Prison: Post-Post-Scriptum on Control Societies." Translated by Simon Pleasance. *Third Text* 18, no. 5 (2004), 435–47.

Pentland, Brian, and Clifford Mawdsley. "Wernicke's Encephalopathy Following 'Hunger Strike.'" *Postgraduate Medical Journal* 58 (1982), 427–28.

Perreault, John. "Earth and Fire: Mendieta's Body of Work." *Ana Mendieta: A Retrospective*, edited by Petra Berreras del Rio and John Perreault, 10–27. New York: New Museum of Contemporary Art, 1987.

Phelan, Peggy. "Marina Abramović: Witnessing Shadows." *Theatre Journal* 56, no. 4 (2004), 569–77.

——. *Mourning Sex: Performing Public Memories*. New York: Routledge, 1997.

——. "On Seeing the Invisible: Marina Abramović's *The House with the Ocean View*." *Marina Abramović: The House with the Ocean View*, edited by Amy Gotzler, 171–79. Milan: Charta, 2003.

——. *Unmarked: The Politics of Performance*. New York: Routledge, 1993.

Piper, Adrian. *Out of Order, Out of Sight*. Vol. 1. Cambridge, Mass.: MIT Press, 1996.

——. "Property and the Limits of the Self." *Political Theory* 8, no. 1 (1980), 39–64.

——. "Two Conceptions of the Self." *Philosophical Studies* 48, no. 2 (1985), 173–97.

"Political Prisoners in Turkey to Begin Hunger Strike on October 20." Devrimci Halk Kurtuluş Partisi-Cephesi Press Release, 18 October 2000.

Pollock, Della, ed. *Exceptional Spaces: Essays in Performance and History*. Chapel Hill: University of North Carolina Press, 1998.

——. "Performing Writing," *The Ends of Performance*, edited by Peggy Phelan and Jill Lane, 73–103. New York: New York University Press, 1998.

Pope, Harrison G., Katharine A. Phillips, and Roberto Olivardia. *The Adonis Complex: The Secret Crisis of Male Body Obsession*. New York: Free Press, 2000.

Popper, Frank. *Art—Action and Participation*. New York: New York University Press, 1975.

"Prison Brief for Turkey." International Centre for Prison Studies (Kings College London) Report, April 2008.

Probyn, Elsbeth. "The Taste of Power." Lecture presented to the CS4 Cultural Studies Colloquium, University of North Carolina at Chapel Hill, 1 October 1999.

Reik, Theodor. *Masochism in Sex and Society*. Translated by Margaret H. Beigel and Gertrud M. Kurth. New York: Black Cat, 1962.

Richardson, Benjamin Ward. "The Philosophy of Fasting." *The Gentleman's Magazine CCXLIX*, edited by Sylvanus Urbanus, 348–66. London: Chatto and Windus, 1880.

Rilke, Rainer Maria. *The Book of Hours*. Translated by Stevie Krayer. Salzburg: Salzburg University Press, 1995.

———. "What Survives." *The Migration of Powers: French Poems*, 43. Translated by A. Poulin. Minneapolis: Graywolf Press, 1984.

Ritter, Naomi. *Art as Spectacle: Images of the Entertainer Since Romanticism*. Columbia: University of Missouri Press, 1968.

Robertson, Richie. *Kafka: A Very Short Introduction*. Oxford: Oxford University Press, 2004.

Robins, Kevin. "Interrupting Identities: Turkey/Europe." *Questions of Cultural Identity*, edited by Stuart Hall and Paul du Gay, 61–86. London: Sage, 1996.

Rosenberg, Charles E. *The Cholera Years: The United States in 1832, 1849, and 1866*. Chicago: University of Chicago Press, 1962.

Roulet, Laura. "Ana Mendieta and Carl Andre: Duet of Leaf and Stone." *Art Journal* 63, no. 3 (2004), 80–101.

Rugoff, Ralph. "Touched by Your Presence." *Frieze* 50 (January–February 2000), 84–89.

Russo, Mary. *The Female Grotesque: Risk, Excess, and Modernity*. New York: Routledge, 1994.

Sachs, Hanns. "On the Genesis of Perversions." *Psychoanalytic Quarterly* 55 (1986), 477–88.

Schjeldahl, Peter. "Chris Burden and the Limits of Art." *New Yorker* 83, no. 12 (2007), 152–53.

Schneider, Rebecca. *The Explicit Body in Performance*. New York: Routledge, 1997.

———. "Performance Remains." *Performance Research* 6, no. 2 (2001), 100–108.

Sedgwick, Eve, and Andrew Parker, eds. *Performativity and Performance*. New York: Routledge, 1995.

Silverman, Kaja. *Male Subjectivity at the Margins*. New York: Routledge, 1992.

———. *World Spectators*. Stanford: Stanford University Press, 2000.

Sinclair, Upton. *The Book of Life: Mind and Body*. Girard, Kan.: Haldeman-Julius, 1922.

"Small Group Isolation in Turkish Prisons: An Avoidable Disaster." Human Rights Watch Briefing Paper, 24 May 2000.

Smith, Neil, and Cindi Katz. "Grounding Metaphor: Towards a Spatialized Politics." *Place and the Politics of Identity*, edited by Michael Keith and Steve Pile, 67–83. New York: Routledge, 1993.

Societas Raffeallo Sanzio. "What the Body Can Do." *Marina Abramović*. Translated by Emanuela Gini, Chris Martin, and Federico Rahola, 139–48. Milan: Charta, 2002.

Sours, John A. *Starving to Death in a Sea of Objects*. Northvale, N.J.: Aronson, 1980.

Spero, Nancy. "Tracing Ana Mendieta." *Artforum International* 30 (April 1992), 75–77.

Spignesi, Angelyn. *Starving Women: A Psychology of Anorexia Nervosa*. Dallas: Spring Publications, 1983.

Spitzack, Carole. "The Spectacle of Anorexia Nervosa." *Text and Performance Quarterly* 13, no. 1 (1993), 1–20.

Spitzer, R. L. "The Diagnostic Status of Homosexuality in DSM-III." *American Journal of Psychiatry* 138 (1981), 210–15.

Stacey, Michelle. *The Fasting Girl: A True Victorian Medical Mystery*. New York: Jeremy P. Tarcher, 2002.

"Tanner's Fast." *Canada Lancet*, 1 September 1880, 27.

TAYAD Komite Nederland. *Documentation on the Death Fast in Turkey*. Rotterdam: TAYAD, 2001.

———. *I Want My Past Back*. Rotterdam: TAYAD, 2001.

Taylor, Brandon. *Avant-Garde and After: Rethinking Art Now*. New York: Abrams, 1995.

Taylor, Diana. *The Archive and the Repertoire: Performing Cultural Memory in the Americas*. Durham, N.C.: Duke University Press, 2003.

Tomova, Analia, and Philip Kumanov. "Sex Differences and Similarities of Hormonal Alterations in Patients with Anorexia Nervosa." *Andrologia* 31 (1999), 143–47.

Treichler, Paula, Lisa Cartwright, and Constance Penley, eds. *The Visible Woman: Imaging Technologies, Gender, and Science*. New York: New York University Press, 1998.

Tucker, Marcia. Preface and Acknowledgements in *Ana Mendieta: A Retrospective*, edited by Petra Barreras del Rio and John Perreault, 6–9. New York: New Museum of Contemporary Art, 1987.

"Turkey Violates Rights of Free Expression." Human Rights Watch Press Release, 15 April 1999.

Turner, Victor. *Ritual Process: Structure and Anti-structure*. Ithaca: Cornell University Press, 1969.

Vandereycken, Walter, and Ron van Deth. *From Fasting Saints to Anorexic Girls: The History of Self-Starvation*. New York: New York University Press, 1994.

Viso, Olga. *Unseen Mendieta: The Unpublished Works of Ana Mendieta*. Munich: Prestel, 2008.

Wabitsch, M., Anne Ballauf, Reinhard Holl, Werner F. Blum, Eberhard Heinz, Helmut Remschmidt, and Johannes Hebebrand. "Serum Leptin, Gonadotropin, and Testosterone Concentrations in Male Patients with Anorexia Nervosa." *Journal of Clinical Endocrinology and Metabolism* 86, no. 7 (2001), 2982–88.

Wagner, Anne. *Three Artists (Three Women): Modernism and the Art of Hesse, Krasner, and O'Keefe*. Berkeley: University of California Press, 1997.

Walmsley, Roy. "World Prison Brief." International Centre for Prison Studies (Kings College London) Report, April 2008.

Wang, Ping. *Aching for Beauty: Footbinding in China*. Minneapolis: University of Minnesota Press, 2000.

Ward, Frazer. "Gray Zone: Watching *Shoot*." *October* 95 (winter 2001), 114–30.

"Wernicke-Korsakoff Syndrome." Family Caregiver Alliance Fact Sheet, November 1998.

"Wernicke's Preventable Encephalopathy." *The Lancet* 313, no. 8126 (1979), 1122–23.

Wescott, James. "Marina Abramović's *The House with the Ocean View*: A View of the House from Some Drops in the Ocean." *TDR: The Drama Review* 47, no. 3 (2003), 129–36.

Wilder, Alexander. "Dr. Tanner and the Forty Days' Fast." *Medical World* 14, no. 12 (1896), 458–61.

Wilson, T. P., and J. P. Geppert, eds. *The Medical Advance IX–X*. Cincinnati: Advance Publishing, 1881.

Wolf, Naomi. *The Beauty Myth: How Images of Beauty Are Used Against Women*. New York: W. Morrow, 1991.

"World Report 1989." Human Rights Watch Briefing Paper, 1989.

index

•

commodification (*cont.*)
self, 164n11; semiotic commodifiability and, 90
Cuba, 25–27, 94, 95–96, 98–100, 140–
43, 148–50. *See also* Guantánamo Bay

Dasein, 2, 14–16, 148. *See also* Heidegger, Martin
death drive, 3, 20, 24, 54–56. *See also*
Derrida, Jacques; Freud, Sigmund
death fast, 115, 130–31, 137, 164
Derrida, Jacques, 24, 53–55
disappearance, 53, 92, 109, 145, 150;
Kafka and, 59, 83; Mendieta and,
95, 97–100, 102; performance and,
23, 25–26, 49, 88, 139–40; self-
starvation and, 2–3, 11–12, 28, 125–
26. *See also* liveness; Phelan, Peggy
duration, 89–90; anorexia and, 38, 49;
of *Bed Piece*, 81; of fasts, 58; of hunger strikes, 114, 131; performances
and, 23, 92–93, 103–4, 107, 166n78;
self-starvation and, 11, 79–80

emaciation, 1–2, 18, 39, 104; children
and, 61; self-starvation and, 9, 28;
slow or gradual, 59, 72–73, 86, 94,
99, 129–31; Spignesi on, 33; symptoms of, 43–44, 47–48
European Union (EU), 111–12, 115–
16, 132, 136, 167n4

Fancher, Mollie, 24–25, 62–66, 68, 69,
161n19
Fanon, Frantz, 9
fasting girls, 24, 72
feeding tube, 27, 53, 140, 143–49
Feldman, Alan, 10, 53, 122–23, 125–
26, 131, 164n24, 169n51. *See also*
Blanketmen Strike; Sands, Bobby
force-feeding, 16, 53, 63, 106–7, 140,
142–43

Foucault, Michel, 24, 109, 122, 127,
132, 134, 148; affinity and, 121; *assujettissement* of, 3, 13; *Discipline and
Punish*, 119–20, 157n27, 168n32;
subjectivation and, 2, 3–9, 14, 16–
17, 23, 36, 145. *See also* interpellation; subjectivation
Freud, Sigmund, 25, 53, 139–40; on
conflict between life and death, 2;
death drive and, 24, 54, 144; ego-
ideal and, 49–50; hysteria and, 45–
46; on instincts, 3, 18, 20–22,
153n4, 155n46; repression and, 12,
14
Fried, Michael, 25, 89–91, 93–94, 109.
See also antitheatrical criticism
F-Type Prison, 112–13, 120, 124, 130,
136–37, 169n54; description of, 26,
115–16; protests against, 111, 117,
122, 126–28, 132

Goldberg, Whoopi, 145–47
Guantánamo Bay (Cuba), 26–27,
140–43, 148–50. *See also* Camp
X-Ray

Halberstam, Judith, 154n26
Hammond, William A., 61–69, 72–73,
78–80
Heidegger, Martin, 2, 3, 14–16, 19,
148, 158n59. *See also* being-toward-
death; Dasein
hope, 30, 66, 99, 133, 139–40, 148,
150–51; despair and, 2, 23; Freud
and, 13; hopelessness and, 58; Orbach on, 36–37
hunger artists, 57–59, 83–84, 108, 140,
150–51
hunger strike, 26–27, 28–29, 35–37,
111–37, 142–43, 148–50
hysteria, 24, 37, 45–46

instinct, 3, 17–18, 20–23, 54–55, 155n4. *See also* Freud, Sigmund

interpellation, 4–7, 13–14, 37, 154n29, 155–56n51. *See also* Althusser, Louis; Foucault, Michel

intersectionality, 155n41, 155–56n51

intersubjectivity, 48–50, 72, 140, 150–51; Abramović and, 92, 108–9; Althusser and, 13, 23; Burden and, 82–84; Feldman and, 125–26; Laplanche and, 20; Orbach and, 37–38; performativity and, 41

John Paul II, 27, 146–47

Jones, Amelia, 60, 97–98, 160n13. *See also* masochism

Kafka, Franz, 57–59, 83–84, 108, 140, 150–51. *See also* hunger artists

Kant, Immanuel, 25, 85–86, 108–9

Kuçuk Armutlu (Istanbul), 112–13, 130–34

Lacan, Jacques, 13–14, 17–18, 31, 48–49, 145–46, 155n46, 170n6. *See also* mirror stage; symbolic order

Laplanche, Jean, 20–23, 155n46

liveness, 23, 26, 28, 91, 93, 139–40, 148–49; Abramović and, 102–3, 108; Burden and, 75–76, 80; Hammond and, 64–65; Mendieta and, 97–98, 101; Phelan and, 49; Piper and, 86; Schiavo and, 146–48. *See also* disappearance; Phelan, Peggy

loss, 3, 54–55, 139; anorexia and, 24, 33, 154–55n38; of bodily integrity, 9–10; love and, 2, 23; performances of, 28, 49; Phelan and, 49; of self, 98; subjectivity and, 147

male anorexia, 24, 30–32, 41–44, 46–53

male gaze, 25

masculinity, 24, 41–44, 46–53, 102, 156n2; endurance and, 60; femininity and, 121, 127; Halberstam and, 154n26; male subjectivity and, 12–13; model of, 25, 80–81; modern art and, 101; shock value of, 98. *See also* Silverman, Kaja

masochism, 22, 25, 60, 75–77, 83, 101–2, 107, 160n13. *See also* Jones, Amelia; Reik, Theodor

Mbembe, Achille, 155n40

Mendieta, Ana, 25–26, 90–101, 102, 108–9

mirror stage, 13, 31, 35, 39, 48, 85–86, 105, 109, 139. *See also* Lacan, Jacques

Moten, Fred, 89–90, 109. *See also* objecthood

Morton, Richard, 42–45, 62, 158n45

Mulvey, Laura, 25

neoliberalism, 99, 140

neurosis, 21–23

objecthood, 3, 9, 26, 88–91, 97, 102, 109

Operation Pedro Pan, 95–96

Operation Return to Life, 114–15, 117, 123–25, 126–28, 130–32, 169n54

Operation Sea Signal, 140

Orbach, Susie, 35–38, 48

performativity, 11, 26, 28, 32, 49, 60, 93, 157–58n41; Austin and, 154n12; Brecht and, 8; Burden and, 78; Butler and, 5–7, 9; Lacan and, 17; masculinity and, 154n26; paradigm of, 40–41; Piper and, 90; Sedgwick and Parker and, 19–20. *See also* Austin, J. L.; Butler, Judith

perversion, 2, 16, 21–23, 104

Phelan, Peggy, 103, 105–6, 108,

Patrick Anderson is associate professor of communication and
a faculty affiliate of critical gender studies and ethnic studies at the
University of California, San Diego. He is a co-editor of *Violence
Performance: Local Roots and Global Routes of Conflict*.

•

Library of Congress Cataloging-in-Publication Data
Anderson, Patrick.
So much wasted : hunger, performance, and the
morbidity of resistance / Patrick Anderson.
p. cm. — (Perverse modernities)
Includes bibliographical references and index.
ISBN 978-0-8223-4819-1 (cloth : alk. paper)
ISBN 978-0-8223-4828-3 (pbk. : alk. paper)
1. Passive resistance. 2. Starvation — Political aspects.
3. Fasting — Political aspects. 4. Performance art.
I. Title. II. Series: Perverse modernities.
HM1281.A534 2010
303.6′1 — dc22
2010022498